On You...

Bed...
Windows...

The Offic...

Special...
Fabulous E...

...home boasts a two-story bay
...ing angled roofline.
...on page 197.
...nd/HomeStyles
...rod & Associates

...ation

A lovely gazebo-shaped entry welcomes guests to this gracious home. See Plan R-2120 on page 201.
Photo: Mark Englund/HomeStyles
Design: Barclay Home Designs

49 Energy-Efficient Homes Under 2,000 Sq. Ft.

145 New Releases: 32 Fresh New Designs

177 Special Section: Sun-Loving Homes with Solar Features

195 Energy-Efficient Homes Over 2,000 Sq. Ft.

EDITORIAL
Brian Boese, Steve Gramins, Laura Lentz, Jason Miller, Pamela Robertson, Mele Willis
PRODUCTION
Todd Monge, Leon Thompson
MARKETING
Dan Brown, Kris Donnelly, Brian Medenwaldt, Shelley Safratowich
TELERELATIONS
Heather Anderson, Jennifer Banks, Laurie Benke, Heidi Bjorlo, Erika Brewer, Bonny Duffney, Carol Green, Mark Kalar, Erin Marsh, Debra Matei, Julie Schaetzel, Karen Strong, Jim Verhaest, Steve Verhaest, Laura Voetberg, Rebecca Wadsworth, Narkeetha Warren
INFORMATION SYSTEMS
John Driscoll, Kevin Gellerman, Brad Olson
ACCOUNTING
Barbara Marquardt, Kellie Pierce, Robert Schultz
ADMINISTRATION
Jeanne Halliwill, Kristy Walsh
HUMAN RESOURCES
Rick Erdmann
COMPANY LEADERS: Jeffrey B. Heegaard, Roger W. Heegaard
STRATEGIC LEADERS: Craig Bryan-Marketing, Nancy Ness-Finance/Administration/Publishing, Wayne Ramaker-Telerelations
OPERATIONAL LEADERS: Eric Englund-Editorial, John Herber-Information Systems, Diana Jasan-Multimedia, Dorothy Jordan-Joint-Venture Marketing, Bruce Krause-Production, Jeanne Marquardt-Accounting, Michael Romain-Telerelations

PUBLISHED BY HOMESTYLES
P.O. Box 75488
St. Paul, MN 55175-0488
TEL: (612) 602-5000 FAX: (612) 602-5001

FOR INFORMATION ON ADVERTISING, CONTACT KEVIN MILLER AT (800) 755-0288

INTERNET ADDRESS: http://homestyles.com

This home's expanse of windows creates exciting views from within and without. See Plan NW-915 on Page 199.
Photo: Mark Englund/HomeStyles
Design: Northwest Home Designing, Inc.

No Pain, No Gain?

Contrary to the oft-quoted words of your elementary-school gym teachers, pain doesn't always mean gain. As you may have learned from running in circles around the track, you can expend a lot of energy and still go nowhere.

Those thinking about building a home have many issues to consider when choosing house plans: style, cost and comfort, as well as efficiency. The process can become frustrating if you're not sure how or where to start, and you may end up feeling as though you've run a mile—and barely moved an inch.

This is particularly true when it comes to heating, cooling and lighting your home. Spending too much energy—and, therefore, money—on these things will not make it a more comfortable place to live if its structure can't maximize your resources.

Energy efficiency is the focus of this collection of home plans by HomeStyles. As you study these pages, you will find a great variety of home sizes and styles, all of which were designed to make the most of your energy dollars. We've taken care to select homes that offer energy-efficient construction (all of the plans in this issue feature 2x6 exterior wall framing)—without sacrificing flair. We've also included a special section of homes with built-in solar features.

You'll enjoy our helpful feature articles. Turn to page four for tips on window placement. The article on page six will serve as an inspiration to anyone who has ever dreamt of his or her own home office.

Best wishes for a successful (and painless) plan search. If you have any questions or comments, please feel free to contact me by letter or by E-mail. I look forward to hearing from you.

Sincerely,

Laura L. Lentz
Editor

HomeStyles Publishing and Marketing Inc.
P.O. Box 75488
St. Paul, MN 55175-0488
E-mail: llentz@homestyles.com

Beautiful Thieves: Windows Steal the Spotlight

When it comes to stealing the spotlight, windows can be slippery thieves. Perhaps you've noticed that no matter how you decorate your home, the magnetic appeal of your windows outshines the rest of your efforts. When guests enter your home for the first time, they are drawn, as if by an invisible force, to these common, yet mysteriously powerful, marvels. Even repeat visitors tend to linger where the view is best, or where a uniquely shaped section of glass creates a fanciful play of light.

Though it is difficult to explain precisely our fascination with windows, it is easy to see that, when carefully incorporated into the design of a home, windows can work as a major visual element. The windows that you choose—and the way they are positioned in your home—can enhance and personalize your interior decor.

David Olds, an architect with St. Paul-based Buetow & Associates, Architects & Engineers, explains that consumers' window choices are often based upon current design trends. Certain styles and placements of windows are continuously swinging in and out of vogue. It is crucial, though, to think about function as well as fashion when you make such a far-reaching decision. How will your windows affect the way you feel about and use the various rooms of your home? Your needs will differ according to the purpose of each room, and you may wish to customize your approach to each space. Determine the desired effect, and situate your windows accordingly.

There is an endless variety of ways that windows can be arranged, and there exist both pros and cons for every option. Olds gives one example of the balancing act of window placement: the choice between high or low window sills. High sills increase privacy within the home, but may tend to create a closed-in feel. Windows with low sills, on the other hand, may decrease privacy somewhat, but they tend to expand a room and increase its feeling of spaciousness, while allowing splendid views of the outdoors. Olds suggests a compromise of using lower sills in the living areas, and higher sills in the sleeping quarters of the home.

Every situation is different, and what is right for one family may not be for another. "The placement of windows is a matter of personal preference," states Olds. "The most important thing is to be flexible."

You may also want to consider energy efficiency when making window choices. In addition to decorative perks, you can reap solar benefits from careful window placement.

Olds asserts that, in addition to its placement, a window's installation will affect your home's energy efficiency for years to come. You'll need to do some homework to ensure that you choose windows that are well constructed. You'll want to make sure that your windows are installed properly, for even the best windows will not function as they should if not precisely framed and insulated.

Long Island architect Charles Koty, of National Home Plans, Inc., explains how window placement

Photo courtesy of Pella Corporation

can also increase the energy efficiency of a home. "In respect to the decorative aspect, windows should face in the direction that allows the best view. In many of our homes, we will have a bay window to bring in the outdoors, especially where there is nice landscaping. In the case of passive solar usage, you would have the large windows facing south, to capture the energy of the sun. On the north side of the home, you would minimize the size of the windows, to help prevent heat loss."

Koty reminds homeowners, "Don't forget that shades should be provided to block sunlight in the summer. Also, deciduous trees in the south provide shading in the summer and lose their leaves in the winter to allow the maximum sunlight into your home."

Combine imagination with careful planning of window placement, and you will create a practical living space in which your most fetching adornments—the windows— can steal the show.

—*Laura Lentz*

Photo courtesy of Pella Corporation

THE Office of Precedent

Over 50 million people will work at home this year. If you decide to join their ranks, you'll be faced with the task of creating a home office that will serve and impress both you and your prospective clients. The questions will pile up like unreturned phone calls: Where will I locate it? What about its layout, design and comfort level? I'm not even sure if my home's electrical system can handle what I'm about to plug in!

don't panic. Start at the beginning—the location—and think carefully. If you'll be holding frequent meetings with clients, do you really want to seat them in a drafty attic or a basement that looks like a horror movie set?

You're better off addressing your needs instead of trying to jam yourself into a "convenient" cubbyhole. Think big. Think future. How large an operation will you have in three years? If you see nothing but growth in the coming years, you'd better be prepared!

Consider the amount of traffic your new endeavors will generate. Do you really want a stampede of clients—however valuable—rumbling through your kitchen or living room? You may need to construct a second entrance, away from the living quarters.

Once you've chosen the location, consider your need for power. Electricity, that is. All the fancy electronic gadgetry in the world won't advance your career if your home office has only one electrical outlet and a single phone jack. If this is the case, you'd better get on the horn to a reputable electrician. Consider adding another phone line, too. One last word on electricity: Buy surge protectors. When your air conditioner, microwave or laser printer kicks into high gear, you'll be glad your precious PC is plugged into a protector.

Now it's time to design the space. To do this, think about how a kitchen or workshop is laid out: all you need is placed within easy reach, never more than a

A GLOSSARY OF BUILDING TERMS:
TO AID IN YOUR SEARCH FOR A HOME, LEARN THE LINGO

Bay - a projection formed by three windows joined at obtuse angles

Bow - a curved projection formed by at least five windows joined at obtuse angles

Clerestory - an outside wall of a room or building that rises above an adjoining roof and contains windows

Dentil - one of a series of small projecting rectangular blocks forming a molding under an overhang, most common in Colonial-style homes

Dormer - a gable-topped structure projecting from a roof, containing a window

Footprint - the outline of a home's foundation; this measures the home's outermost points and is used for site planning

Gable - the vertical triangular end of a building or part of a building, from the eaves to the ridge

Gable roof - a roof consisting of two rectanglular planes sloping up to a ridge, forming gables on both ends

Gambrel roof - a roof with a lower, steeper slope and an upper, less steep slope on each of its two sides

Hip roof - a roof with sloping ends and sloping sides that meet at a ridge

Keystone - a wedge-shaped detail at the crown of an arch

Lanai - a patio or veranda

Loggia - a roofed open gallery, often on an upper level

Palladian window - a window arrangement with a half-round window on top of a wider rectangular window

Pediment - a triangular space formed in the middle of a gable; also used as a decoration above a door

Porte cochere - a covered, drive-through structure that extends from the side of a home, providing shelter for people getting in and out of vehicles

Portico - a roof supported by columns; often used at an entry

Quoin - a large, square stone set into the corner of a masonry building; distinguished from the adjoining walls by material, texture or projection

Sidelight - a vertical window beside a door or another window

Transom window - a narrow horizontal window above a window or door, named for the cross bar on which it rests

Tray ceiling - a recessed ceiling resembling an upside-down tray; also referred to as a stepped ceiling

Turret - a small tower usually on the corner of a building, most common in Victorian-style homes

Vaulted ceiling - a ceiling that slopes up to a peak

Volume ceiling - any ceiling higher than the standard 8 feet

step or two away. How can this principle be applied to your office?

Your physical characteristics play a role, too. Are you tall? Left-handed? Are you physically challenged? Answering questions like these will allow you to make intelligent choices when it comes to the layout of your business space.

You can define your space easily and inexpensively. Try the light touch by placing throw rugs strategically. Or use barriers such as plants, screens, panels or bookcases. Above all else, remember that you are in charge. If you seek professional help, you don't have to adhere to an expert's idea of what is best for you. Listen to the advice, then choose the arrangement that respects your needs for comfort and productivity.

Paint your world, but don't get carried away. It's wise to stick with neutral colors. Keep in mind that potential clients will be seated in your space. Do you really want them surrounded by a distracting personal statement? Best to save the shocking hot pink surprise for the basement bathroom.

Finally, make yourself comfortable. Furnish your home office with adjustable work surfaces and chairs. Speaking of the latter, consider giving the folks at Biomechanics Corporation of America a

call (1-800-248-3746). They've got an Intelligent Seat that actually conforms to your tuckus.

In a short while, your home office doors will open for business. What kind of space those doors introduce is up to you. With a little forethought and hard work, you too can create your own office of precedent.

—*Jason Miller*

Sources: Compute, *November 1991;* The Home Office Book: How to Set Up and Use an Efficient Personal Workspace in the Computer Age, *by Mark Alvarez;* Popular Science, *May 1992.*
Photos courtesy of Bruce Hardwood Floors.

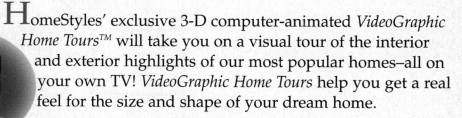

Planned to Perfection

- This attractive and stylish home offers an interior design that is planned to perfection.
- The covered entry and vaulted foyer create an impressive welcome.
- The vaulted Great Room features a corner fireplace, a wet bar and lots of windows. The adjoining dining room offers a bay window and access to a covered patio.
- The gourmet kitchen includes an island cooktop, a garden window above the sink and a built-in desk. The attached nook is surrounded by windows that overlook a delightful planter.
- The master suite boasts a tray ceiling that rises to 9½ ft. and a peaceful reading area that accesses a private patio. The superb master bath features a garden tub and a separate shower.
- Two secondary bedrooms share a compartmentalized bath.

Plan S-4789

Bedrooms: 3	Baths: 2

Living Area:	
Main floor	1,665 sq. ft.
Total Living Area:	**1,665 sq. ft.**
Standard basement	1,665 sq. ft.
Garage	400 sq. ft.
Exterior Wall Framing:	2x6

Foundation Options:

Standard basement

Crawlspace

Slab

(All plans can be built with your choice of foundation and framing. A generic conversion diagram is available. See order form.)

BLUEPRINT PRICE CODE:	**B**

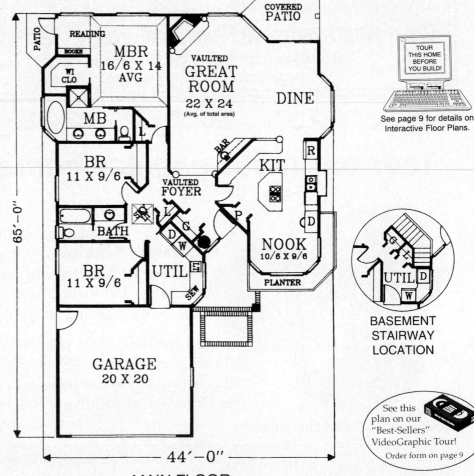

MAIN FLOOR

See page 9 for details on Interactive Floor Plans.

BASEMENT STAIRWAY LOCATION

See this plan on our "Best-Sellers" VideoGraphic Tour! Order form on page 9

HOW JIM BRANDENBURG LOOKS AT THE WORLD.

At his home near the Canadian border in northern Minnesota, award-winning nature photographer Jim Brandenburg photographs wolves right from his window. What kind of windows give him the wide, expansive views he needs yet are still tight enough to seal out the bitter cold and strong, winter winds? Jim Brandenburg has Marvin windows. To learn more about the windows that are as efficient as they are beautiful, call 1-800-346-5128 (1-800-263-6161 in Canada) or mail the coupon for a free brochure.

Complete and mail to:
Marvin Windows & Doors
Warroad, MN 56763.

Name _____

Address _____

City _____ State _____

Zip _____ Phone (____) _____
Z36970ZA

MARVIN
WINDOWS & DOORS
Made to order. Made for you.

Denzel Washington

Put this card in the hands of a child and there'll be no room for a gun. A needle. Or a knife.

It's only a piece of paper, but that little membership card has helped keep millions of kids off drugs, out of gangs and in school. To learn how you can help the Boys & Girls Clubs, call: **1-800-854-Club.**

BOYS & GIRLS CLUBS OF AMERICA

The **Positive** Place For Kids

THE HOMESTYLES

WHAT OUR PLANS INCLUDE

HomeStyles construction blueprints are detailed, clear and concise. All blueprints are designed by licensed architects or members of the American Institute of Building Design (AIBD), and each plan is designed to meet nationally recognized building codes (either the Uniform Building Code, Standard Building Code or Basic Building Code) at the time and place they were drawn.

The blueprints for most home designs include the following elements, but the presentation of these elements may vary depending on the size and complexity of the home and the style of the individual designer:

1. *Exterior Elevations* show the front, rear and sides of the house, including exterior materials, details and measurements.

2. *Foundation Plans* include drawings for a full, daylight or partial basement, crawlspace, slab, or pole foundation. All necessary notations and dimensions are included. (Foundation options will vary for each plan. If the home you want does not have the type of foundation you desire, a generic foundation conversion diagram is available from HomeStyles.)

3. *Detailed Floor Plans* show the placement of interior walls and the dimensions for rooms, doors, windows, stairways, etc., of each level of the house.

4. *Cross Sections* show details of the house as though it were cut in slices from the roof to the foundation. The cross sections specify the home's construction, insulation, flooring and roofing details.

5. *Interior Elevations* show the specific details of cabinets (kitchen, bathroom, and utility room), fireplaces, built-in units, and other special interior features, depending on the nature and complexity of the item. **Note:** *To save money and to accommodate your own style and taste, we suggest contacting local cabinet and fireplace distributors for sizes and styles.*

6. *Roof Details* show slope, pitch and location of dormers, gables and other roof elements, including clerestory windows and skylights. These details may be shown on the elevation sheet or on a separate diagram. **Note:** *If trusses are used, we suggest using a local truss manufacturer to design your trusses to comply with your local codes and regulations.*

7. *Schematic Electrical Layouts* show the suggested locations for switches, fixtures and outlets. These details may be shown on the floor plan or on a separate diagram.

8. *General Specifications* provide general instructions and information regarding structure, excavating and grading, masonry and concrete work, carpentry and wood, thermal and moisture protection, and specifications about drywall, tile, flooring, glazing, caulking and sealants.

PLANS PACKAGE

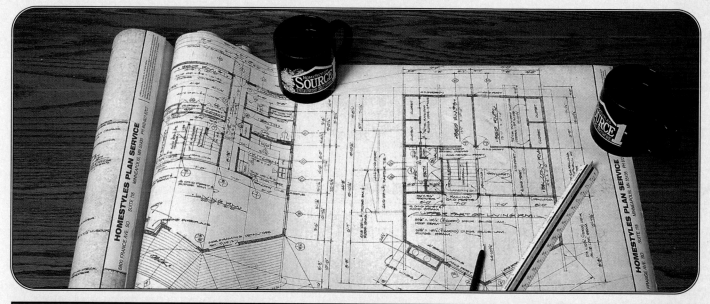

OTHER HELPFUL BUILDING AIDS

Every set of plans that you order will contain the details your builder needs. However, HomeStyles provides additional guides and information that you may order, as follows:

1. *Reproducible Set* is useful if you plan to make changes to the stock home plan you've chosen. This set consists of line drawings produced on erasable, reproducible paper for the purpose of modification. When alterations are complete, working copies can be made.

2. *Mirror-Reversed Plans* are used when building the home in reverse of the illustrated floor plan. Reversed plans are available for an additional one-time surcharge. Since the lettering and dimensions will read backwards, we recommend that you order only one or two reversed sets in addition to the regular-reading sets.

3. *Itemized List of Materials* details the quantity, type and size of materials needed to build your home. (This list is helpful in acquiring an accurate construction estimate.)

4. *Description of Materials* describes the type and quality of materials suggested for the home. This form may be required for obtaining FHA or VA financing.

5. *Typical "How-To" Diagrams — Plumbing, Wiring, Solar Heating, and Framing and Foundation Conversion Diagrams.* Each of these diagrams details the basic tools and techniques needed to plumb; wire; install a solar heating system; convert plans with 2x4 exterior walls to 2x6 (or vice versa); or adapt a plan for a basement, crawlspace or slab foundation. ***Note: These diagrams are generic and not specific to any one plan.**

NOTE: Due to regional variations, local availability of materials, local codes, methods of installation, and individual preferences, it is impossible to include much detail on heating, plumbing, and electrical work on your plans. The duct work, venting, and other details will vary depending on the type of heating and cooling system (forced air, hot water, electric, solar) and the type of energy (gas, oil, electricity, solar) that you use. These details and specifications are easily obtained from your builder, contractor, and/or local suppliers.

PLEASE READ BEFORE YOU ORDER

WHO WE ARE

The HomeStyles Designers' Network is a consortium of over 50 leading residential designers. All the plans presented in this book are designed by licensed architects or members of the American Institute of Building Design (AIBD), and each plan is designed to meet nationally recognized building codes (either the Uniform Building Code, Standard Building Code or Basic Building Code) in effect at the time and place that they were drawn.

BLUEPRINT PRICES

Our sales volume allows us to offer quality blueprints at a fraction of the cost it takes to develop them. Custom designs cost thousands of dollars, usually 5 to 15% of the cost of construction. Design costs for a $100,000 home, for example, can range from $5,000 to $15,000.

Our pricing schedule is based on "Total heated living space." Garages, porches, decks and unfinished basements are not included.

EXCHANGE INFORMATION

We want you to be happy with your blueprint purchase. If, for some reason, the blueprints that you ordered cannot be used, we will be pleased to exchange them within 30 days of the purchase date. Please note that a handling fee will be assessed for all exchanges. For more information, call us toll-free. **Note: Reproducible sets cannot be exchanged for any reason.**

LICENSE AGREEMENT, COPY RESTRICTIONS, COPYRIGHT

When you purchase a HomeStyles blueprint or reproducible set, we, as Licensor, grant you, as Licensee, the right to use these documents **to construct a single unit.** All of the plans in the publication are protected under the Federal Copyright Act, Title XVII of the United States Code and Chapter 37 of the Code of Federal Regulations. Each HomeStyles designer retains title and ownership of the original documents.

The blueprints licensed to you cannot be resold or used by any other person, copied, or reproduced by any means.

When you purchase a reproducible set, you reserve the right to modify and reproduce the plan. Reproducible sets cannot be resold or used by any other person.

ESTIMATING BUILDING COSTS

Building costs vary widely depending on style, size, type of finishing materials you select, and the local rates for labor and building materials. A local average cost per square foot of construction can give you a rough estimate. To get the average cost per square foot in your area, you can call a local contractor, your state or local builders association, the National Association of Home Builders (NAHB), or the AIBD. A more accurate estimate will require a professional review of the working blueprints and the types of materials you will be using.

FOUNDATION OPTIONS AND EXTERIOR CONSTRUCTION

Depending on your location and climate, your home will be built with either a slab, crawlspace or basement foundation; the exterior walls will either be 2x4 or 2x6. Most professional contractors and builders can easily adapt a home to meet the foundation and exterior wall requirements that you desire.

If the home that you select does not offer the foundation or exterior wall requirements that you prefer, HomeStyles offers a typical foundation and framing conversion diagram. (See order form.)

HOW MANY BLUEPRINTS SHOULD I ORDER?

A single set of blueprints is sufficient to study and review a home in greater detail. However, if you are planning to get cost estimates or are planning to build, you will need a minimum of 4 sets. If you will be modifying your home plan, we recommend ordering a reproducible set.

To help determine the exact number of sets you will need, please refer to the Blueprint Checklist below:

BLUEPRINT CHECKLIST

____**Owner (1 Set)**
____**Lending Institution (usually 1 set for conventional mortgage; 3 sets for FHA or VA loans)**
____**Builder (usually requires at least 3 sets)**
____**Building Permit Department (at least 1 set)**

REVISIONS, MODIFICATIONS AND CUSTOMIZING

The tremendous variety of designs available from HomeStyles allows you to choose the home that best suits your lifestyle, budget and building site. Through your choice of siding, roof, trim, decorating, color, etc., your home can be customized easily.

Minor changes and material substitutions can be made by any professional builder without the need for expensive blueprint revisions. However, if you will be making major changes, we strongly recommend that you order a reproducible set and seek the services of an architect or professional designer.

**Every state, county and municipality has its own codes, zoning requirements, ordinances, and building regulations. Modifications may be necessary to comply with your specific requirements -- snow loads, energy codes, seismic zones, etc.

COMPLIANCE WITH CODES

Depending on where you live, you may need to modify your plans to comply with local building requirements -- snow loads, energy codes, seismic zones, etc. All HomeStyles plans are designed to meet the specifications of seismic zones I or II. HomeStyles authorizes the use of our blueprints expressly conditioned upon your obligation and agreement to strictly comply with all local building codes, ordinances, regulations, and requirements -- including permits and inspections at the time of construction.

ARCHITECTURAL AND ENGINEERING SEALS

The increased concern over energy costs and safety has prompted many cities and states to require an architect or engineer to review and "seal" a blueprint prior to construction. There may be a fee for this service. Please contact your local lumber yard, municipal building department, builders association, or local chapter of the AIBD or American Institute of Architects (AIA).

Note: (Plans for homes to be built in Nevada may have to be re-drawn and sealed by a Nevada-licensed design professional.)

BLUEPRINT ORDER FORM

Ordering your dream home plans is as easy as 1-2-3!

COMPLETE THIS ORDER FORM IN JUST 3 EASY STEPS, THEN MAIL IN YOUR ORDER, OR CALL 1-888-626-2026 FOR FASTER SERVICE!

Please read the ordering information below:

1 BLUEPRINTS & ACCESSORIES

Price Code	1 Set	4 Sets	7 Sets	Reproducible Set*
AAA	$245	$295	$330	$430
AA	$285	$335	$370	$470
A	$365	$415	$450	$550
B	$405	$455	$490	$590
C	$445	$495	$530	$630
D	$485	$535	$570	$670
E	$525	$575	$610	$710
F	$565	$615	$650	$750
G	$605	$655	$690	$790
H	$645	$695	$730	$830
I	$685	$735	$770	$870

Prices subject to change

A Reproducible Set is produced on erasable paper for the purpose of modification. Only available for plans with these prefixes: A, AG, AGH, AH, AHP, APS, AX, B, BOD, BRF, C, CC, CDG, CPS, DCL, DD, DW, E, EOF, FB, G, GA, GL, GSA, H, HDS, HFL, HOM, IDG, J, JWA, K, KD, KLF, L, LRD, LS, M, NW, OH, PH, PI, RD, S, SDG, SG, SUL, SUN, THD, TS, U, UDA, UDG, V.

Additional Sets: Additional sets of the plan ordered are $40 each. Save money by ordering the 4-set or 7-set package shown above.

Mirror-Reversed Plans: A $50 surcharge. From the total number of sets you ordered above, choose the number of these that you want to be reversed. Pay only $50. *Note: All writing on mirror-reversed plans is backward. We recommend ordering one or two reversed sets in addition to the regular-reading sets.*

Itemized List of Materials: Available for $50; each additional set is $15. Details the quantity, type and size of materials needed to build your home.

Description of Materials: Sold only in set of two for $50. (For use in obtaining FHA or VA financing.)

Typical How-To Diagrams: One set $20. Two sets $30. Three sets $40. All four sets only $45. Generic guides on plumbing, wiring, and solar heating, plus information on how to convert from one foundation or exterior framing to another. *Note: These diagrams are not specific to any one plan.*

2 SHIPPING & HANDLING

Add shipping and handling costs according to chart below:

	1-3 sets	4-6 sets	7 sets or more	Reproducible Set
U.S. Regular (5-6 business days)	$17.50	$20.00	$22.50	$17.50
U.S. Express (2-3 business days)	$29.50	$32.50	$35.00	$29.50
Canada Regular (2-3 weeks)	$20.00	$22.50	$25.00	$20.00
Canada Express (5-6 business days)	$35.00	$40.00	$45.00	$35.00
Overseas/Airmail (7-10 business days)	$57.50	$67.50	$77.50	$57.50

3 PAYMENT INFORMATION

Choose the method of payment you prefer. Send check, money order or credit card information, along with name and address to: ➡

COMPLETE THIS FORM

Plan Number: HD9- _____   **Price Code** ____

Foundation _____
(Carefully review the foundation option(s) available for your plan — basement, crawlspace, pole, pier, or slab. If several options are offered, choose only one.)

No. of Sets:

1
- ☐ One Set
- ☐ Four Sets
- ☐ Seven Sets
- ☐ One Reproducible Set

➡ $_____ (See Blueprint Chart at left)

Additional Sets _____ (Quantity) $_____ ($40 each)

Mirror-Reversed Sets _____ (Quantity) $_____ ($50 surcharge)

Itemized List of Materials _____ (Quantity) $_____ ($50; $15 for each additional)
Available for plans with these prefixes: AH, AHP, APS*, AX*, B*, BOD*, C, CAR, CC, CDG*, CPS, DD*, DW, E, G, GSA, H, HFL, HOM, I*, IDG, J, K, LMB*, LRD, NW*, P, PH, R, S, SG*, SUN, THD, U, UDA, UDG, VL.
Not available on all plans. Please call before ordering.

Description of Materials $_____ ($50 for two sets)
Available for plans with these prefixes: AHP, C, DW, H, J, K, P, PH, SUL, VL.

Typical How-To Diagrams $_____ (All four only $45)
(One set $20. Two sets $30. Three sets $40.)
- ☐ Plumbing   ☐ Wiring   ☐ Solar Heating   ☐ Framing & Foundation Conversion

SUBTOTAL	$_____
SALES TAX*	$_____ *MN residents add 6.5% sales tax
SHIPPING/HANDLING	$_____ (See chart at left)
TOTAL	$_____
GRAND TOTAL	$_____

2

3
- ☐ Check/Money Order enclosed (in U.S. funds)
- ☐ VISA   ☐ MasterCard   ☐ AmEx   ☐ Discover

Credit Card # _____   **Exp. Date** _____

Name _____

Address _____

City _____ **State** _____ **Country** _____

ZIP _____ **Daytime Phone (** ____ **)** _____

Please check if you are a builder : ☐   **Home Phone (** ____ **)** _____

Source Code HD9

MAIL COUPON TO:	HomeStyles Plan Service P.O. Box 75488 St. Paul, MN 55175-0488	OR FAX TO: (612) 602-5002

FOR FASTER SERVICE CALL 1-888-626-2026

Comfortable L-Shaped Ranch

- From the covered entry to the beautiful and spacious family gathering areas, this comfortable ranch-style home puts many extras into a compact space.
- Straight off the central foyer, an inviting fireplace and a bright bay window highlight the living and dining area, while sliding glass doors open to a wide backyard terrace.
- The combination kitchen/family room features a large eating bar. The nearby mudroom offers a service entrance, laundry facilities, access to the garage and room for a half-bath.
- In the isolated sleeping wing, the master bedroom boasts a private bath and plenty of closet space. Two additional bedrooms share another full bath.

Plan K-276-R

Bedrooms: 3	Baths: 2+
Living Area:	
Main floor	1,245 sq. ft.
Total Living Area:	**1,245 sq. ft.**
Standard basement	1,245 sq. ft.
Garage	499 sq. ft.
Exterior Wall Framing:	2x4 or 2x6

Foundation Options:

Standard basement
Crawlspace
Slab
(All plans can be built with your choice of foundation and framing. A generic conversion diagram is available. See order form.)

BLUEPRINT PRICE CODE:	A

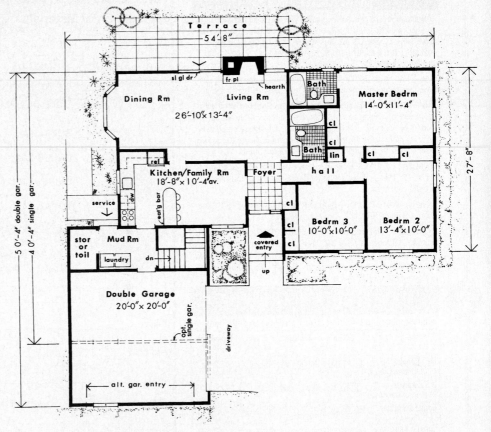

MAIN FLOOR

See this plan on our "Best-Sellers" VideoGraphic Tour! Order form on page 9

IT'S THE GIFT OF A LIFE-TIME.

Making a bequest to the American Heart Association says something special about you. It's a gift of health for future generations — an unselfish act of caring.

Your gift will fund research and educational programs to fight heart attack, stroke, high blood pressure and other cardiovascular diseases. And bring others the joy and freedom of good health.

To learn more about how you can leave a legacy for the future, call 1-800-AHA-USA1. Do it today.

American Heart Association℠
Fighting Heart Disease and Stroke

Remember that warm glow your family shared by the campfire?

Unexpected Amenities

- Surprising interior amenities are found within the casual exterior of this good-looking design.
- A dramatic fireplace warms the comfortable formal areas. The living and dining rooms share a 20-ft. cathedral ceiling and high windows that flank the fireplace. Sliding glass doors access the outdoors.

- The efficient walk-through kitchen provides plenty of counter space, in addition to a windowed sink and a pass-through to the living areas.
- A large bedroom, a full bath and an oversized utility room complete the main floor. The utility room offers space for a washer and dryer, plus a sink and an extra freezer.
- Upstairs, the spacious and secluded master suite boasts a walk-in closet, a private bath and lots of storage space. A railed loft area overlooks the living and dining rooms.

Plan I-1249-A

Bedrooms: 2	**Baths:** 2

Living Area:	
Upper floor	297 sq. ft.
Main floor	952 sq. ft.
Total Living Area:	**1,249 sq. ft.**
Standard basement	952 sq. ft.
Exterior Wall Framing:	2x6

Foundation Options:
Standard basement
Crawlspace
(All plans can be built with your choice of foundation and framing. A generic conversion diagram is available. See order form.)

BLUEPRINT PRICE CODE: **A**

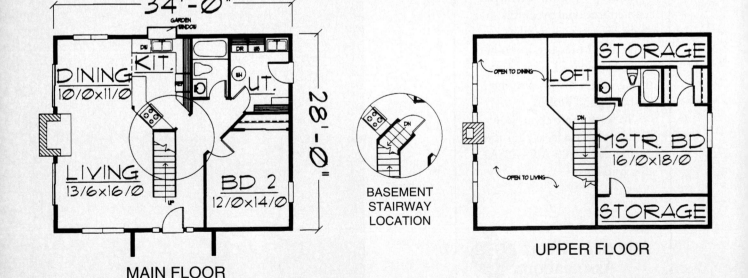

MAIN FLOOR

BASEMENT STAIRWAY LOCATION

UPPER FLOOR

Plan I-1249-A

PRICES AND DETAILS
ON PAGES 12-15

Need to Make Plan Changes?

Y ou've purchased your dream home plans, but the bids coming back from local builders are giving you sticker shock . . .

Your family has narrowed down the choices in your search for the perfect dream home plan to build, but there are a few things you wish were different about the plans . . .

Sound familiar? You're not alone. Most home plans buyers love their design, but need to make some changes, whether to add or delete square footage, make regional changes to satisfy code requirements or just rearrange rooms to better meet their family's lifestyle needs.

The good news is that any plan can be modified to your exact requirements. Your family doesn't have to settle for "close." To modify a plan, you need to purchase a reproducible plan set from HomeStyles, which allows changes to be made from the original.

Once you have a reproducible copy of your dream home plan, you can have the plans modified at an additional cost either locally by a design professional or nationally by a company like **LifeStyle HomeDesign Services** of St. Paul, Minnesota. LifeStyle offers quick, cost-effective modifications to any plan, many of which are drawn on a computer and can be changed easily.

Make your dream home perfect. Call LifeStyle toll-free at **1-888-2MODIFY** for a free, no-obligation quote for the cost, and expected delivery time for modifications.

Want the power of a nationally recognized home design and modification company working for you? Get to know **LifeStyle**.

Bring it home to the family room.

There's something about a warm glowing campfire that draws everyone together. And now thanks to Heat-N-Glo's new gas fireplace Model 6000 XLS, a realistic campfire can come to life at a moment's notice right in the comfort of your home. In fact, the flames created by the 6000 XLS are so real they've earned a patent.

It's also nice to know that the warm glow provided by the 6000 XLS is more than a visual delight because this fireplace is rated as a furnace. Our heating models burn at over 75% efficiency. And with our direct vent technology, you can place it practically anywhere because there's no need for a chimney.

Heat-N-Glo's 6000 XLS uses outside air for combustion and the sealed burning chamber means the air you breath stays clean. No drafts, just warmth.

 Before you buy a gas fireplace, gas insert, gas stove or log set... **See and feel the Glo of our new CampFyre products.**

Call 1-800-669-4328 for a free Heat-N-Glo brochure, because nothing draws a family together like warmth.

QUALITY FIREPLACE PRODUCTS SINCE 1975

No One Builds A Better Fire.

E-mail us at: hng@winternet.com
Visit our Web site at: http:/www.winternet.com/~hng

Covered Porch Invites Visitors

- This nice home welcomes visitors with its covered front porch and its wide-open living areas.
- Detailed columns, railings and shutters decorate the front porch that guides guests to the central entry.
- Just off the entry, the bright living room merges with the dining room. The side wall is lined with glass, including a glass door that opens to the yard.
- The angled kitchen features a serving counter facing the dining room. A handy laundry closet and access to a storage area and the garage are nearby.
- An angled hall leads to the bedroom wing. The master suite offers a private bath, a walk-in closet and a dressing area with a vanity. Two additional bedrooms and another full bath are located down the hall.

Plan E-1217

Bedrooms: 3	Baths: 2
Living Area:	
Main floor	1,266 sq. ft.
Total Living Area:	**1,266 sq. ft.**
Garage and storage	550 sq. ft.
Exterior Wall Framing:	2x6

Foundation Options:
Crawlspace
Slab
(All plans can be built with your choice of foundation and framing. A generic conversion diagram is available. See order form.)

BLUEPRINT PRICE CODE:	A

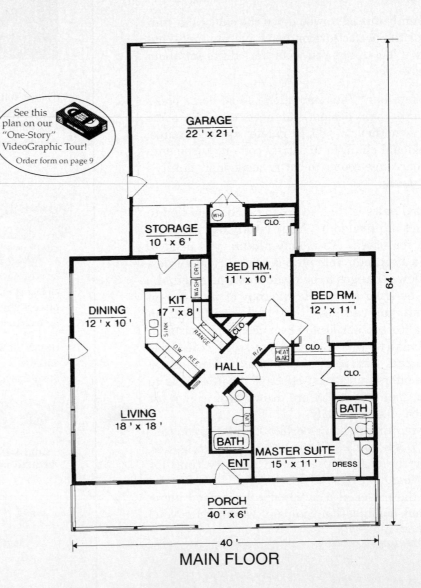

See this plan on our "One-Story" VideoGraphic Tour! Order form on page 9

MAIN FLOOR

Plan E-1217

A Chalet for Today

- With its wraparound deck and soaring windows, this chalet-style home is ideal for recreational living and scenic sites.
- The living and dining rooms are combined to take advantage of the dramatic 23-ft. cathedral ceiling, the rugged stone fireplace and the view through the spectacular windows.
- A quaint balcony above adds to the warm country feeling of the living area, which extends to the expansive deck.

- The open kitchen features a bright corner sink and a nifty breakfast bar that adjoins the living area.
- The handy main-floor laundry area is close to two bedrooms and a full bath.
- A 17-ft. sloped ceiling crowns the quiet study, which is a feature rarely found in a home of this size and style.
- The master suite and a storage area encompass the upper floor. A 13-ft., 8-in. cathedral ceiling, a whirlpool bath and sweeping views from the balcony give this space an elegant feel.
- The basement option includes a tuck-under garage, additional storage space and a separate utility area.

Plan AHP-9340

Bedrooms: 3+	Baths: 2
Living Area:	
Upper floor	332 sq. ft.
Main floor	974 sq. ft.
Total Living Area:	**1,306 sq. ft.**
Basement	624 sq. ft.
Tuck-under garage	350 sq. ft.
Exterior Wall Framing:	2x4 or 2x6

Foundation Options:

Standard basement
Daylight basement
Crawlspace
Slab

(All plans can be built with your choice of foundation and framing. A generic conversion diagram is available. See order form.)

BLUEPRINT PRICE CODE: **A**

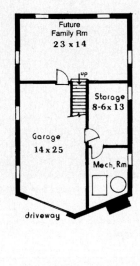

BASEMENT

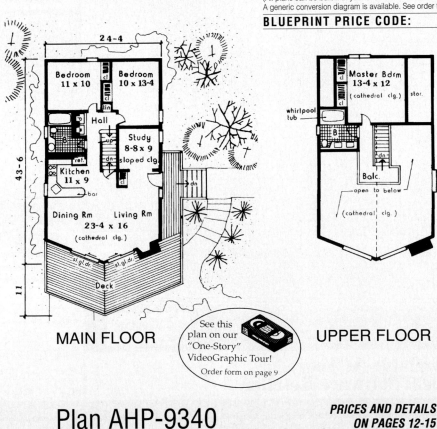

MAIN FLOOR

See this plan on our "One-Story" VideoGraphic Tour!
Order form on page 9

UPPER FLOOR

Plan AHP-9340

PRICES AND DETAILS ON PAGES 12-15

Unique, Dramatic Floor Plan

- An expansive and impressive Great Room, warmed by a wood stove, features an island kitchen that's completely open in design.
- A passive solar sun room is designed to collect and store heat from the sun, while also providing a good view of the surroundings.
- Upstairs, you'll see a glamorous master suite with a private bath and a huge walk-in closet.
- The daylight basement adds a sunny sitting room, a third bedroom and a large recreation room.

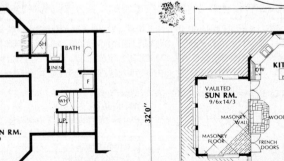

UPPER FLOOR

See this plan on our "Two-Story" VideoGraphic Tour!
Order form on page 9

Plans P-536-2A & -2D

Bedrooms: 2-3	Baths: 2-3
Space:	
Upper floor:	642 sq. ft.
Main floor:	863 sq. ft.
Total living area:	**1,505 sq. ft.**
Basement:	863 sq. ft.
Garage:	445 sq. ft.
Exterior Wall Framing:	2x4

Foundation options:	Plan #
Daylight basement	P-536-2D
Crawlspace	P-536-2A

(Foundation & framing conversion diagram available — see order form.)

Blueprint Price Code:	
Plan P-536-2A	B
Plan P-536-2D	C

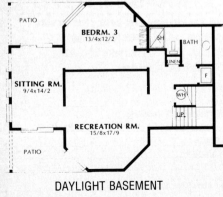

DAYLIGHT BASEMENT

MAIN FLOOR

Rustic Comfort

- Rustic charm highlights the exterior of this design, while the interior is filled with all the latest comforts.
- The wide, covered porch opens to a roomy entry, where two 7-ft.-high openings with decorative railings view into the dining room.
- Straight ahead lies the sunken living room, which features a 16-ft.-high vaulted ceiling with exposed beams. The fireplace is faced with floor-to-ceiling fieldstone, adding to the rustic look. A rear door opens to a large patio with luscious plant areas.

- The large and functional U-shaped kitchen features a china niche with glass shelves. Other bonuses include the adjacent sewing/hobby room, the oversized utility room and the storage area and built-in workbench in the side-entry garage.
- The secluded master suite hosts a sunken sleeping area with built-in bookshelves. One step up is a cozy sitting area that is defined by brick columns and a railed room divider. Double doors open to the deluxe bath, which offers a niche with glass shelves.
- Across the home, two more bedrooms share a second full bath.

Plan E-1607

Bedrooms: 3	Baths: 2
Living Area:	
Main floor	1,600 sq. ft.
Total Living Area:	**1,600 sq. ft.**
Standard basement	1,600 sq. ft.
Garage	484 sq. ft.
Storage	132 sq. ft.
Exterior Wall Framing:	2x6

Foundation Options:
Standard basement
Crawlspace
Slab
(All plans can be built with your choice of foundation and framing. A generic conversion diagram is available. See order form.)

BLUEPRINT PRICE CODE:	B

See this plan on our "Country & Traditional" Video Tour! Order form on page 9

MAIN FLOOR

Plan E-1607

PRICES AND DETAILS **ON PAGES 12-15**

Masterful Master Suite

- This gorgeous home features front and rear covered porches and a master suite so luxurious it deserves its own wing.
- The expansive entry welcomes visitors into a spacious, skylighted living room, which boasts a handsome fireplace. The adjacent formal dining room overlooks the front porch.
- Designed for efficiency, the kitchen features an angled snack bar, a bayed eating area and views of the porch. An all-purpose utility room is conveniently located off the kitchen.
- The kitchen, eating area, living room and dining room are all heightened by 12-ft. ceilings.
- The sumptuous and secluded master suite features a tub and a separate shower, a double-sink vanity, a walk-in closet with built-in shelves and a compartmentalized toilet.
- The two secondary bedrooms share a hall bath at the other end of the home. The rear bedroom offers porch access.
- The garage features built-in storage and access to unfinished attic space.

Plan E-1811

Bedrooms: 3	Baths: 2
Living Area:	
Main floor	1,800 sq. ft.
Total Living Area:	**1,800 sq. ft.**
Garage and storage	634 sq. ft.
Exterior Wall Framing:	2x6

Foundation Options:

Crawlspace

Slab

(All plans can be built with your choice of foundation and framing. A generic conversion diagram is available. See order form.)

BLUEPRINT PRICE CODE:	B

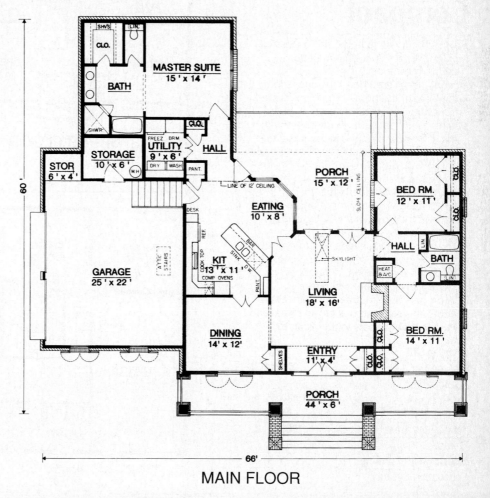

MAIN FLOOR

Photo courtesy of Breland & Farmer Designers, Inc.

Stylish and Compact

- This country-style home has a classic exterior and a space-saving and compact interior.
- A quaint covered porch extends along the front of the home. The oval-glassed front door opens to the entry, which leads to the spacious living room with a handsome fireplace, windows at either end and access to a big screened porch.
- The formal dining room flows from the living room and is easily served by the convenient U-shaped kitchen.
- A nice-sized laundry room and a full bath are nearby. The two-car garage offers a super storage area.
- The deluxe master suite features a huge walk-in closet. A separate dressing area leads to an adjoining, dual-access bath.
- The upper floor offers two more bedrooms and another full bath. Each bedroom has generous closet space and independent access to attic space.

Plan E-1626

Bedrooms: 3	Baths: 2
Living Area:	
Upper floor	464 sq. ft.
Main floor	1,136 sq. ft.
Total Living Area:	**1,600 sq. ft.**
Garage	462 sq. ft.
Exterior Wall Framing:	2x6

Foundation Options:

Crawlspace
Slab

(All plans can be built with your choice of foundation and framing. A generic conversion diagram is available. See order form.)

BLUEPRINT PRICE CODE:	**B**

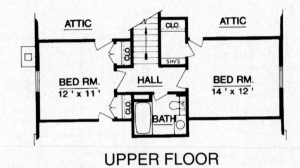

UPPER FLOOR

**NOTE:
The above photographed home may have been modified by the homeowner. Please refer to floor plan and/or drawn elevation shown for actual blueprint details.

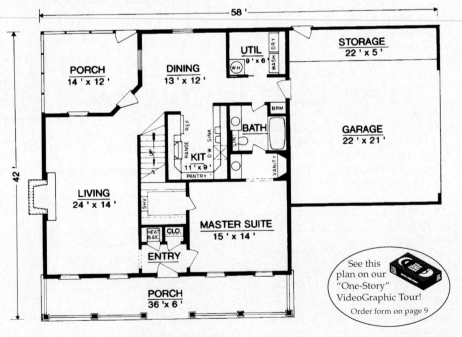

MAIN FLOOR

See this plan on our "One-Story" VideoGraphic Tour!
Order form on page 9

Panoramic Prow View

- This glass-filled prow gable design is almost as spectacular as the panoramic view from inside.
- French doors open from the front deck to the dining room. A stunning window wall illuminates the adjoining living room, which flaunts a 20-ft.-high cathedral ceiling.

- The open, corner kitchen is perfectly angled to service the dining room and the family room, while offering views of the front and rear decks.
- A handy utility/laundry room opens to the rear deck. Two bedrooms share a full bath, to complete the main floor.
- A dramatic, open-railed stairway leads up to the secluded master bedroom, which boasts a dressing room and a private bath with a dual-sink vanity and a separate tub and shower.

Plan NW-196	
Bedrooms: 3	**Baths:** 2
Living Area:	
Upper floor	394 sq. ft.
Main floor	1,317 sq. ft.
Total Living Area:	**1,711 sq. ft.**
Exterior Wall Framing:	2x6
Foundation Options:	

Crawlspace
(All plans can be built with your choice of foundation and framing. A generic conversion diagram is available. See order form.)

BLUEPRINT PRICE CODE:	B

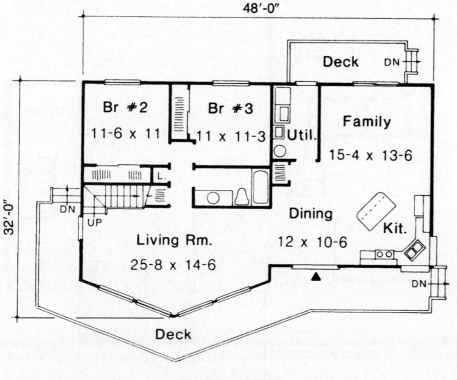

MAIN FLOOR

UPPER FLOOR

Free-Flowing Floor Plan

- A fluid floor plan with open indoor/outdoor living spaces characterizes this exciting luxury home.
- The stylish columned porch opens to a spacious living room and dining room expanse that overlooks the outdoor spaces. The breathtaking view also includes a dramatic corner fireplace.
- The dining area opens to a bright kitchen with an angled eating bar. The overall spaciousness of the living areas is increased with high 12-ft. ceilings.
- A sunny, informal eating area adjoins the kitchen, and an angled set of doors opens to a convenient main-floor laundry room near the garage entrance.
- The vaulted master bedroom has a walk-in closet and a sumptuous bath with an oval tub.
- A separate wing houses two additional bedrooms and another full bath.
- Attic space is accessible from stairs in the garage and in the bedroom wing.

REAR VIEW

Plan E-1710

Bedrooms: 3	Baths: 2
Living Area:	
Main floor	1,792 sq. ft.
Total Living Area:	**1,792 sq. ft.**
Standard basement	1,792 sq. ft.
Garage	484 sq. ft.
Storage	96 sq. ft.
Exterior Wall Framing:	2x6

Foundation Options:

Standard basement
Crawlspace
Slab
(All plans can be built with your choice of foundation and framing. A generic conversion diagram is available. See order form.)

BLUEPRINT PRICE CODE:	**B**

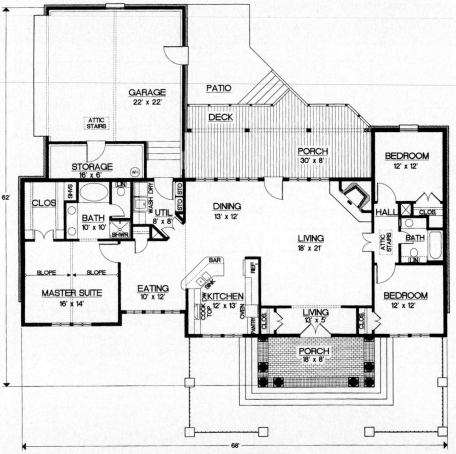

MAIN FLOOR

Plan E-1710

Outstanding One-Story

- This sharp one-story home has an outstanding floor plan, attractively enhanced by a stately brick facade.
- A vestibule introduces the foyer, which flows between the formal living spaces at the front of the home.
- The large living room features a 14-ft., 8-in. sloped ceiling and dramatic, high windows. The spacious dining room has easy access to the kitchen.

- The expansive family room is the focal point of the home, with a 16-ft. beamed cathedral ceiling, a slate-hearth fireplace and sliding glass doors to a backyard terrace.
- The adjoining kitchen has a snack bar and a sunny dinette framed by a curved window wall that overlooks the terrace.
- Included in the sleeping wing is a luxurious master suite with a private bath. A skylighted dressing room and a big walk-in closet are also featured.
- The two secondary bedrooms share a hall bath that has a dual-sink vanity. A half-bath is near the mud/laundry room.

Plan K-278-M	
Bedrooms: 3	**Baths:** 2½
Living Area:	
Main floor	1,803 sq. ft.
Total Living Area:	**1,803 sq. ft.**
Standard basement	1,778 sq. ft.
Garage and storage	586 sq. ft.
Exterior Wall Framing:	2x4 or 2x6
Foundation Options:	
Standard basement	
Slab	

(All plans can be built with your choice of foundation and framing. A generic conversion diagram is available. See order form.)

BLUEPRINT PRICE CODE: B

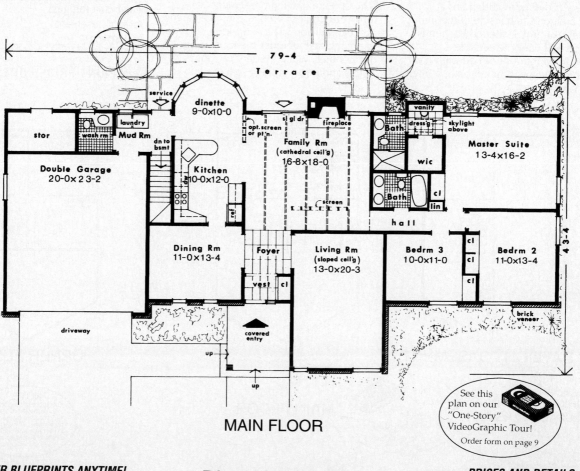

MAIN FLOOR

See this plan on our "One-Story" VideoGraphic Tour! Order form on page 9

Photo by Bob Hallinen

Soaring Design

- Dramatic windows soar to the peak of this prowed chalet, offering unlimited views of outdoor scenery.
- The spacious living room flaunts a fabulous fireplace, a soaring 26-ft. vaulted ceiling, a striking window wall and sliding glass doors to a wonderful wraparound deck.
- An oversized window brightens a dining area on the left side of the living room. The sunny, L-shaped kitchen is spacious and easily accessible.
- The secluded main-floor bedroom has convenient access to a full bath, a linen closet, a good-sized laundry room and the rear entrance.
- A central, open-railed staircase leads to the upper floor, which contains two more bedrooms and a full bath.
- A skylighted balcony is the high point of this design, offering a railed overlook into the living room below and sweeping outdoor vistas through the wall of windows.
- The optional daylight basement provides another fireplace in a versatile recreation room. The extra-long, tuck-under garage includes plenty of room for hobbies, while the service room offers additional storage space.

Plans H-930-1 & -1A

Bedrooms: 3	Baths: 2
Living Area:	
Upper floor	710 sq. ft.
Main floor	1,210 sq. ft.
Daylight basement	605 sq. ft.
Total Living Area:	**1,920/2,525 sq. ft.**
Tuck-under garage/shop	605 sq. ft.
Exterior Wall Framing:	2x6
Foundation Options:	**Plan #**
Daylight basement	H-930-1
Crawlspace	H-930-1A

(All plans can be built with your choice of foundation and framing. A generic conversion diagram is available. See order form.)

BLUEPRINT PRICE CODE:	**B/D**

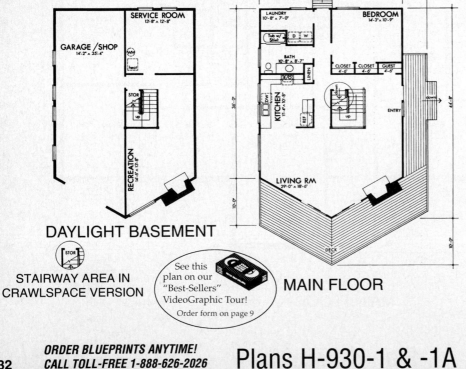

DAYLIGHT BASEMENT

STAIRWAY AREA IN CRAWLSPACE VERSION

See this plan on our "Best-Sellers" VideoGraphic Tour! Order form on page 9

MAIN FLOOR

UPPER FLOOR

NOTE: The above photographed home may have been modified by the homeowner. Please refer to floor plan and/or drawn elevation shown for actual blueprint details.

Plans H-930-1 & -1A

PRICES AND DETAILS ON PAGES 12-15

Open, Flowing Floor Plan

- Open, flowing rooms punctuated with wonderful windows enhance this spacious four-bedroom home.
- The two-story-high foyer is brightened by an arched window above. To the left lies the living room, which flows into the family room. An inviting fireplace and windows overlooking a rear terrace highlight the family room.
- The centrally located kitchen serves both the formal dining room and the dinette, with a view of the family room beyond. Sliding glass doors in the dinette open to a lovely terrace.
- Upstairs, the master suite features an arched window and a walk-in closet with a dressing area. The private master bath includes a dual-sink vanity, a skylighted whirlpool tub and a separate shower.
- The three remaining bedrooms share another skylighted bath.

Plan AHP-9020

Bedrooms: 4	Baths: 2½
Living Area:	
Upper floor	1,021 sq. ft.
Main floor	1,125 sq. ft.
Total Living Area:	**2,146 sq. ft.**
Standard basement	1,032 sq. ft.
Garage	480 sq. ft.
Exterior Wall Framing:	2x6

Foundation Options:

Standard basement
Crawlspace
Slab

(All plans can be built with your choice of foundation and framing. A generic conversion diagram is available. See order form.)

BLUEPRINT PRICE CODE: C

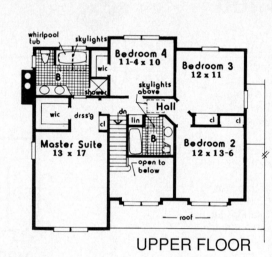

See this plan on our "Two-Story" VideoGraphic Tour!
Order form on page 9

UPPER FLOOR

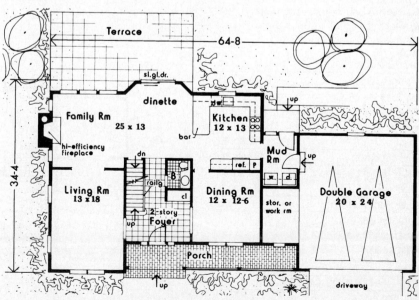

MAIN FLOOR

Old-Fashioned Charm

- A trio of dormers add old-fashioned charm to this modern design.
- Both the living room and the dining room offer 12-ft.-high vaulted ceilings and flow together to create a sense of even more spaciousness.
- The open kitchen/nook/family room features a sunny alcove, a walk-in pantry and a woodstove.
- A first-floor den and a walk-through utility room are other big bonuses.
- Upstairs, the master suite includes an enormous walk-in closet and a deluxe bath with a refreshing spa tub and a separate shower and water closet.
- Two more bedrooms, each with a window seat, and a bonus room complete this stylish design.

See this plan on our "Country & Traditional" Video Tour!

Order form on page 9

NOTE:
The above photographed home may have been modified by the homeowner. Please refer to floor plan and/or drawn elevation shown for actual blueprint details.

Plan CDG-2004

Bedrooms: 3+	Baths: 2½
Living Area:	
Upper floor	928 sq. ft.
Main floor	1,317 sq. ft.
Bonus area	192 sq. ft.
Total Living Area:	**2,437 sq. ft.**
Partial daylight basement	780 sq. ft.
Garage	537 sq. ft.
Exterior Wall Framing:	2x6

Foundation Options:

Partial daylight basement
Crawlspace

(All plans can be built with your choice of foundation and framing. A generic conversion diagram is available. See order form.)

BLUEPRINT PRICE CODE: C

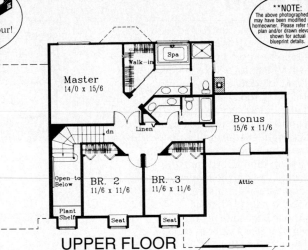

UPPER FLOOR

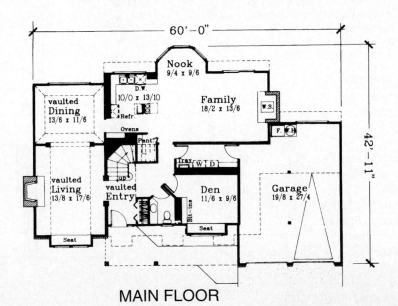

MAIN FLOOR

Plan E-2004

Bedrooms: 3	Baths: 2

Space:

Total living area:	2,023 sq. ft.
Garage:.	484 sq. ft.
Storage & Porches:	423 sq. ft.

Exterior Wall Framing: 2x6

Foundation options:
Crawlspace.
Slab.
(Foundation & framing conversion diagram available — see order form.)

Blueprint Price Code: C

Exciting Floor Plan In Traditional French Garden Home

- Creative, angular design permits an open floor plan.
- Living and dining rooms open to a huge covered porch.
- Kitchen, living and dining rooms feature impressive 12' ceilings accented by extensive use of glass.
- Informal eating nook faces a delightful courtyard.
- Luxurious master bath offers a whirlpool tub, shower, and walk-in closet.
- Secondary bedrooms also offer walk-in closets.

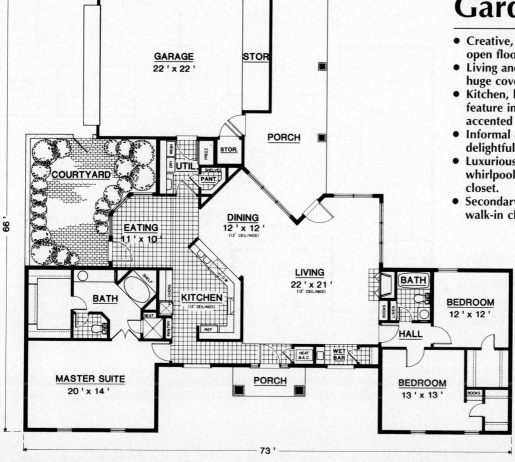

**NOTE:
The above photographed home may have been modified by the homeowner. Please refer to floor plan and/or drawn elevation shown for actual blueprint details.

See this plan on our "One-Story" VideoGraphic Tour!
Order form on page 9

High Luxury in One Story

- Beautiful arched windows lend a luxurious feeling to the exterior of this one-story home.
- Twelve-foot-high ceilings add volume to both the wide entry area and the central living room, which boasts a large fireplace and access to a covered porch and the patio beyond.
- Double doors separate the formal dining room from the corridor-style kitchen. Features of the kitchen include a pantry, a trash compactor, garage access and an angled eating bar with double sinks and a dishwasher. The sunny, bayed eating area is perfect for casual family meals.
- The plush master suite has amazing amenities: patio access, a walk-in closet, a skylighted, angled whirlpool tub, a separate shower, and private access to the laundry/utility room.
- Three bedrooms and a full bath are situated on the opposite side of the home.

Plan E-2302

Bedrooms: 4	Baths: 2
Living Area:	
Main floor	2,396 sq. ft.
Total Living Area:	**2,396 sq. ft.**
Standard basement	2,396 sq. ft.
Garage	484 sq. ft.
Exterior Wall Framing:	2x6

Foundation Options:
Standard basement
Crawlspace
Slab
(Typical foundation & framing conversion diagram available—see order form.)

BLUEPRINT PRICE CODE:	C

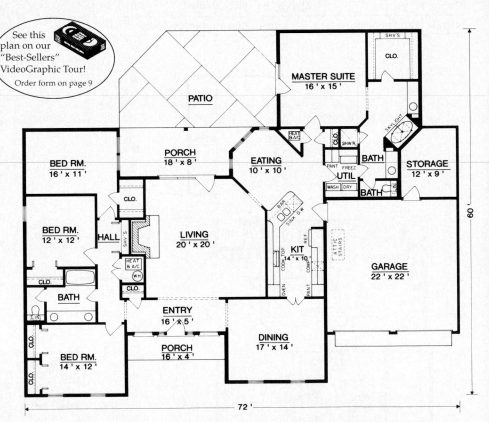

See this plan on our "Best-Sellers" VideoGraphic Tour!
Order form on page 9

MAIN FLOOR

Innovative Floor Plan

- The wide, covered front porch, arched windows and symmetrical lines of this traditional home conceal the modern, innovative floor plan found within.
- A two-story-high foyer guides guests to the front-oriented formal areas, which have views to the front porch.
- The hotspot of the home is the Great Room, with one of the home's three fireplaces and a media wall. Flanking doors open to a large backyard deck.
- The island kitchen and glassed-in eating nook overlook the deck and access a handy mudroom. High 9-ft. ceilings add to the aura of warmth and hospitality found on the main floor of this home.
- Another of the fireplaces is offered in the master suite. This private oasis also boasts a 13-ft.-high cathedral ceiling and a delicious bath with a garden tub.
- Upstairs, one bedroom has a sloped ceiling and a private bath. Three more bedrooms share another full bath.

Plan AHP-9360

Bedrooms: 5	Baths: 3½
Living Area:	
Upper floor	970 sq. ft.
Main floor	1,735 sq. ft.
Total Living Area:	**2,705 sq. ft.**
Standard basement	1,550 sq. ft.
Garage and utility area	443 sq. ft.
Exterior Wall Framing:	2x6

Foundation Options:
Standard basement
Crawlspace
Slab
(All plans can be built with your choice of foundation and framing. A generic conversion diagram is available. See order form.)

BLUEPRINT PRICE CODE:	D

See this plan on our "Country & Traditional" Video Tour! Order form on page 9

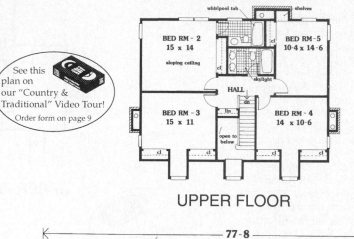

UPPER FLOOR

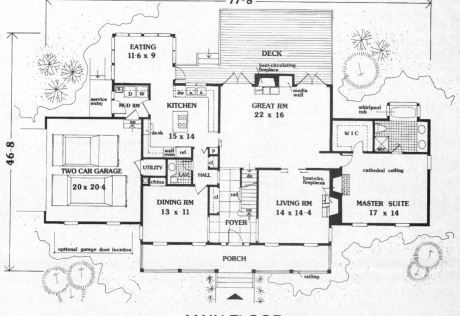

MAIN FLOOR

You Asked for It!

- Our most popular plan in recent years, E-3000, has now been downsized for affordability, without sacrificing character or excitement.
- Exterior appeal is created with a covered front porch with decorative columns, triple dormers and rail-topped bay windows.
- The floor plan has combined the separate living and family rooms available in E-3000 into one spacious family room with corner fireplace, which flows into the dining room through a columned gallery.
- The kitchen serves the breakfast room over an angled snack bar, and features a huge pantry.
- The stunning main-floor master suite offers a private sitting area, a walk-in closet and a dramatic, angled bath.
- There are two large bedrooms upstairs accessible via a curved staircase with bridge balcony.

Plan E-2307

Bedrooms: 3	Baths: 2½
Living Area:	
Upper floor	595 sq. ft.
Main floor	1,765 sq. ft.
Total Living Area:	**2,360 sq. ft.**
Standard basement	1,765 sq. ft.
Garage	484 sq. ft.
Storage	44 sq. ft.
Exterior Wall Framing:	2x6

Foundation Options:

Standard basement
Crawlspace
Slab

(All plans can be built with your choice of foundation and framing. A generic conversion diagram is available. See order form.)

BLUEPRINT PRICE CODE:	C

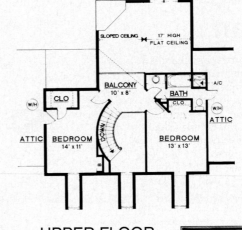

See this plan on our "Best-Sellers" VideoGraphic Tour!
Order form on page 9

UPPER FLOOR

MAIN FLOOR

Spectacular Design

- The spectacular brick facade of this home conceals a stylish floor plan. Endless transoms crown the windows that wrap around the rear of the home, flooding the interior with natural light.
- The foyer opens to a huge Grand Room with a 14-ft. ceiling. French doors access a delightful covered porch.
- A three-sided fireplace warms the three casual rooms, which share a high 12-ft. ceiling. The Gathering Room is surrounded by tall windows; the Good Morning Room features porch access; and the island kitchen offers a double oven, a pantry and a snack bar.
- Guests will dine in style in the formal dining room, with its 13-ft. tray ceiling and trio of tall, arched windows.
- Curl up with a good book in the quiet library, which has an airy 10-ft. ceiling.
- A 12-ft. ceiling enhances the fantastic master suite, which is wrapped in windows. The superb master bath boasts a step-up garden tub, a separate shower, two vanities, a makeup table and a bidet.
- Two sleeping suites on the other side of the home have 10-ft. ceilings and share a unique bath with private vanities.

Plan EOF-8

Bedrooms: 3+	Baths: 3½
Living Area:	
Main floor	3,392 sq. ft.
Total Living Area:	**3,392 sq. ft.**
Garage	871 sq. ft.
Exterior Wall Framing:	2x6

Foundation Options:

Slab

(All plans can be built with your choice of foundation and framing. A generic conversion diagram is available. See order form.)

BLUEPRINT PRICE CODE:	E

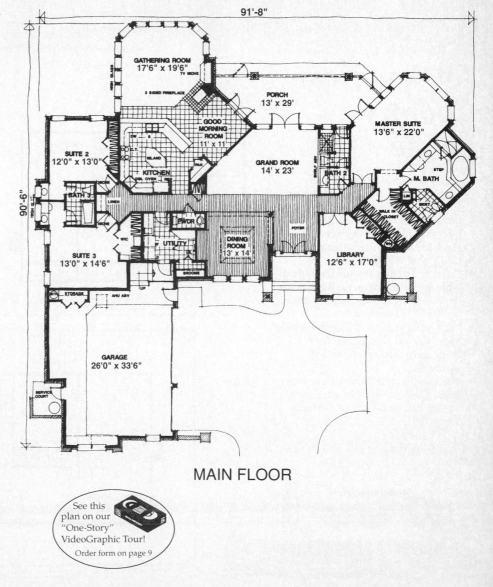

MAIN FLOOR

See this plan on our "One-Story" VideoGraphic Tour!
Order form on page 9

All-American Country Home

- Romantic, old-fashioned and spacious living areas combine to create this modern home.
- Off the entryway is the generous living room with fireplace and French doors which open onto the traditional rear porch.
- Country kitchen features an island table for informal occasions, while the adjoining family room is ideal for family gatherings.
- Practically placed, a laundry/mud room lies off the garage for immediate disposal of soiled garments.
- This plan is available with garage (H-3711-1) or without garage (H-3711-2) and with or without basement.

PLANS H-3711-2 & H-3711-2A
(WITHOUT GARAGE)

**NOTE:
The above photographed home may have been modified by the homeowner. Please refer to floor plan and/or drawn elevation shown for actual blueprint details.

PLANS H-3711-1 & H-3711-1A
(WITH GARAGE)

UPPER FLOOR

WALK-IN CLOSET 7'-6" x 7'-6"
BATH
BATH
BEDROOM 13'-3" x 11'-0"
LINEN 6'-0"
STOR.
CLOSET 4'-9"
CLOSET 4'-9"
UP TO ATTIC
up   down
CLOSET 4'-9"
BEDROOM 13'-0" x 19'-0"
BEDROOM 15'-0" x 10'-0"
BEDROOM 10'-0" x 13'-3"

MAIN FLOOR

74'-0"
FRENCH DRS.
DINING 11'-9" x 13'-3"
DW
LAUNDRY 13'-0" x 7'-6"
STORAGE 15'-8" x 13'-6"
PANTRY
ISLAND
COUNTRY KITCHEN 15'-0" x 27'-0"
REF.
WH
down
GARAGE 23'-6" x 21'-6"
44'-0"
LIVING ROOM 13'-0" x 27'-0"
up   down
ENTRY
CLOS. 3'-0"
LAV.
FAMILY ROOM
8' WIDE COVERED PORCH

Plans H-3711-1/1A & -2/2A

Bedrooms: 4	Baths: 2½

Space:

Upper floor:	1,176 sq. ft.
Main floor:	1,288 sq. ft.

Total living area:	2,464 sq. ft.
Basement:	approx. 1,288 sq. ft.
Garage:	505 sq. ft.

Exterior Wall Framing:	2x6

Foundation options:
Standard basement (Plans H-3711-1 & -2).
Crawlspace (Plans H-3711-1A & -2A).
(Foundation & framing conversion diagram available — see order form.)

Blueprint Price Code:	C

See this plan on our "Best-Sellers" VideoGraphic Tour!
Order form on page 9

Plans H-3711-1/1A & -2/2A
PRICES AND DETAILS
ON PAGES 12-15

Shaded Kiss

- Columned porches give this brick and stucco home a shaded kiss of Old World charm and grace. Dormer windows and a soaring roofline complete the facade.
- The magic continues inside, with a massive living room that boasts a cozy fireplace to satisfy your passion for romance. French doors grant passage to a secluded porch.
- Privacy reigns in the isolated master suite, which offers a sitting area and a built-in desk. Double doors introduce the luxurious bath with style. There, you'll find a marvelous oval tub, a separate shower, and a walk-in closet and vanity for each of you.
- Like to entertain? Give your meals that personal touch in the formal dining room! For casual cuisine, try the eating nook at the other end of the kitchen, or gather around the island for munchies.
- Upstairs, a balcony hall lets the kids enjoy the porch before heading to bed. The upper porch is railed for their safety and your peace of mind.

Plan E-2604

Bedrooms: 4	Baths: 2½
Living Area:	
Upper floor	855 sq. ft.
Main floor	1,750 sq. ft.
Total Living Area:	**2,605 sq. ft.**
Standard basement	1,655 sq. ft.
Garage and storage	569 sq. ft.
Exterior Wall Framing:	2x6

Foundation Options:

Standard basement
Crawlspace
Slab

(All plans can be built with your choice of foundation and framing. A generic conversion diagram is available. See order form.)

BLUEPRINT PRICE CODE: D

NOTE: The above photographed home may have been modified by the homeowner. Please refer to floor plan and/or drawn elevation shown for actual blueprint details.

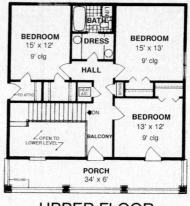

UPPER FLOOR

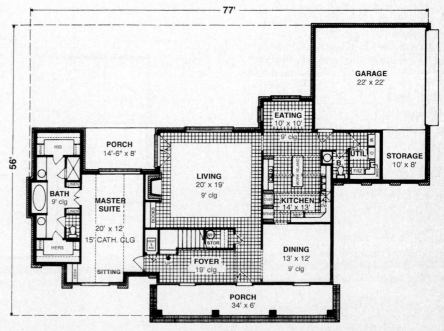

MAIN FLOOR

Photo by Gil Ford

Spacious and Stately

- This popular home design boasts a classic Creole exterior and a symmetrical layout, with 9-ft.-high ceilings on the main floor.
- French doors lead from the formal living and dining rooms to the large family room. The central fireplace is flanked by French doors that open to a covered rear porch and an open-air deck.
- The kitchen is reached easily from the family room, the dining room and the rear entrance. An island cooktop and a window-framed eating area are other features found here.
- The real seller, though, is the main-floor master suite with its spectacular bath. Among its many extras are a built-in vanity, a spa tub and a 16-ft. sloped ceiling with a skylight.
- Three upstairs bedrooms, each with double closets and private bath access, make this the perfect family-sized home.

Plan E-3000

Bedrooms: 4	Baths: 3½
Living Area:	
Upper floor	1,027 sq. ft.
Main floor	2,008 sq. ft.
Total Living Area:	**3,035 sq. ft.**
Standard basement	2,008 sq. ft.
Garage	484 sq. ft.
Storage	96 sq. ft.
Exterior Wall Framing:	2x6

Foundation Options:

Standard basement

Crawlspace

Slab

(All plans can be built with your choice of foundation and framing. A generic conversion diagram is available. See order form.)

BLUEPRINT PRICE CODE:	E

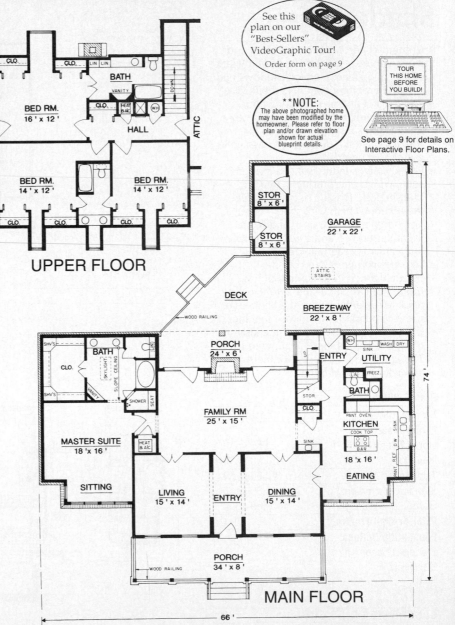

See this plan on our "Best-Sellers" VideoGraphic Tour! Order form on page 9

NOTE: The above photographed home may have been modified by the homeowner. Please refer to floor plan and/or drawn elevation shown for actual blueprint details.

TOUR THIS HOME BEFORE YOU BUILD! See page 9 for details on Interactive Floor Plans.

UPPER FLOOR

MAIN FLOOR

ORDER BLUEPRINTS ANYTIME! CALL TOLL-FREE 1-888-626-2026

Plan E-3000

PRICES AND DETAILS ON PAGES 12-15

Versatile Sun Room

- This cozy country-style home offers an inviting front porch and an interior just as welcoming.
- The spacious living room features a warming fireplace and windows that overlook the porch.
- The living room opens to a dining area, where French doors access a covered porch and a sunny patio.
- The island kitchen has a sink view, plenty of counter space, and a handy pass-through to the adjoining sun room. The bright sun room is large enough to serve as a formal dining room, a family room or a hobby room.
- The private master suite is secluded to the rear. A garden spa tub, dual walk-in closets and separate dressing areas are nice features found in the master bath.

Plan J-90014

Bedrooms: 3	Baths: 2½
Living Area:	
Main floor	2,190 sq. ft.
Total Living Area:	**2,190 sq. ft.**
Standard basement	2,190 sq. ft.
Garage	465 sq. ft.
Storage	34 sq. ft.
Exterior Wall Framing:	2x6

Foundation Options:

Standard basement
Crawlspace
Slab

(All plans can be built with your choice of foundation and framing. A generic conversion diagram is available. See order form.)

BLUEPRINT PRICE CODE: C

MAIN FLOOR

75-6

55-2

MASTER BEDROOM 21-4 x 13-2

PATIO

PORCH 21-0 x 3-10

BEDROOM 11-6 x 14-0

KITCHEN 11-0 x 14-0

DINING 10-0 x 14-0

SUNROOM 11-6 x 17-0

MASTER BATH 10-3 x 9-10

STOR.

UTILITY 11-6 x 5-5

BEDROOM 11-6 x 14-0

LIVING 21-0 x 15-0

GARAGE 21-4 x 20-8

PORCH 39-0 x 6-0

See this plan on our "One-Story" VideoGraphic Tour!
Order form on page 9

Luxurious Interior

- This luxurious home is introduced by an exciting tiled entry with a 17½-ft. vaulted ceiling and a skylight.
- The highlight of the home is the expansive Great Room and dining area, with its fireplace, planter, 17½-ft. vaulted ceiling and bay windows. The fabulous wraparound deck with a step-up hot tub is the perfect complement to this large entertainment space.
- The kitchen features lots of counter space, a large pantry and an adjoining bay-windowed breakfast nook.
- The exquisite master suite flaunts a sunken garden tub, a separate shower, a dual-sink vanity, a walk-in closet and private access to the deck area.
- The game room downstairs is perfect for casual entertaining, with its warm woodstove, oversized wet bar and patio access. Two bedrooms, a full bath and a large utility area are also included.

Plan P-6595-3D

Bedrooms: 3	Baths: 2½
Living Area:	
Main floor	1,530 sq. ft.
Daylight basement	1,145 sq. ft.
Total Living Area:	**2,675 sq. ft.**
Garage	462 sq. ft.
Exterior Wall Framing:	2x6

Foundation Options:

Daylight basement

(All plans can be built with your choice of foundation and framing. A generic conversion diagram is available. See order form.)

BLUEPRINT PRICE CODE:	D

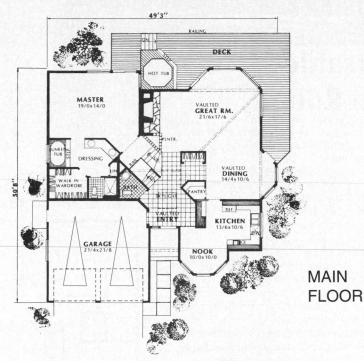

MAIN FLOOR

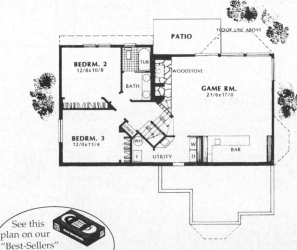

DAYLIGHT BASEMENT

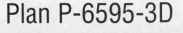

See this plan on our "Best-Sellers" VideoGraphic Tour! Order form on page 9

Floor Plans

GREAT ROOM BELOW

BR
11/6 X 10/6

STR

ATTIC

LIMITED STOR

BALCONY

OPEN TO FOYER

BATH

S

D

DEN
10 X 11/6

BR
10/6 X 11/6

UPPER FLOOR

**NOTE:
The above photographed home may have been modified by the homeowner. Please refer to floor plan and/or drawn elevation shown for actual blueprint details.

HOT TUB

DECK

VAULTED MBR
17/6 X 13/6

VAULTED GREAT ROOM
19 X 15/6 AVG

DINE
12/6 X 12

WI CLO

WI CLO

MB

FOYER

UTIL

W D

KIT
R

GARAGE
23/6 X 23/6

MAIN FLOOR

52'

50'

Vaulted Great Room

- While the exterior has traditional overtones, this plan is thoroughly modern both inside and out.
- The vaulted Great Room with adjacent kitchen and dining room gives the home an open and spacious feeling.
- The vaulted master suite on the first floor includes walk-in closets and a sumptuous master bath.
- The upper floor includes two more bedrooms, which share a continental bath.
- Also note the den and balcony overlooking the foyer and Great Room below.
- A huge deck with a hot tub can be reached easily from the master suite, the Great Room or the dining room.

Plan S-2100

Bedrooms: 3	Baths: 2½
Living Area:	
Upper floor:	660 sq. ft.
Main floor	1,440 sq. ft.
Total Living Area:	**2,100 sq. ft.**
Standard basement	1,440 sq. ft.
Garage	552 sq. ft.
Exterior Wall Framing:	2x6

Foundation Options:
Standard basement
Crawlspace
Slab
(Typical foundation & framing conversion diagram available—see order form.)

BLUEPRINT PRICE CODE: C

See this plan on our "Two-Story" VideoGraphic Tour!
Order form on page 9

Vaulted Ceilings Expand Interior

- A dignified exterior and a gracious, spacious interior combine to make this an outstanding plan for today's families.
- A step down from the vaulted entry, the living room offers a 12-ft.-high vaulted ceiling brightened by an arch-top boxed window and a nice fireplace.
- The vaulted dining room ceiling rises to more than 15 ft., and sliding glass doors open to a unique central atrium.
- The island kitchen shares a snack bar with the bayed nook and provides easy service to the dining room.
- The spacious family room boasts a sloped ceiling that peaks at 18 ft. and a woodstove that warms the entire area.
- The master suite is first-class all the way, with a spacious sleeping room and an opulent bath, which features a walk-in closet, a sunken garden tub, a separate shower and a skylighted dressing area with a dual-sink vanity.
- Two secondary bedrooms have window seats and share another full bath.

Plans P-7697-4A & -4D

Bedrooms: 3	Baths: 2

Living Area:

Main floor (crawlspace version)	2,003 sq. ft.
Main floor (basement version)	2,030 sq. ft.
Total Living Area:	**2,003/2,030 sq. ft.**
Daylight basement	2,015 sq. ft.
Garage	647 sq. ft.
Exterior Wall Framing:	**2x6**

Foundation Options:	**Plan #**
Daylight basement	P-7697-4D
Crawlspace	P-7697-4A

(All plans can be built with your choice of foundation and framing. A generic conversion diagram is available. See order form.)

BLUEPRINT PRICE CODE: C

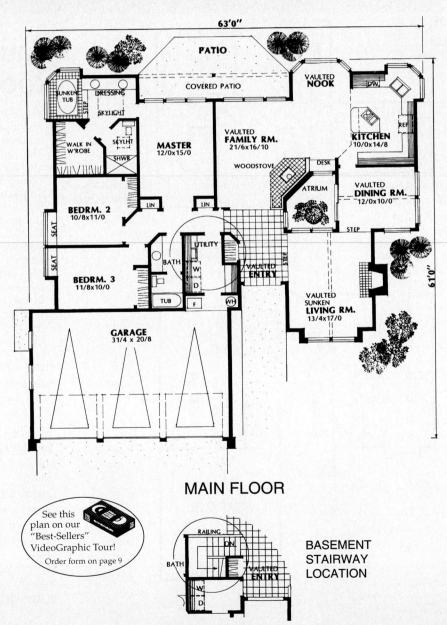

MAIN FLOOR

See this plan on our "Best-Sellers" VideoGraphic Tour! Order form on page 9

BASEMENT STAIRWAY LOCATION

Plans P-7697-4A & -4D

PRICES AND DETAILS ON PAGES 12-15

Dynamic Design

- Angled walls, vaulted ceilings and lots of glass set the tempo for this dynamic home.
- The covered front entry opens to a raised foyer and a beautiful staircase with a bayed landing.
- One step down, a spectacular see-through fireplace with a raised hearth and built-in wood storage is visible from both the bayed dining room and the stunning Great Room.
- The Great Room also showcases an 18-ft.-high vaulted ceiling, wraparound windows and access to a deck or patio.
- The adjoining nook has a door to the deck and is served by the kitchen's snack bar. The kitchen is enhanced by a 9-ft. ceiling, corner windows and a pass-through to the dining room.
- Upstairs, the master suite offers a 10-ft.-high coved ceiling, a splendid bath, a large walk-in closet and a private deck.

Plan S-41587

Bedrooms: 3+	**Baths:** 3

Living Area:	
Upper floor	1,001 sq. ft.
Main floor	1,550 sq. ft.
Total Living Area:	**2,551 sq. ft.**
Basement	1,550 sq. ft.
Garage (three-car)	773 sq. ft.
Exterior Wall Framing:	2x6

Foundation Options:
Daylight basement
Standard basement
Crawlspace
Slab
(All plans can be built with your choice of foundation and framing. A generic conversion diagram is available. See order form.)

BLUEPRINT PRICE CODE: D

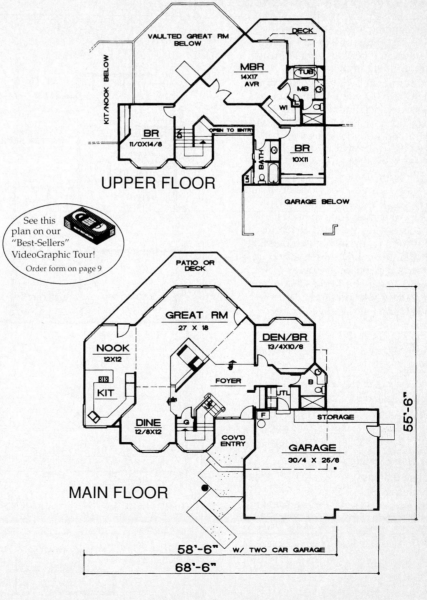

See this plan on our "Best-Sellers" VideoGraphic Tour!
Order form on page 9

Full of Surprises

- While dignified and reserved on the outside, this plan presents intriguing angles, vaulted ceilings and surprising spaces throughout the interior.
- The elegant, vaulted living room flows from the expansive foyer and includes a striking fireplace and a beautiful bay.
- The spacious island kitchen offers wide corner windows above the sink and easy service to both the vaulted dining room and the skylighted nook.
- The adjoining vaulted family room features a warm corner woodstove and sliding doors to the backyard patio.
- The superb master suite includes a vaulted sleeping area and an exquisite private bath with a skylighted dressing area, a large walk-in closet, a step-up spa tub and a separate shower.
- Three secondary bedrooms are located near another full bath and a large laundry room with garage access.

Plans P-7711-3A & -3D

Bedrooms: 4	Baths: 2
Living Area:	
Main floor (crawlspace version)	2,510 sq. ft.
Main floor (basement version)	2,580 sq. ft.
Total Living Area:	**2,510/2,580 sq. ft.**
Daylight basement	2,635 sq. ft.
Garage	806 sq. ft.
Exterior Wall Framing:	**2x6**
Foundation Options:	**Plan #**
Daylight basement	P-7711-3D
Crawlspace	P-7711-3A

(All plans can be built with your choice of foundation and framing. A generic conversion diagram is available. See order form.)

BLUEPRINT PRICE CODE:	**D**

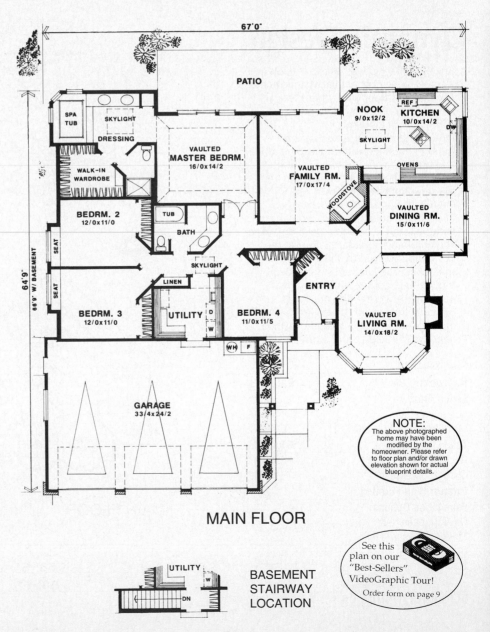

MAIN FLOOR

NOTE:
The above photographed home may have been modified by the homeowner. Please refer to floor plan and/or drawn elevation shown for actual blueprint details.

BASEMENT STAIRWAY LOCATION

See this plan on our "Best-Sellers" VideoGraphic Tour! Order form on page 9

Scenic Hideaway

- The perfect complement to any scenic hideaway spot, this A-frame is as affordable as it is adorable.
- A large deck embraces the front of the chalet, providing ample space for outdoor dining and recreation. Inside, vaulted ceilings and high windows lend a feeling of spaciousness.
- The living room is dramatically expanded by a 17-ft.-high vaulted ceiling and soaring windows facing the deck. This room also boasts a woodstove with a masonry hearth.
- The galley kitchen is well organized and includes a stacked washer/dryer unit and easy outdoor access. Nearby is a skylighted full bath.
- The romantic bedroom/loft overlooks the living room and features a 16-ft. ceiling. Windows at both ends of the room provide stunning views.
- On both floors, areas with limited headroom are utilized effectively for storage.

Plan H-968-1A	
Bedrooms: 1	**Baths:** 1
Living Area:	
Upper floor	144 sq. ft.
Main floor	391 sq. ft.
Total Living Area:	**535 sq. ft.**
Exterior Wall Framing:	2x6
Foundation Options:	
Crawlspace	

(All plans can be built with your choice of foundation and framing. A generic conversion diagram is available. See order form.)

BLUEPRINT PRICE CODE: AA

MAIN FLOOR

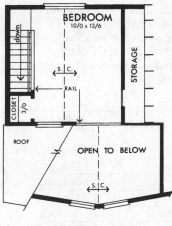

UPPER FLOOR

Relax in the Country

- This country home provides plenty of room to relax, with its covered porches and wide-open living spaces.
- Just off the front porch, the living room boasts a soothing fireplace with a raised brick hearth. The 18-ft. cathedral ceiling is shared with the adjoining dining room, which offers French-door access to the backyard porch.
- The walk-through kitchen features a handy pantry, plus a laundry closet that houses a stackable washer and dryer.
- A convenient pocket door leads to the secluded full bath.
- The master bedroom boasts two closets and private access to the bath.
- An open stairway with an oak handrail leads up to another bedroom, with a cozy seat under an arched window arrangement. Other features include a 9-ft. ceiling, a pair of closets and access to extra storage space.

Plan J-90016

Bedrooms: 2	Baths: 1
Living Area:	
Upper floor	203 sq. ft.
Main floor	720 sq. ft.
Total Living Area:	**923 sq. ft.**
Standard basement	720 sq. ft.
Exterior Wall Framing:	2x6

Foundation Options:

Standard basement
Crawlspace
Slab

(All plans can be built with your choice of foundation and framing. A generic conversion diagram is available. See order form.)

BLUEPRINT PRICE CODE:	AA

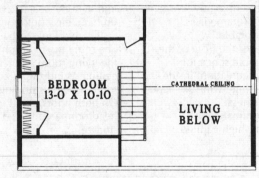

UPPER FLOOR

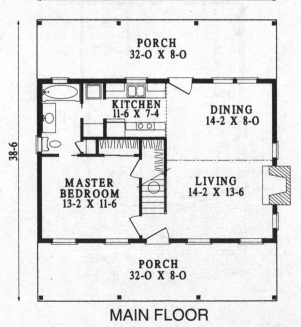

MAIN FLOOR

Build It Yourself

- Everything you need for a leisure or retirement retreat is neatly packaged in this affordable, easy-to-build design.
- The basic rectangular shape features a unique wraparound deck, entirely covered by a projecting roofline.
- A central fireplace and a vaulted ceiling that rises to 10 ft. visually enhance the cozy living and dining rooms.
- The efficient kitchen offers convenient service to the adjoining dining room. In the crawlspace version, the kitchen also includes a snack bar.
- Two main-floor bedrooms share a large full bath.
- The daylight-basement option is suitable for building on a sloping lot and consists of an extra bedroom, a general-purpose area and a garage.

Plans H-833-7 & -7A

Bedrooms: 2+	Baths: 1
Living Area:	
Main floor	952 sq. ft.
Daylight basement	676 sq. ft.
Total Living Area:	**952/1,628 sq. ft.**
Tuck-under garage	276 sq. ft.
Exterior Wall Framing:	2x6
Foundation Options:	**Plan #**
Daylight basement	H-833-7
Crawlspace	H-833-7A

(All plans can be built with your choice of foundation and framing. A generic conversion diagram is available. See order form.)

BLUEPRINT PRICE CODE:	**AA/B**

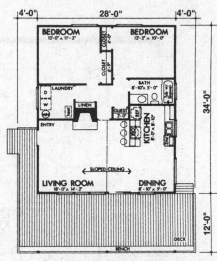

MAIN FLOOR
Crawlspace version

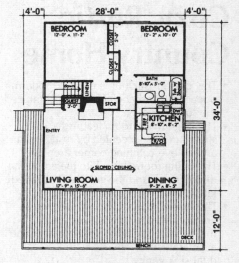

MAIN FLOOR
Basement version

See this plan on our "Two-Story" VideoGraphic Tour!
Order form on page 9

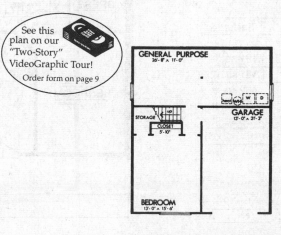

DAYLIGHT BASEMENT

Cozy, Rustic Country Home

- This cozy, rustic home offers a modern, open interior that efficiently maximizes the square footage.
- The large living room features a 13-ft. sloped ceiling accented by rustic beams and an eye-catching corner fireplace.
- The living room flows into the adjoining dining room and the efficient U-shaped kitchen for a spacious, open feel.
- The master and secondary bedrooms are separated by the activity areas. The master suite includes a private bath and a separate dressing area with a dual-sink vanity.
- The secondary bedrooms share another full bath.

Plan E-1109

Bedrooms: 3	Baths: 2
Living Area:	
Main floor	1,191 sq. ft.
Total Living Area:	**1,191 sq. ft.**
Garage	462 sq. ft.
Storage	55 sq. ft.
Utility	55 sq. ft.
Exterior Wall Framing:	2x6

Foundation Options:

Crawlspace

Slab

(All plans can be built with your choice of foundation and framing. A generic conversion diagram is available. See order form.)

BLUEPRINT PRICE CODE: A

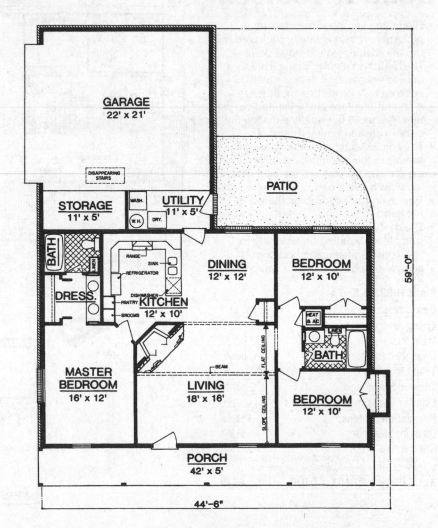

MAIN FLOOR

Plan E-1109

PRICES AND DETAILS
ON PAGES 12-15

Compact and Efficient

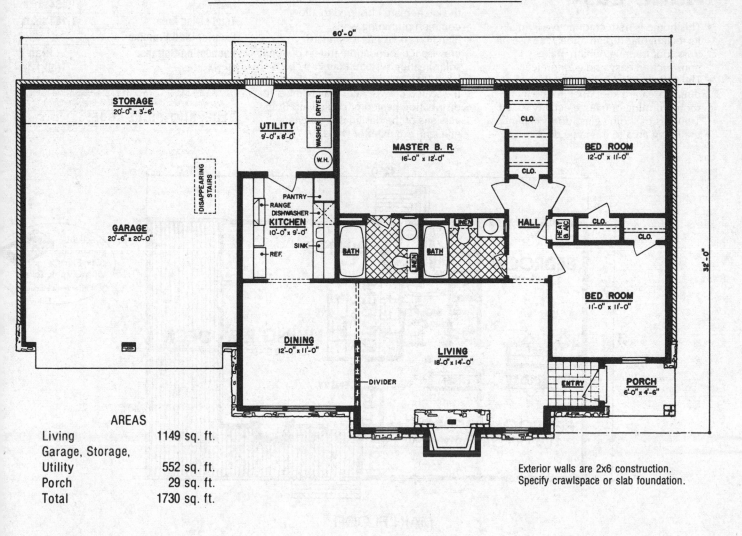

STORAGE
20'-0" x 3'-6"

GARAGE
20'-6" x 20'-0"

DISAPPEARING STAIRS

UTILITY
9'-0" x 8'-0"

WASHER
DRYER
W.H.

PANTRY
RANGE
DISHWASHER
KITCHEN
10'-0" x 9'-0"
SINK
REF.

MASTER B. R.
16'-0" x 12'-0"

CLO.
CLO.

BED ROOM
12'-0" x 11'-0"

BATH
LINEN
BATH
LINEN

HALL
HEAT & A/C
CLO.
CLO.

BED ROOM
11'-0" x 11'-0"

DINING
12'-0" x 11'-0"

DIVIDER

LIVING
18'-0" x 14'-0"

ENTRY

PORCH
6'-0" x 4'-6"

60'-0"

32'-0"

AREAS

Living	1149 sq. ft.
Garage, Storage, Utility	552 sq. ft.
Porch	29 sq. ft.
Total	1730 sq. ft.

Exterior walls are 2x6 construction.
Specify crawlspace or slab foundation.

ORDER BLUEPRINTS ANYTIME!
CALL TOLL-FREE 1-888-626-2026

Blueprint Price Code A
Plan E-1102

PRICES AND DETAILS
ON PAGES 12-15

53

Active Living Made Easy

- This home is perfect for active living. Its rectangular design allows the use of truss roof framing, which makes construction easy and economical.
- The galley-style kitchen and the sunny dining area are kept open to the living room, forming one huge activity space. Two sets of sliding glass doors expand the living area to the large deck.

- The secluded master bedroom offers a private bath, while the remaining bedrooms share a hall bath.
- The two baths, the laundry facilities and the kitchen are clustered to allow common plumbing walls.
- Plan H-921-1A has a standard crawlspace foundation and an optional solar-heating system. Plan H-921-2A has a Plen-Wood system, which utilizes the sealed crawlspace as a chamber for distributing heated or cooled air. Both versions of the design call for energy-efficient 2x6 exterior walls.

Plans H-921-1A & -2A	
Bedrooms: 3	**Baths:** 2
Living Area:	
Main floor	1,164 sq. ft.
Total Living Area:	**1,164 sq. ft.**
Exterior Wall Framing:	2x6
Foundation Options:	**Plan #**
Crawlspace	H-921-1A
Plen-Wood crawlspace	H-921-2A

(All plans can be built with your choice of foundation and framing. A generic conversion diagram is available. See order form.)

BLUEPRINT PRICE CODE:	**A**

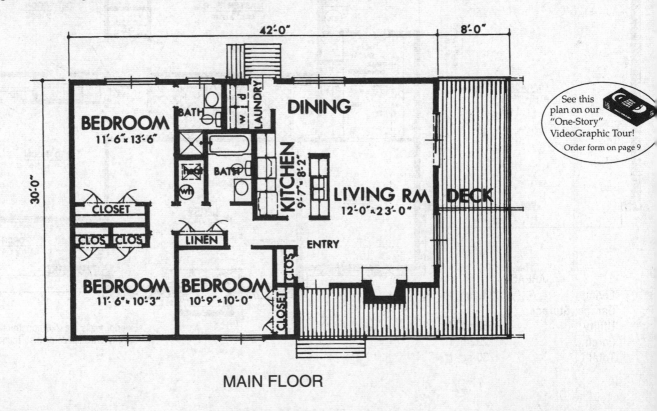

See this plan on our "One-Story" VideoGraphic Tour!
Order form on page 9

MAIN FLOOR

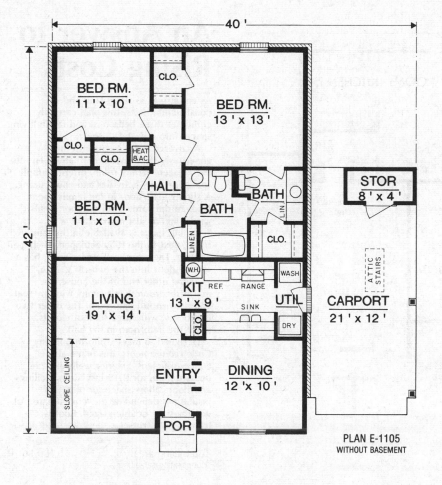

BED RM.
11' x 10'

CLO.

BED RM.
13' x 13'

CLO.

CLO.

HEAT
& AC

STOR
8' x 4'

HALL

BATH

BED RM.
11' x 10'

BATH

LIN

CLO.

LINEN

ATTIC
STAIRS

W.H

WASH

LIVING
19' x 14'

KIT
13' x 9'

REF.

RANGE

UTIL

CARPORT
21' x 12'

SINK

DRY

SLOPE CEILING

CLO.

ENTRY

DINING
12' x 10'

POR

40'

42'

PLAN E-1105
WITHOUT BASEMENT

Simple, Economical to Build

AREAS

Living   1168 sq. ft.
Carport, Storage,
 Stoops   316 sq. ft.
Total   1484 sq. ft.

Exterior walls are 2x6 construction.
Specify crawlspace or slab foundation.

Blueprint Price Code A
Plan E-1105

ORDER BLUEPRINTS ANYTIME!
CALL TOLL-FREE 1-888-626-2026

PRICES AND DETAILS
ON PAGES 12-15

55

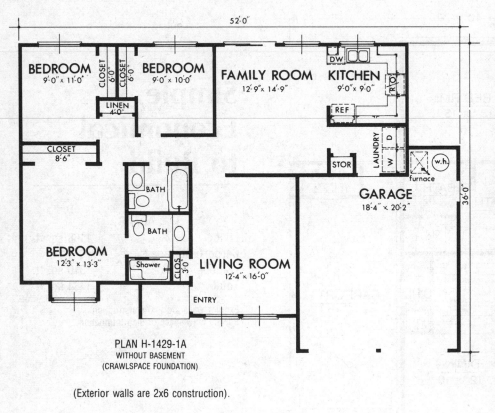

52'-0"

BEDROOM
9'-0" x 11'-0"

CLOSET 6'-0"

CLOSET 6'-0"

BEDROOM
9'-0" x 10'-0"

FAMILY ROOM
12'-9" x 14'-9"

KITCHEN
9'-0" x 9'-0"

DW

REF

LINEN
4'-0"

CLOSET
8'-6"

BATH

BATH

LAUNDRY

W | D

STOR

w.h.

furnace

BEDROOM
12'-3" x 13'-3"

Shower

CLOS. 3'-0"

LIVING ROOM
12'-4" x 16'-0"

GARAGE
18'-4" x 20'-2"

36'-0"

ENTRY

PLAN H-1429-1A
WITHOUT BASEMENT
(CRAWLSPACE FOUNDATION)

(Exterior walls are 2x6 construction).

An Answer to Rising Costs

As an answer to rising land and construction costs, this plan carefully combines three bedrooms and family living spaces into only 1,180 sq. ft.

A covered entry opens into the generously sized living room and then into the adjacent family room, offering ample space for daily activities and entertaining. A sliding glass door in the family room leads to the yard — for outdoor meals, gardening, or just relaxing.

Dining space is available in the family room, next to the fully equipped, U-shaped kitchen. The adjacent laundry room has a service door into the two-car garage.

At the other end of the house, the master bedroom has a sunny window seat and its own full bathroom. The other two bedrooms, with large six-foot closets, share the bathroom in the hall.

Designed to meet Uniform Building Code requirements, this home also is energy efficient. Exterior walls are 2x6 construction, for R-19 insulation. Ceilings and floors allow space for plenty of insulation, depending on your climate. All windows are double-glazed. Roof is framed with trusses.

Total living area: 1,180 sq. ft.
(Not counting garage)

Blueprint Price Code A
Plan H-1429-1A

**PRICES AND DETAILS
ON PAGES 12-15**

Compact Home with Rustic Look

- While it may resemble a hunting lodge on the outside, this home is cozy and modern inside.
- The spacious living room offers sloped ceilings, a great fireplace and hearth and a view through the open dining room to the rear of the home.
- The kitchen is designed for convenience, featuring a broom closet and a double pantry.
- The master suite is luxurious for a compact home, with its large closet, compartmentalized bath and dressing room with double vanity.
- Two secondary bedrooms are on the opposite side of the home for privacy and share another full bath.
- Note the unusual wrap-around arrangement of the utility/storage area and garage.

Plan E-1106

Bedrooms: 3	Baths: 2

Space:	
Main floor	1,187 sq. ft.

Total Living Area	1,187 sq. ft.

Garage	440 sq. ft.
Utility & Storage	108 sq. ft.
Porch	99 sq. ft.

Exterior Wall Framing	2x6

Foundation options:
Crawlspace
Slab
(Foundation & framing conversion diagram available—see order form.)

Blueprint Price Code	A

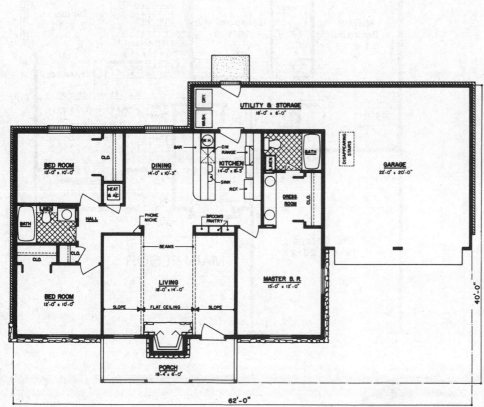

Appealing Farmhouse

- This appealing farmhouse design features a shady and inviting front porch with decorative railings.
- Inside, 14-ft. vaulted ceilings expand the living and dining rooms.
- This large area is brightened by bay windows and warmed by a unique two-way fireplace. Sliding glass doors lead to a sunny backyard patio.
- The functional kitchen includes a pantry closet, plenty of cabinet space and a serving bar to the dining room.
- The master bedroom boasts a mirrored dressing area, a private bath and abundant closet space.
- Two additional bedrooms share another full bath. The third bedroom includes a cozy window seat.

Plan NW-521

Bedrooms: 3	Baths: 2
Living Area:	
Main floor	1,187 sq. ft.
Total Living Area:	**1,187 sq. ft.**
Garage	448 sq. ft.
Exterior Wall Framing:	2x6

Foundation Options:

Crawlspace

(All plans can be built with your choice of foundation and framing. A generic conversion diagram is available. See order form.)

BLUEPRINT PRICE CODE: A

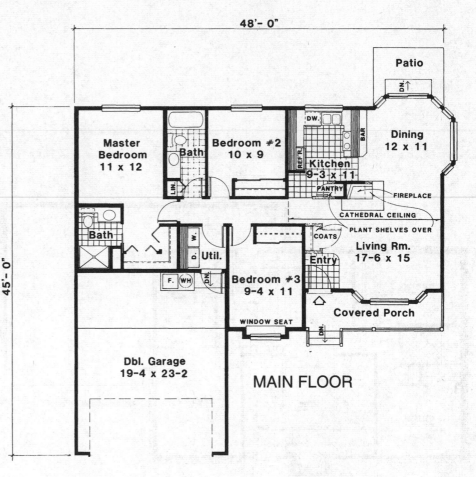

MAIN FLOOR

See this plan on our "Best-Sellers" VideoGraphic Tour! Order form on page 9

ORDER BLUEPRINTS ANYTIME! CALL TOLL-FREE 1-888-626-2026

Plan NW-521

PRICES AND DETAILS ON PAGES 12-15

Compact Design Offers Secluded Entry

- This efficient and economical design offers a stylish exterior and an interior that provides for comfortable living.
- The living and dining area is huge for a home of this size, and the corner fireplace is a real eye-catcher.
- The efficient U-shaped kitchen is open to the dining room and includes a floor-to-ceiling pantry as well as abundant cabinet space.
- The master suite boasts a private bath and a large walk-in closet. Two other bedrooms share another full bath.
- A small side porch accesses the dining room as well as a large utility and storage area.

Plan E-1214

Bedrooms: 3	Baths: 2

Space:	
Main floor	1,200 sq. ft.
Total Living Area	**1,200 sq. ft.**
Porches	60 sq. ft.
Utility & Storage	100 sq. ft.
Exterior Wall Framing	**2x6**

Foundation options:

Crawlspace
Slab
(Foundation & framing conversion diagram available—see order form.)

Blueprint Price Code	**A**

Plan E-1214

Compact Cabin

- An open stairway in the entryway of this compact two-story cabin leads to an open loft hall above.
- The Great Room to the left offers a cathedral ceiling and an inviting fireplace that welcomes guests.
- A screened porch to the rear of the adjoining dining room is close to the kitchen for convenient outdoor dining; a private sun deck off the master bedroom is located above.
- The kitchen features a counter bar and nearby toilet and laundry facilities.

DECK

WALK IN CLOS

W I C

MASTER BEDROOM
12'-0 × 15'-0

BATH

lin

BEDROOM
11'-0 × 11'-4

LOFT

DN

UPPER PART GREAT ROOM
skyl

UPPER FLOOR

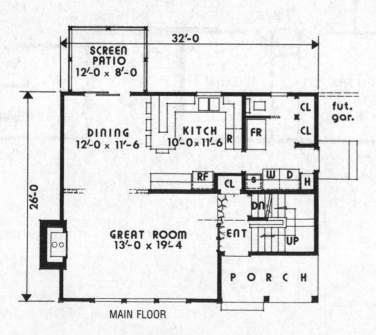

32'-0

SCREEN PATIO
12'-0 × 8'-0

fut. gar.

DINING
12'-0 × 11'-6

KITCH
10'-0 × 11'-6

R

FR

CL

CL

26'-0

RF

CL

S

W

D

H

DN

GREAT ROOM
13'-0 × 19'-4

ENT

UP

P O R C H

MAIN FLOOR

Plan CPS-1077-SE

Bedrooms: 2	Baths: 1½

Space:	
Upper floor:	528 sq. ft.
Main floor:	760 sq. ft.

Total living area:	1,288 sq. ft.
Basement:	760 sq. ft.

Exterior Wall Framing:	2x6

Foundation options:
Standard basement.
(Foundation & framing conversion diagram available — see order form.)

Blueprint Price Code:	A

Plan CPS-1077-SE

PRICES AND DETAILS
ON PAGES 12-15

FRONT VIEW

Sunshine Floods Rustic Design

- The main floor is virtually one huge room divided into areas for lounging, eating and cooking.
- A spacious deck, spanning the entire rear of the home, provides for outdoor living and entertaining.
- Upstairs, one large bedroom serves as a master suite, while the balcony room can be used for a variety of purposes, if not needed as a second bedroom.
- Five huge skylight windows across the rear slope of the roof flood the entire home with sunlight and solar heat, achieving a dramatic effect throughout the home.

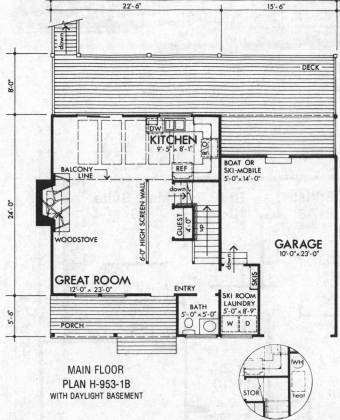

MAIN FLOOR
PLAN H-953-1B
WITH DAYLIGHT BASEMENT

PLAN H-953-1A
WITHOUT BASEMENT

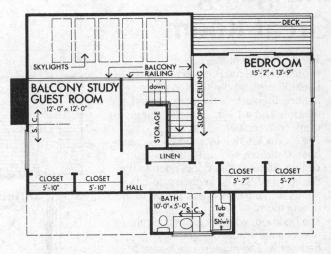

UPPER FLOOR

Plans H-953-1A & -1B	
Bedrooms: 2	**Baths:** 1½
Space:	
Upper floor	689 sq. ft.
Main floor	623 sq. ft.
Total Living Area	**1,312 sq. ft.**
Basement	540 sq. ft.
Garage	319 sq. ft.
Storage	70 sq. ft.
Exterior Wall Framing	**2x6**
Foundation options:	**Plan #**
Daylight Basement	H-953-1B
Crawlspace	H-953-1A
(Foundation & framing conversion diagram available—see order form.)	
Blueprint Price Code	**A**

REAR VIEW

Intriguing Great Room

- The focal point of this open, economical home is its comfortable Great Room and dining area. An inviting fireplace, a dramatic arched window and a 13-ft. vaulted ceiling spark conversation.
- The roomy kitchen incorporates a sunny breakfast room with a 10-ft. vaulted ceiling. Sliding glass doors open to the backyard deck. The kitchen also has a pantry and a handy pass-through to the dining room.
- The bedroom wing includes a lovely master suite and two secondary bedrooms. The master suite boasts a private bath with a separate tub and shower, while the secondary bedrooms share another full bath.
- The washer and dryer are conveniently located near the bedroom wing and the entrance from the garage.

Plan B-90008

Bedrooms: 3	Baths: 2
Living Area:	
Main floor	1,325 sq. ft.
Total Living Area:	**1,325 sq. ft.**
Standard basement	1,325 sq. ft.
Garage	390 sq. ft.
Exterior Wall Framing:	2x6

Foundation Options:

Standard basement
(All plans can be built with your choice of foundation and framing. A generic conversion diagram is available. See order form.)

BLUEPRINT PRICE CODE:	A

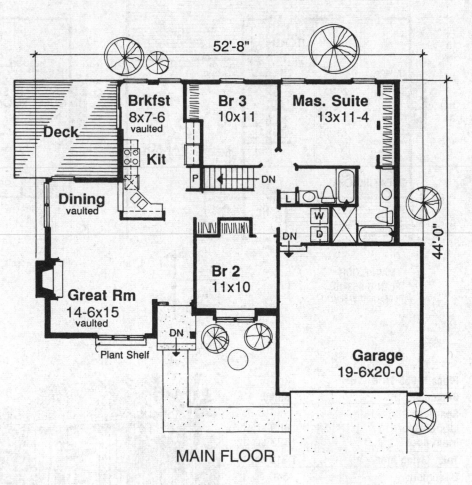

MAIN FLOOR

Plan B-90008

PRICES AND DETAILS
ON PAGES 12-15

FRONT VIEW

Compact Plan Fits Narrow Building Site

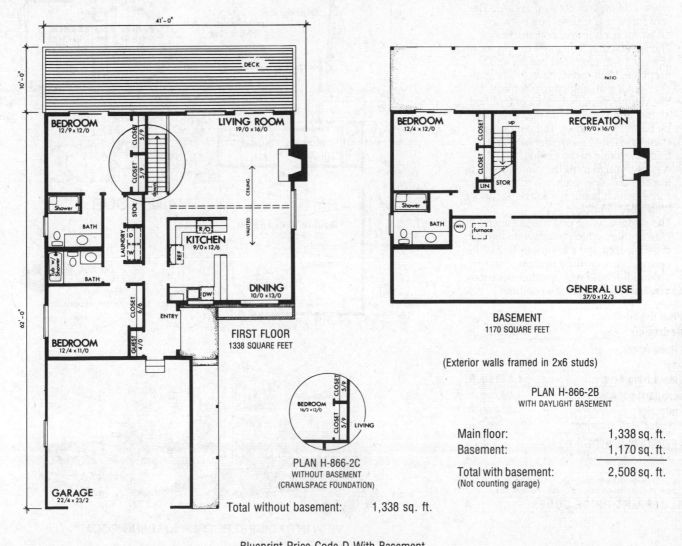

41'-0"

10'-0"

DECK

BEDROOM
12/9 x 12/0

CLOSET 5/9
CLOSET 5/9

LIVING ROOM
19/0 x 16/0

Shower

BATH

STOR

LAUNDRY

CEILING

VAULTED

Tub w/ Shower

BATH

KITCHEN
9/0 x 12/6

R/O

REF

DINING
10/0 x 13/0

62'-0"

CLOSET 6/6

DW

ENTRY

BEDROOM
12/4 x 11/0

GUEST 4/0

FIRST FLOOR
1338 SQUARE FEET

GARAGE
22/4 x 23/2

BEDROOM
16/2 x 12/0

CLOSET 5/9
CLOSET 5/9

LIVING

PLAN H-866-2C
WITHOUT BASEMENT
(CRAWLSPACE FOUNDATION)

Total without basement: 1,338 sq. ft.

BEDROOM
12/4 x 12/0

CLOSET

up

RECREATION
19/0 x 16/0

LIN

STOR

Shower

BATH

WH

furnace

GENERAL USE
37/0 x 12/3

BASEMENT
1170 SQUARE FEET

(Exterior walls framed in 2x6 studs)

PLAN H-866-2B
WITH DAYLIGHT BASEMENT

Main floor:	1,338 sq. ft.
Basement:	1,170 sq. ft.
Total with basement:	2,508 sq. ft.
(Not counting garage)	

Blueprint Price Code D With Basement
Blueprint Price Code A Without Basement

High-Profile Contemporary

- This design does away with wasted space, putting the emphasis on quality rather than on size.
- The angled floor plan minimizes hall space and creates smooth traffic flow while adding architectural appeal. The roof framing is square, however, to allow for economical construction.
- The spectacular living and dining rooms share a 16-ft. cathedral ceiling and a fireplace. Both rooms have lots of glass overlooking an angled rear terrace.
- The dining room includes a glass-filled alcove and sliding patio doors topped by transom windows. Tall windows frame the living room fireplace and trace the slope of the ceiling.
- A pass-through joins the dining room to the combination kitchen and family room, which features a snack bar and a clerestory window.
- The sleeping wing provides a super master suite, which boasts a skylighted dressing area and a luxurious bath. The optional den, or third bedroom, shares a second full bath with another bedroom that offers a 14-ft. sloped ceiling.

Plan K-688-D

Bedrooms: 2+	Baths: 2½
Living Area:	
Main floor	1,340 sq. ft.
Total Living Area:	**1,340 sq. ft.**
Standard basement	1,235 sq. ft.
Garage	484 sq. ft.
Exterior Wall Framing:	2x4 or 2x6

Foundation Options:
Standard basement
Slab
(All plans can be built with your choice of foundation and framing. A generic conversion diagram is available. See order form.)

BLUEPRINT PRICE CODE: A

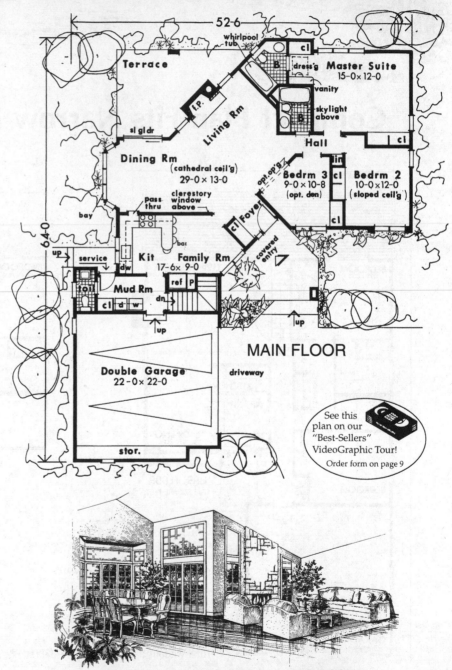

MAIN FLOOR

See this plan on our "Best-Sellers" VideoGraphic Tour! Order form on page 9

VIEW INTO DINING ROOM AND LIVING ROOM

FRONT VIEW

(Exterior walls are 2x6 construction)

PLAN H-931-1
WITH BASEMENT

PLAN H-931-1A
WITHOUT BASEMENT
(CRAWLSPACE FOUNDATION)

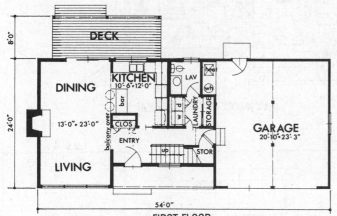

FIRST FLOOR
714 SQUARE FEET

SECOND FLOOR
644 SQUARE FEET

A Studio Garret and Open Planning

A new wave of popularity in singles homes has encouraged the design of another dwelling suitable for singles or couples who desire a small, compact, private dwelling instead of an apartment. A skylighted 10'-3" x 23' studio room that can be used for multiple purposes, including over-flow sleeping, is located over the garage.

One of the singular features of this home is a balcony bedroom that measures 18'-8" x 12' and has a deep walk-in wardrobe closet and linen shelves, plus a private bathroom. This balcony overlooks the living room.

Downstairs, this exciting plan offers a pleasing traffic pattern circulating around a spacious entry flanked by an open staircase. The functional kitchen includes an L-shaped cabinet arrangement with an eating bar separating kitchen and dining-living area.

The living-dining room spans one end of the house and includes access to a covered outdoor deck space. An expansive fireplace is placed midway on the long wall of the living room. The plumbing center is well located, with the washer-dryer and laundry room cabinetry placed on a wall common to the kitchen and lower bathroom plumbing. Extra storage room and space for the water heater and central heating system are included in this area. A large double garage is accessible from the central hallway.

Exterior walls are designed with 2x6 studs for R-19 insulation.

First floor: 714 sq. ft.
Second floor: 644 sq. ft.

Total living area: 1,358 sq. ft.
(Not counting basement or garage)

Blueprint Price Code A

Plans H-931-1 & H-931-1A

PRICES AND DETAILS
ON PAGES 12-15

All in One!

- This plan puts all of today's most luxurious home-design features into one attractive, economical package.
- The covered front porch and the gabled roofline, accented by an arched window and a round louver vent, give the exterior a homey yet stylish appeal.
- Just inside the front door, the ceiling rises up to 11 ft., making an impressive greeting. A skylight and French doors framing the fireplace flood the living room with light.
- The living room flows into a nice-sized dining room, also with an 11-ft. ceiling, which in turn leads to the large eat-in kitchen. Here you'll find lots of counter space, a handy laundry closet and a eating area that opens to a terrace.
- The bedroom wing includes a wonderful master suite, with a sizable sleeping area and a dressing area with two closets. Glass blocks above the dual-sink vanity let in light yet maintain privacy. A whirlpool tub and a separate shower complete the suite.
- The larger of the two remaining bedrooms boasts an 11-ft.-high ceiling and an arched window.

Plan HFL-1680-FL

Bedrooms: 3	Baths: 2

Living Area:	
Main floor	1,367 sq. ft.
Total Living Area:	**1,367 sq. ft.**
Standard basement	1,367 sq. ft.
Garage	431 sq. ft.
Exterior Wall Framing:	**2x6**

Foundation Options:

Standard basement

(All plans can be built with your choice of foundation and framing. A generic conversion diagram is available. See order form.)

BLUEPRINT PRICE CODE: A

VIEW INTO LIVING ROOM

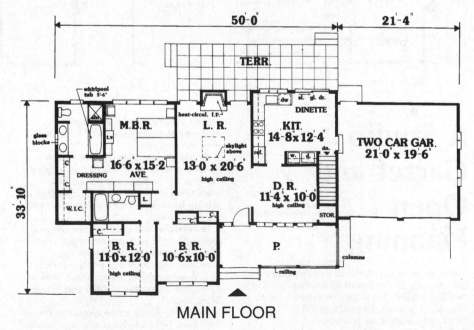

MAIN FLOOR

   Plan HFL-1680-FL

FRONT VIEW

Practical Country Residence

Skylights on a steep pitched roof, vertical siding, and a covered deck provide a pleasing overall appearance for this home.

This practical country residence is designed with excellent room orientation around the entry hall.

Welcoming kitchen adjacent to the entry is totally equipped with modern appliances, abundant cabinet space, and breakfast bar.

Comfortable living room features a fireplace, and sliding glass doors opening to a private rear deck. Attractive vaulted ceiling and balcony railings add to the interior beauty of the living room.

A compact hallway provides access to the bedrooms and a centrally located bathroom. Washer and dryer are installed in an individual closet.

Stairway leads to a second floor where a bedroom loft awaits overnight visitors. Private bathroom and spacious closet serve this area.

First floor:	993 sq. ft.
Second floor:	383 sq. ft.
Total living area:	1,376 sq. ft.

(Not counting basement or garage)
(Exterior walls framed in 2x6 studs)

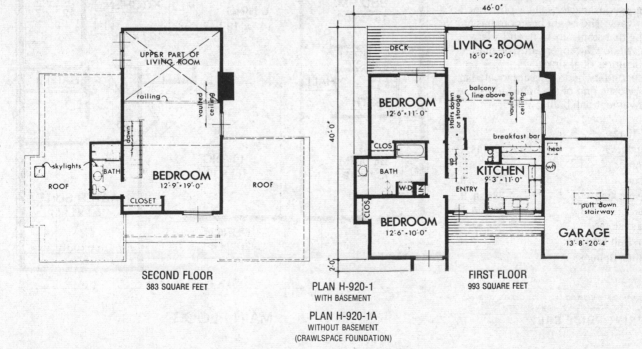

SECOND FLOOR
383 SQUARE FEET

PLAN H-920-1
WITH BASEMENT

PLAN H-920-1A
WITHOUT BASEMENT
(CRAWLSPACE FOUNDATION)

FIRST FLOOR
993 SQUARE FEET

Blueprint Price Code A

Plan H-920-1 & -1A

PRICES AND DETAILS
ON PAGES 12-15

Easy Living

- This cozy one-story design makes the most of its square footage by neatly incorporating features usually found only in much larger homes.
- Off the covered porch is a spacious living room with a dramatic corner fireplace, a ceiling that slopes to 13 ft., 6 in. and a long view to the backyard patio.
- The living room unfolds to a lovely dining room with a patio door.
- The adjoining kitchen features a snack bar for convenient serving and quick meals. The efficient, U-shaped kitchen also offers a pantry and a broom closet, plus a nearby utility/storage room.
- The gorgeous master suite is positioned for privacy. The bright bedroom has a ceiling that slopes to 11 ft. and a large front window arrangement. The master bath features dual sinks.
- The secondary bedrooms are located at the opposite end of the home and share a convenient hall bath.

Plan E-1311

Bedrooms: 3	Baths: 2
Living Area:	
Main floor	1,380 sq. ft.
Total Living Area:	**1,380 sq. ft.**
Garage	440 sq. ft.
Utility and storage	84 sq. ft.
Exterior Wall Framing:	2x6

Foundation Options:

Crawlspace
Slab
(All plans can be built with your choice of foundation and framing. A generic conversion diagram is available. See order form.)

BLUEPRINT PRICE CODE:	A

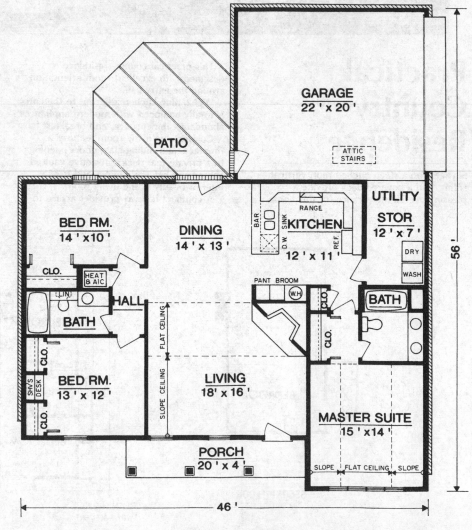

MAIN FLOOR

Plan E-1311

PRICES AND DETAILS
ON PAGES 12-15

Three Looks for One Great Plan

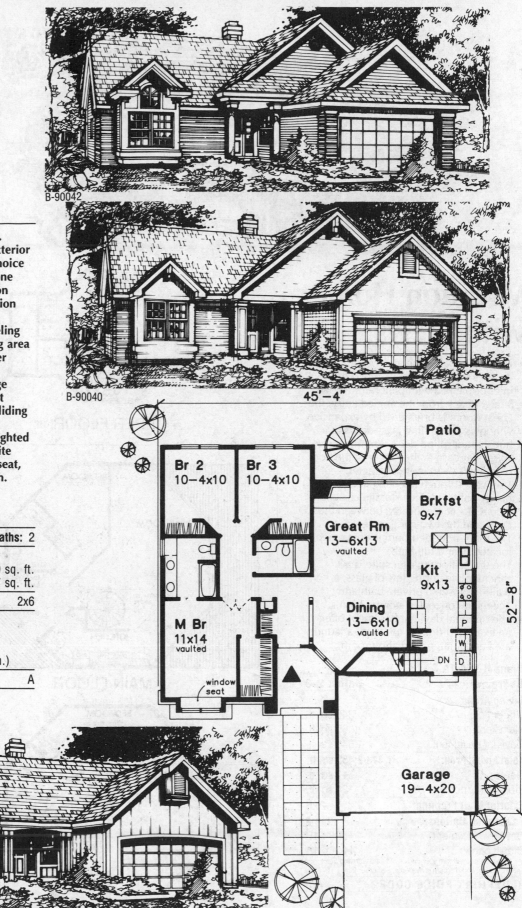

B-90042

B-90040

B-90047

- This well-planned 1,390 sq. ft. ranch offers three different exterior looks to give homebuyers a choice and chance to find the right one for them. (Note: Each elevation sold separately. Specify elevation when ordering.)
- The entry opens to an airy-feeling Great Room and formal dining area with vaulted ceiling and corner fireplace.
- The kitchen, with handy garage access, overlooks the breakfast room and rear patio beyond sliding doors.
- The three bedrooms are highlighted by a double-doored master suite with vaulted ceiling, window seat, walk-in closet and private bath.

Plans B-90040, B-90042, B-90047

Bedrooms: 3	Baths: 2
Space:	
Total living area:	1,390 sq. ft.
Garage:	387 sq. ft.
Exterior Wall Framing:	2x6
Foundation options: Standard basement. (Foundation & framing conversion diagram available — see order form.)	
Blueprint Price Code:	A

Floor plan labels:
- 45'—4"
- 52'—8"
- Patio
- Br 2 10—4x10
- Br 3 10—4x10
- Great Rm 13—6x13 vaulted
- Brkfst 9x7
- Kit 9x13
- M Br 11x14 vaulted
- Dining 13—6x10 vaulted
- window seat
- DN
- P W D
- Garage 19—4x20

Vacation Home with Views

- The octagonal shape and window-filled walls of this home create a powerful interior packed with panoramic views.
- Straight back from the angled entry, the Great Room is brightened by expansive windows and sliding glass doors to a huge wraparound deck. An impressive spiral staircase at the center of the floor plan lends even more character.
- The walk-through kitchen offers a handy pantry. A nice storage closet and a coat closet are located between the entry and the two-car garage.
- The main-floor bedroom is conveniently located near a full bath.
- The upper-floor master suite is a sanctuary, featuring lots of glass, a walk-in closet, a private bath and access to concealed storage rooms.
- The optional daylight basement offers an extra bedroom, a full bath, a laundry area and a large recreation room.

Plans H-964-1A & -1B

Bedrooms: 2+	Baths: 2-3
Living Area:	
Upper floor	346 sq. ft.
Main floor	1,067 sq. ft.
Daylight basement	1,045 sq. ft.
Total Living Area:	**1,413/2,458 sq. ft.**
Garage	512 sq. ft.
Storage (upper floor)	134 sq. ft.
Exterior Wall Framing:	**2x6**
Foundation Options:	**Plan #**
Daylight basement	H-964-1B
Crawlspace	H-964-1A

(All plans can be built with your choice of foundation and framing. A generic conversion diagram is available. See order form.)

BLUEPRINT PRICE CODE:	**A/C**

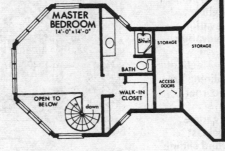

UPPER FLOOR

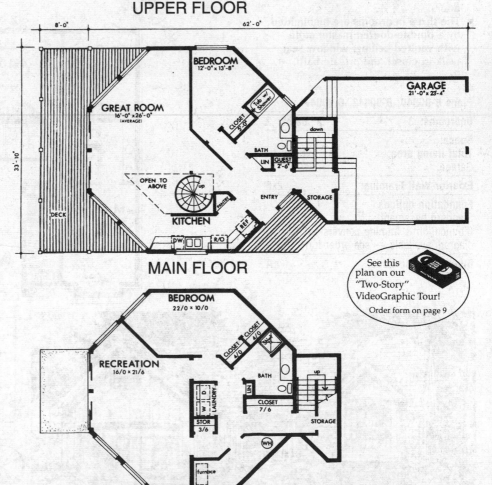

MAIN FLOOR

See this plan on our "Two-Story" VideoGraphic Tour!
Order form on page 9

DAYLIGHT BASEMENT

Street Privacy

- If privacy from street traffic or noise is a concern, this unique home design will fit the bill. The views are oriented to the rear, leaving the front of the home quiet and protected.
- The covered entry porch opens to a spacious living room that overlooks a back porch and patio area. A dramatic corner fireplace is an inviting feature.
- A functional snack bar separates the kitchen from the adjoining dining room, which boasts a lovely bay window.
- Just off the kitchen, a deluxe utility room doubles as a mudroom. The area includes a pantry, a broom closet, a storage closet and laundry facilities.
- The private master suite has an angled window wall, a large walk-in closet and a nice-sized bath with twin sinks.
- Two more bedrooms share another full bath on the opposite end of the home.

Plan E-1424

Bedrooms: 3	Baths: 2
Living Area:	
Main floor	1,415 sq. ft.
Total Living Area:	**1,415 sq. ft.**
Garage	484 sq. ft.
Storage	60 sq. ft.
Exterior Wall Framing:	2x6

Foundation Options:

Crawlspace

Slab

(All plans can be built with your choice of foundation and framing. A generic conversion diagram is available. See order form.)

BLUEPRINT PRICE CODE: A

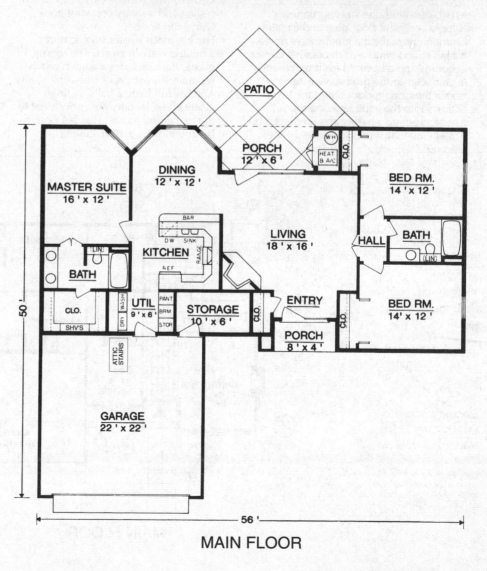

MAIN FLOOR

Off to a Great Start!

- This beautiful one-story's charming looks, efficient floor plan and elegant amenities make it a great starter home.
- Half-round windows, decorative corner quoins and a covered front porch add character to the distinctive exterior.
- Past the double-door entry, the foyer flows into the vaulted living room, which boasts a handsome fireplace and a ceiling that slopes to nearly 14 feet.

- The adjoining formal dining room is brightened by French doors to a covered patio. A convenient pass-through provides service from the kitchen, which enjoys a 10-ft. vaulted ceiling and a sunny breakfast nook with patio access.
- The luxurious master suite features a double walk-in closet. The roomy master bath includes a garden tub, a separate shower and a dual-sink vanity.
- Another full bath, a hallway linen closet and a laundry are convenient to the remaining rooms. The den or third bedroom offers a 10-ft. ceiling.

Plan B-93009

Bedrooms: 2+	Baths: 2
Living Area:	
Main floor	1,431 sq. ft.
Total Living Area:	**1,431 sq. ft.**
Standard basement	1,431 sq. ft.
Garage	380 sq. ft.
Exterior Wall Framing:	2x6

Foundation Options:

Standard basement
(All plans can be built with your choice of foundation and framing. A generic conversion diagram is available. See order form.)

BLUEPRINT PRICE CODE:	A

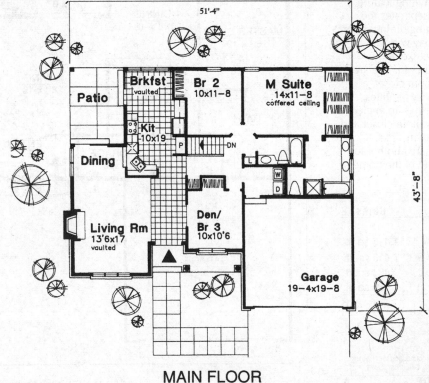

MAIN FLOOR

Plan B-93009

PRICES AND DETAILS
ON PAGES 12-15

Wide Angles Add Style

- The comfortably-sized living areas of this gorgeous home are stylishly enhanced by wide, interesting angles.
- Past the covered front porch, the sidelighted front door brightens the living room just ahead.
- The spacious living room is warmed by a dramatic corner fireplace and opens to an angled, covered back porch.
- A stunning bayed dining room merges with the kitchen and its functional angled snack bar. Laundry facilities and access to the garage are nearby.
- The master suite is removed from the secondary bedrooms and features double doors to a deluxe private bath with an angled spa tub, a dual-sink vanity and a large walk-in closet.
- Another full bath serves the two additional bedrooms at the opposite end of the home.

Plan E-1426

Bedrooms: 3	**Baths:** 2

Living Area:	
Main floor	1,420 sq. ft.
Total Living Area:	**1,420 sq. ft.**
Garage and storage	540 sq. ft.
Exterior Wall Framing:	2x6

Foundation Options:

Crawlspace
Slab
(All plans can be built with your choice of foundation and framing. A generic conversion diagram is available. See order form.)

BLUEPRINT PRICE CODE: A

MAIN FLOOR

Charming Traditional

- The attractive facade of this traditional home features decorative fretwork and louvers in the gables, plus eye-catching window and door treatments.
- The entry area features a commanding view of the living room, which boasts a 12½-ft. ceiling and a corner fireplace. A rear porch and patio are visible through French doors.
- The bayed dining room shares an eating bar with the U-shaped kitchen. The nearby utility room includes a pantry and laundry facilities.
- The quiet master suite includes a big walk-in closet and a private bath with a dual-sink vanity.
- On the other side of the home, double doors close off the two secondary bedrooms from the living areas. A full bath services this wing.

Plan E-1428

Bedrooms: 3	Baths: 2

Living Area:	
Main floor	1,415 sq. ft.
Total Living Area:	**1,415 sq. ft.**
Garage	484 sq. ft.
Storage	60 sq. ft.
Exterior Wall Framing:	2x6

Foundation Options:

Crawlspace
Slab
(All plans can be built with your choice of foundation and framing. A generic conversion diagram is available. See order form.)

BLUEPRINT PRICE CODE: A

MAIN FLOOR

Economical One-Level Comfort

- This charming one-level home was designed with economy in mind.
- The plan is based on the Great Room concept, which makes the most of available square footage and creates an open feeling throughout the house.
- A dining area is defined by the sunny bay windows in the Great Room near the kitchen.
- The open-plan kitchen is combined with a sunny nook for an open, airy feeling.
- The private area of the home features a master suite which is impressive for a home of this size. It features two walk-in closets as well as a private bath with double-bowl vanity.
- Two secondary bedrooms share another full bath.
- A utility area in the garage entryway includes space for a washer and dryer.

Plan S-52191

Bedrooms: 3	Baths: 2
Space:	
Main floor	1,441 sq. ft.
Total Living Area	**1,441 sq. ft.**
Basement	1,441 sq. ft.
Garage	473 sq. ft.
Exterior Wall Framing	2x6

Foundation options:

Standard Basement

Crawlspace

(Foundation & framing conversion diagram available—see order form.)

Blueprint Price Code	**A**

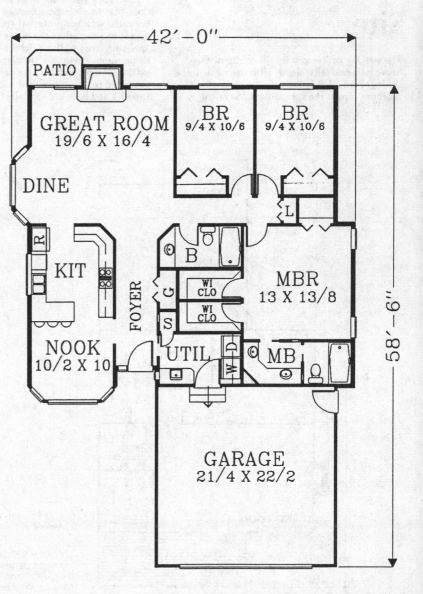

Contemporary Blends with Site

The striking contemporary silhouette of this home paradoxically blends with the rustic setting. Perhaps it is the way the shed rooflines repeat the spreading limbs of the surrounding evergreens, or the way the foundation conforms to the grade much as do the rocks in the foreground. Whatever the reason, the home "belongs."

Aesthetics aside, one must examine the floor plan to determine genuine livability. From the weather-protected entry there is access to any part of the house without annoying cross traffic. Kitchen, dining and living room, the active "waking-hours" section of the residence, are enlarged and enhanced by the convenient outdoor deck. Laundry and bath are located inconspicuously along the hall leading to the main floor bedroom. A huge linen closet is convenient to this area. The additional bedrooms are located upstairs on the 517 sq. ft. second level. A romantic feature of the second floor is the balcony overlooking the living area.

Plans including a full basement are available at your option. A large double garage completes the plan and is an important adjunct, especially if the home is built without a basement, because it can provide much needed storage space.

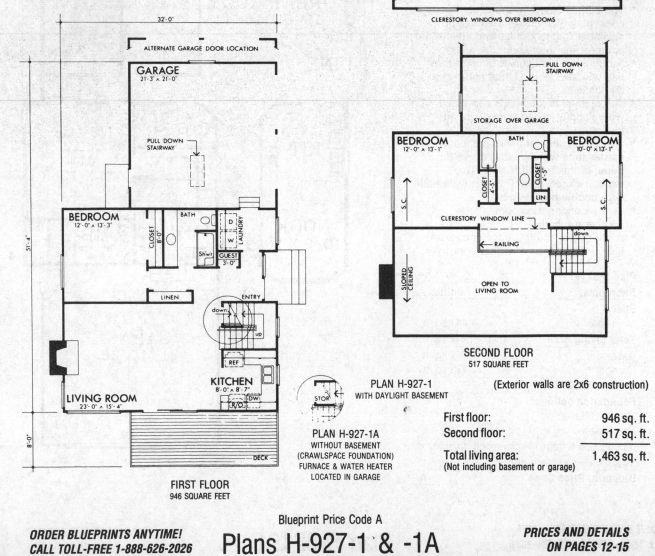

FIRST FLOOR
946 SQUARE FEET

PLAN H-927-1
WITH DAYLIGHT BASEMENT

PLAN H-927-1A
WITHOUT BASEMENT
(CRAWLSPACE FOUNDATION)
FURNACE & WATER HEATER
LOCATED IN GARAGE

SECOND FLOOR
517 SQUARE FEET

(Exterior walls are 2x6 construction)

First floor:	946 sq. ft.
Second floor:	517 sq. ft.
Total living area: (Not including basement or garage)	1,463 sq. ft.

Blueprint Price Code A

Plans H-927-1 & -1A

PRICES AND DETAILS
ON PAGES 12-15

FRONT VIEW

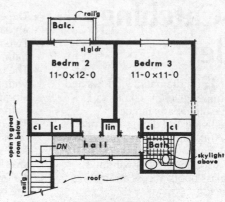

REAR VIEW

More for Less

- Big in function but small in square footage, this passive-solar plan can be built as a single-family home or as part of a multiple-unit complex.
- The floor plan flows visually from its open foyer to its high-ceilinged Great Room, where a high-efficiency fireplace is flanked by glass. Sliding glass doors open to a brilliant south-facing sun room that overlooks a backyard terrace.
- The eat-in kitchen has a pass-through to a bright dining area that opens to a nice side terrace.
- The master bedroom boasts a pair of tall windows, a deluxe private bath and three roomy closets.
- A handy laundry closet and a half-bath are located at the center of the floor plan, near the garage.
- Upstairs, a skylighted bath serves two more bedrooms, one with a private, rear-facing balcony.

See this plan on our "Two-Story" VideoGraphic Tour!
Order form on page 9

Plan K-507-S

Bedrooms: 3	Baths: 2½
Living Area:	
Upper floor	397 sq. ft.
Main floor	915 sq. ft.
Sun room	162 sq. ft.
Total Living Area:	**1,474 sq. ft.**
Standard basement	915 sq. ft.
Garage	400 sq. ft.
Exterior Wall Framing:	2x4 or 2x6

Foundation Options:
Standard basement
Slab
(All plans can be built with your choice of foundation and framing. A generic conversion diagram is available. See order form.)

BLUEPRINT PRICE CODE: A

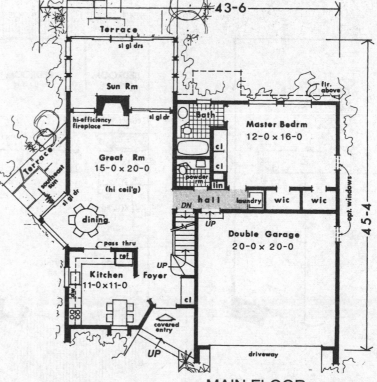

UPPER FLOOR

MAIN FLOOR

Eye-Catching Chalet

- Steep rooflines, dramatic windows and wide cornices give this chalet a distinctive alpine appearance.
- The large living and dining area offers a striking 20-ft.-high vaulted ceiling and a breathtaking view of the outdoors through a soaring wall of windows. Sliding glass doors access an inviting wood deck.

- The efficient U-shaped kitchen shares an eating bar with the dining area.
- Two main-floor bedrooms share a hall bath, and laundry facilities are nearby.
- The upper floor hosts a master bedroom with a 12-ft. vaulted ceiling, plenty of storage space and easy access to a full bath with a shower.
- The pièce de résistance is a balcony with a 12-ft. vaulted ceiling, offering sweeping outdoor views as well as an overlook into the living/dining area below. Additional storage areas flank the balcony.

Plans H-886-3 & -3A	
Bedrooms: 3	**Baths:** 2
Living Area:	
Upper floor	486 sq. ft.
Main floor	994 sq. ft.
Total Living Area:	**1,480 sq. ft.**
Daylight basement	715 sq. ft.
Tuck-under garage	279 sq. ft.
Exterior Wall Framing:	2x6
Foundation Options:	**Plan #**
Daylight basement	H-886-3
Crawlspace	H-886-3A

(All plans can be built with your choice of foundation and framing. A generic conversion diagram is available. See order form.)

BLUEPRINT PRICE CODE:	**A**

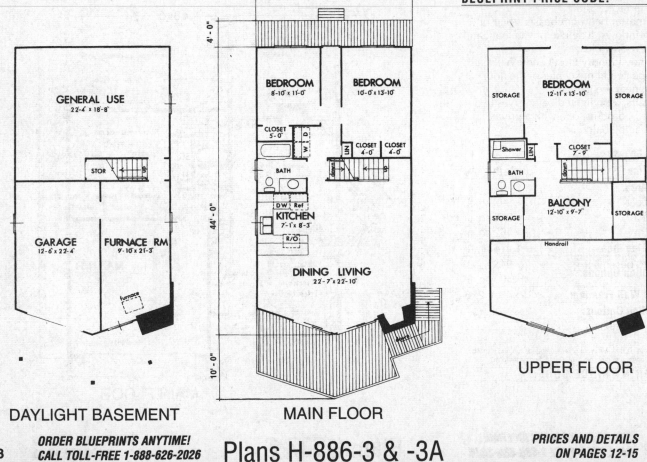

DAYLIGHT BASEMENT

MAIN FLOOR

UPPER FLOOR

Plans H-886-3 & -3A

PRICES AND DETAILS
ON PAGES 12-15

Classic Country-Style

- The classic covered front porch with decorative railings and columns make this home reminiscent of an early 20th-century farmhouse.
- Dormers give the home the appearance of a two-story, even though it is designed for single-level living.
- The huge living room features a ceiling that slopes up to 13 feet. A corner fireplace radiates warmth to both the living room and the dining room.
- The dining room overlooks a backyard patio and shares a versatile serving bar with the open kitchen. A large utility room is just steps away.
- The master bedroom boasts a roomy bath with a dual-sink vanity. The two smaller bedrooms at the other end of the home share a full bath.

Plan E-1412

Bedrooms: 3	Baths: 2
Living Area:	
Main floor	1,484 sq. ft.
Total Living Area:	**1,484 sq. ft.**
Garage	440 sq. ft.
Exterior Wall Framing:	2x6

Foundation Options:

Crawlspace
Slab

(All plans can be built with your choice of foundation and framing. A generic conversion diagram is available. See order form.)

BLUEPRINT PRICE CODE: A

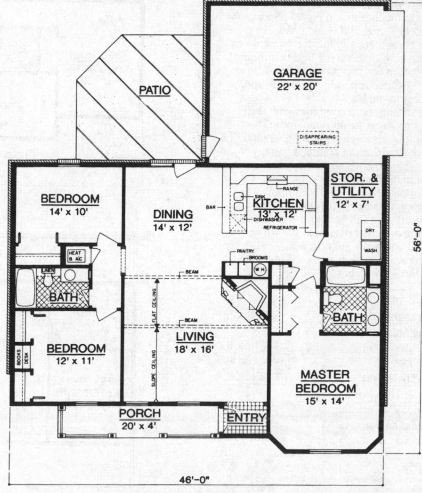

MAIN FLOOR

Compact, Cozy, Inviting

- Full-width porches at the front and the rear of this home add plenty of space for outdoor living and entertaining.
- The huge, centrally located living room is the core of this three-bedroom home. The room features a corner fireplace, a 16-ft. sloped, open-beam ceiling and access to the back porch.
- The dining room combines with the kitchen to create an open, more spacious atmosphere. A long, central work island and a compact laundry closet are other space-saving features.
- The main-floor master suite offers a private bath with dual vanities and a large walk-in closet. Two additional bedrooms, a full bath and an intimate sitting area that overlooks the living room and entry are upstairs.
- A separate two-car garage is included with the blueprints.

Plan E-1421

Bedrooms: 3	Baths: 2
Living Area:	
Upper floor	561 sq. ft.
Main floor	924 sq. ft.
Total Living Area:	**1,485 sq. ft.**
Standard basement	924 sq. ft.
Exterior Wall Framing:	2x6

Foundation Options:

Standard basement

Crawlspace

Slab

(All plans can be built with your choice of foundation and framing. A generic conversion diagram is available. See order form.)

BLUEPRINT PRICE CODE: A

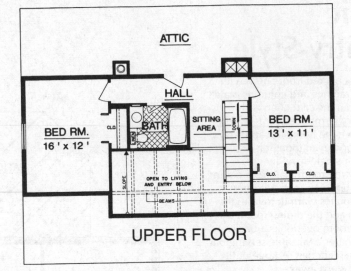

UPPER FLOOR

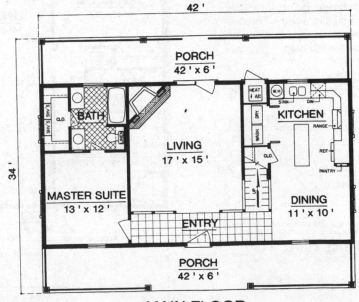

MAIN FLOOR

ORDER BLUEPRINTS ANYTIME!
CALL TOLL-FREE 1-888-626-2026

Plan E-1421

PRICES AND DETAILS
ON PAGES 12-15

Open Plan
for Narrow Lot

- This home's smart floor plan provides plenty of open spaces while fitting nicely on a narrow lot.
- The two-story foyer welcomes guests and provides a nice view through the living area and into the backyard.
- The sunken living room features a 16-ft. ceiling, a gas fireplace framed by windows and a corner niche that is designed to house a wet bar or an entertainment center.
- Bathed in sunlight, the adjacent dining bay opens to a rear covered patio through a French door and is easily serviced by the modern kitchen.
- A half-bath and a utility room with a built-in desk complete the main floor.
- Upstairs, a railed bridge overlooks the living room and the foyer.
- The master bedroom showcases a private covered deck that is reached through an elegant French door. The master bath has a unique glass-block wall and a dual-sink vanity.
- The two remaining bedrooms each have a custom window seat. A full bath is nearby.

Plan NW-366-ND

Bedrooms: 3	Baths: 2½
Living Area:	
Upper floor	703 sq. ft.
Main floor	788 sq. ft.
Total Living Area:	**1,491 sq. ft.**
Garage	485 sq. ft.
Exterior Wall Framing:	2x6

Foundation Options:

Crawlspace

(All plans can be built with your choice of foundation and framing. A generic conversion diagram is available. See order form.)

BLUEPRINT PRICE CODE: **A**

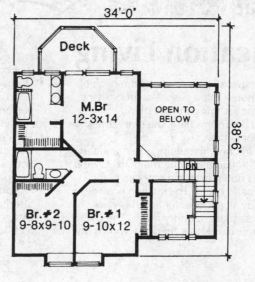

UPPER FLOOR

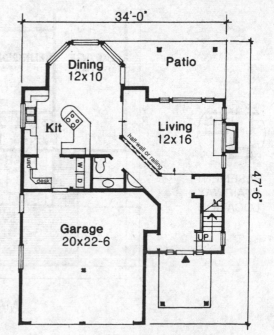

MAIN FLOOR

REAR VIEW

Vacation Living

- An expansive deck across the back of the home sets a casual outdoor living theme for this compact plan.
- Two bedrooms flank the entry and share a roomy bath.
- The kitchen, the dining room and the 16½-ft. vaulted living room are several steps down from the entry level for a dramatic effect. The kitchen provides a handy snack counter and has easy access to the laundry room. The living room's handsome fireplace warms the entire area. Sliding glass doors extend functions to the outdoors.
- Upstairs, a hideaway bedroom includes an 11½-ft. open-beam vaulted ceiling, a personal bath, a walk-in closet and a romantic private deck.
- The optional daylight basement (not shown) features a large recreation room with a fireplace and sliding glass doors to a patio underneath the rear deck.
- A fourth bedroom and a third bath are also included, in addition to large area that could be used for a hobby room or a children's play area.

FRONT OF HOME

Plans H-877-1 & -1A	
Bedrooms: 3+	Baths: 2-3
Living Area:	
Upper floor	320 sq. ft.
Main floor	1,200 sq. ft.
Daylight basement	1,200 sq. ft.
Total Living Area:	1,520/2,720 sq. ft.
Garage	155 sq. ft.
Exterior Wall Framing:	2x6
Foundation Options:	Plan #
Daylight basement	H-877-1
Crawlspace	H-877-1A

(All plans can be built with your choice of foundation and framing. A generic conversion diagram is available. See order form.)

BLUEPRINT PRICE CODE:	B/D

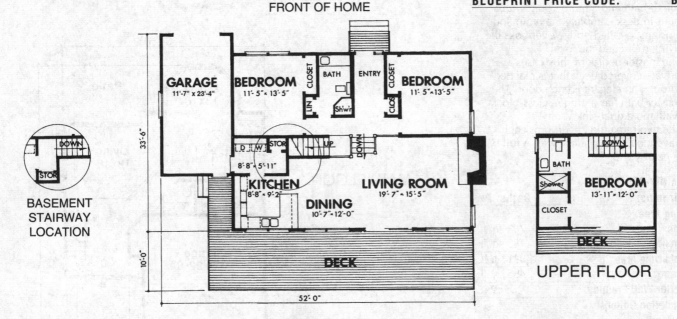

BASEMENT STAIRWAY LOCATION

MAIN FLOOR

UPPER FLOOR

Plans H-877-1 & -1A

PRICES AND DETAILS ON PAGES 12-15

Luxury in a Small Package

- The elegant exterior of this design sets the tone for the luxurious spaces within.
- The foyer opens to the centrally located living room, which features a 15-ft. cathedral ceiling, a handsome fireplace and access to a lovely rear terrace.
- The unusual kitchen design includes an angled snack bar that lies between the bayed breakfast den and the formal dining room. Sliding glass doors open to another terrace.
- The master suite is a dream come true, with its romantic fireplace, built-in desk and 9-ft.-high tray ceiling. The private bath includes a whirlpool tub and a dual-sink vanity.
- Another full bath serves the remaining two bedrooms, one of which boasts a cathedral ceiling and a beautiful arched window.

Plan AHP-9300

Bedrooms: 3	Baths: 2
Living Area:	
Main floor	1,513 sq. ft.
Total Living Area:	**1,513 sq. ft.**
Standard basement	1,360 sq. ft.
Garage	400 sq. ft.
Exterior Wall Framing:	2x4 or 2x6

Foundation Options:

Standard basement
Crawlspace
Slab
(All plans can be built with your choice of foundation and framing. A generic conversion diagram is available. See order form.)

BLUEPRINT PRICE CODE:	B

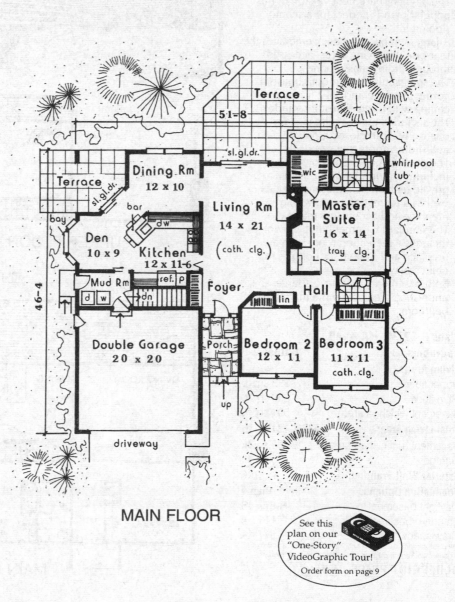

MAIN FLOOR

See this plan on our "One-Story" VideoGraphic Tour!
Order form on page 9

Hillside Design Fits Contours

- The daylight-basement version of this popular plan is perfect for a scenic, sloping lot.
- A large, wraparound deck embraces the rear-oriented living areas, accessed through sliding glass doors.
- The spectacular living room boasts a corner fireplace and a 19-ft. vaulted ceiling with three clerestory windows.
- The secluded master suite upstairs offers a walk-in closet, a private bath and sliding doors to a sun deck.
- The daylight basement (not shown) includes a fourth bedroom with a private bath and a walk-in closet, as well as a recreation room with a fireplace and access to a rear patio.
- The standard basement (not shown) includes a recreation room with a fireplace and a room for hobbies or child's play.
- Both basements also have a large unfinished area below the main-floor bedrooms.

REAR VIEW

UPPER FLOOR

STAIRWAY AREA IN CRAWLSPACE VERSION

Plans H-877-4, -4A & -4B

Bedrooms: 3+	Baths: 2-3
Living Area:	
Upper floor	333 sq. ft.
Main floor	1,200 sq. ft.
Basement (finished area)	591 sq. ft.
Total Living Area:	**1,533/2,124 sq. ft.**
Basement (unfinished area)	493 sq. ft.
Garage	480 sq. ft.
Exterior Wall Framing:	2x6
Foundation Options:	**Plan #**
Daylight basement	H-877-4B
Standard basement	H-877-4
Crawlspace	H-877-4A

(All plans can be built with your choice of foundation and framing. A generic conversion diagram is available. See order form.)

BLUEPRINT PRICE CODE:	**B/C**

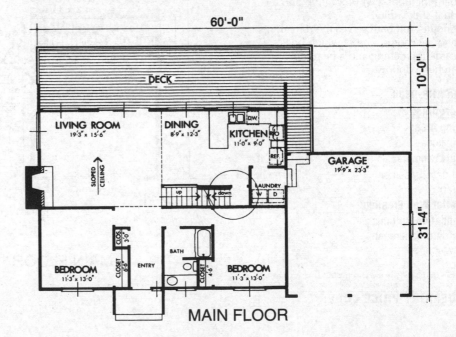

MAIN FLOOR

Plans H-877-4, -4A & -4B
PRICES AND DETAILS ON PAGES 12-15

Space-Saving Floor Plan

- Easy, affordable living is the basis for this great town and country design.
- The welcoming porch and the graceful arched window give the home its curb appeal. Inside, the floor plan provides large, highly livable spaces rather than several specialized rooms.
- The foyer opens to the spacious living room. A column separates the foyer from the formal dining room, which features a bay window and an alcove that is perfect for a china hutch. The country kitchen is large enough to accommodate family and guests alike.
- A beautiful open staircase leads to the second floor, where there are three bedrooms and two baths. The master bedroom offers a tray ceiling and a luxurious bath with a sloped ceiling and a corner shower.

Plan AX-92320

Bedrooms: 3	Baths: 2½
Living Area:	
Upper floor	706 sq. ft.
Main floor	830 sq. ft.
Total Living Area:	**1,536 sq. ft.**
Standard basement	754 sq. ft.
Garage	510 sq. ft.
Exterior Wall Framing:	2x6

Foundation Options:
Standard basement
Slab

(Typical foundation & framing conversion diagram available—see order form.)

BLUEPRINT PRICE CODE: B

FRONT VIEW

REAR VIEW

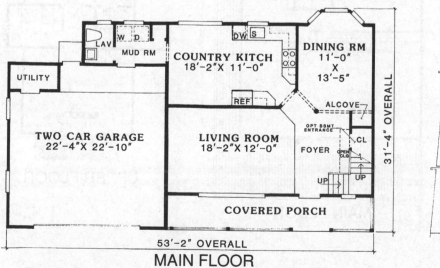

MAIN FLOOR

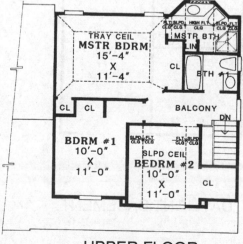

UPPER FLOOR

Romantic Retreat

- The romance and appeal of the Alpine chalet have remained constant over time. With more than 1,500 sq. ft. of living area, this chalet would make a great full-time home or vacation retreat.
- The L-shaped living room, dining room and kitchen flow together for casual living. This huge area is warmed by a

freestanding fireplace and surrounded by an ornate deck, which is accessed through sliding glass doors.
- The main-level bedroom, with its twin closets and adjacent bath, could serve as a nice master suite.
- Upstairs, two large bedrooms share another full bath. One bedroom features a walk-in closet, while the other boasts its own private deck.
- The daylight basement offers laundry facilities, plenty of storage space and an extra-long garage.

Plan H-858-2

Bedrooms: 3	**Baths:** 2

Living Area:	
Upper floor	576 sq. ft.
Main floor	960 sq. ft.
Total Living Area:	**1,536 sq. ft.**
Daylight basement	530 sq. ft.
Tuck-under garage	430 sq. ft.
Exterior Wall Framing:	2x6

Foundation Options:

Daylight basement
(All plans can be built with your choice of foundation and framing. A generic conversion diagram is available. See order form.)

BLUEPRINT PRICE CODE:	**B**

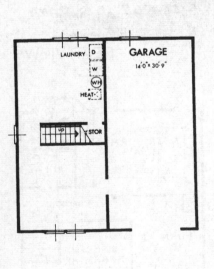

DAYLIGHT BASEMENT

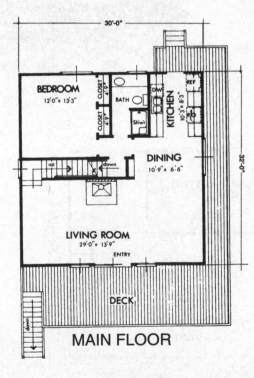

MAIN FLOOR

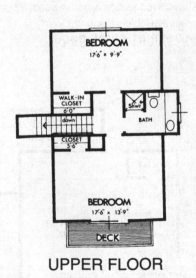

UPPER FLOOR

Plan H-858-2

PRICES AND DETAILS
ON PAGES 12-15

Narrow Lot Excitement

- A stylish entry invites guests into this exciting, narrow-lot, two-story home.
- The excitement continues inside with a two-story entry foyer and a view into the living room with fireplace and the dining room with sliders to the rear terrace.
- The U-shaped kitchen opens to a family eating/lounging area with side terrace.
- Upstairs, there are three large bedrooms and two full baths.
- The master bedroom offers two walk-in closets and a whirlpool tub in its private bath.

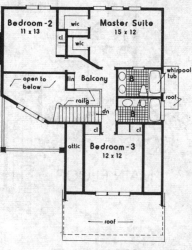

UPPER FLOOR

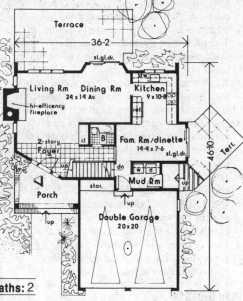

MAIN FLOOR

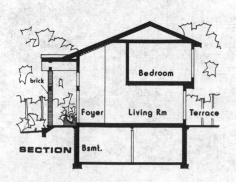

Plan AHP-9010	
Bedrooms: 3	**Baths:** 2
Space:	
Upper Floor	826 sq. ft.
Main floor	794 sq. ft.
Total Living Area	**1,620 sq. ft.**
Basement	794 sq. ft.
Garage	444 sq. ft.
Exterior Wall Framing	2x6
Foundation options:	
Standard Basement	
Slab	
(Foundation & framing conversion diagram available—see order form.)	
Blueprint Price Code	B

Distinctive One-Story

- Bright, bold windows and eye-catching masonry details give this modern one-story home its distinctive look.
- The vaulted living room, located just past the inviting, light-filled entry, boasts a 13-ft., 8-in. vaulted ceiling. The attractive fireplace, flanked by floor-to-ceiling windows, serves as the focal point of the room.
- The formal dining room, separated from the living room by columns, accesses a large rear deck through French doors.
- The modern kitchen includes a sunny breakfast area with access to a covered portion of the rear deck. A convenient laundry room is nearby.
- The luxurious master suite features a soaring 12-ft.-high ceiling and a bright sitting area with deck access. The master bath has a spa tub, a dual-sink vanity and a walk-in closet.
- Two additional bedrooms share a second full bath and are serviced by a hallway linen closet.

Plan B-91014

Bedrooms: 2+	Baths: 2
Living Area:	
Main floor	1,633 sq. ft.
Total Living Area:	**1,633 sq. ft.**
Standard basement	1,633 sq. ft.
Garage	448 sq. ft.
Exterior Wall Framing:	2x6

Foundation Options:

Standard basement

(All plans can be built with your choice of foundation and framing. A generic conversion diagram is available. See order form.)

BLUEPRINT PRICE CODE: B

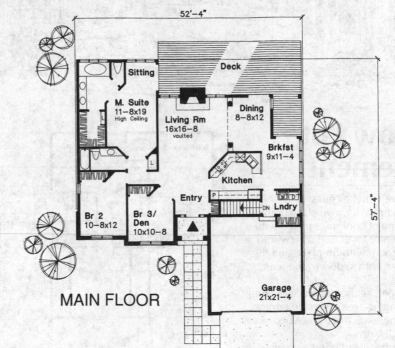

MAIN FLOOR

REAR VIEW

Plan B-91014

Garden Room Enhances Contemporary

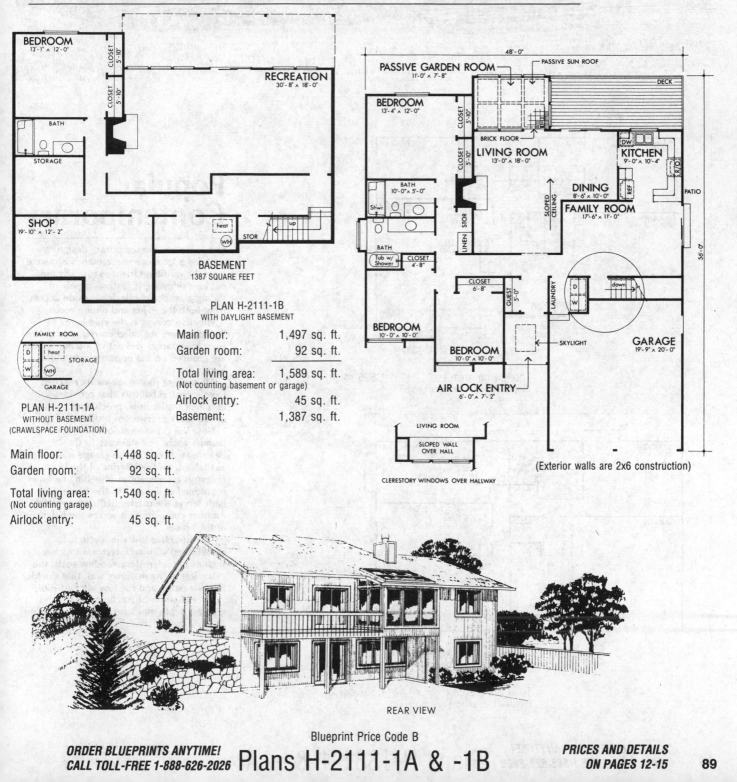

BEDROOM
13'-1" × 12'-0"

CLOSET 5'-10"

CLOSET 5'-10"

RECREATION
30'-8" × 18'-0"

BATH

STORAGE

SHOP
19'-10" × 12'-2"

heat
WH

up

STOR

BASEMENT
1387 SQUARE FEET

PLAN H-2111-1B
WITH DAYLIGHT BASEMENT

Main floor:	1,497 sq. ft.
Garden room:	92 sq. ft.
Total living area:	1,589 sq. ft.
(Not counting basement or garage)	
Airlock entry:	45 sq. ft.
Basement:	1,387 sq. ft.

FAMILY ROOM

D
heat
W
WH
STORAGE

GARAGE

PLAN H-2111-1A
WITHOUT BASEMENT
(CRAWLSPACE FOUNDATION)

Main floor:	1,448 sq. ft.
Garden room:	92 sq. ft.
Total living area:	1,540 sq. ft.
(Not counting garage)	
Airlock entry:	45 sq. ft.

48'-0"

PASSIVE GARDEN ROOM
11'-0" × 7'-8"

PASSIVE SUN ROOF

DECK

BEDROOM
13'-4" × 12'-0"

CLOSET 5'-10"

CLOSET 5'-10"

BRICK FLOOR

LIVING ROOM
13'-0" × 18'-0"

KITCHEN
9'-0" × 10'-4"

DW

R/O

REF

PATIO

BATH
10'-0" × 5'-0"

Shwr

LINEN

STOR

SLOPED CEILING

DINING
8'-6" × 10'-0"

FAMILY ROOM
17'-6" × 11'-0"

BATH

Tub w/ Shower

CLOSET
4'-8"

CLOSET
6'-8"

GUEST
5'-0"

LAUNDRY

D
W

down

56'-0"

BEDROOM
10'-0" × 10'-0"

SKYLIGHT

GARAGE
19'-9" × 20'-0"

BEDROOM
10'-0" × 10'-0"

AIR LOCK ENTRY
6'-0" × 7'-2"

LIVING ROOM

SLOPED WALL OVER HALL

CLERESTORY WINDOWS OVER HALLWAY

(Exterior walls are 2x6 construction)

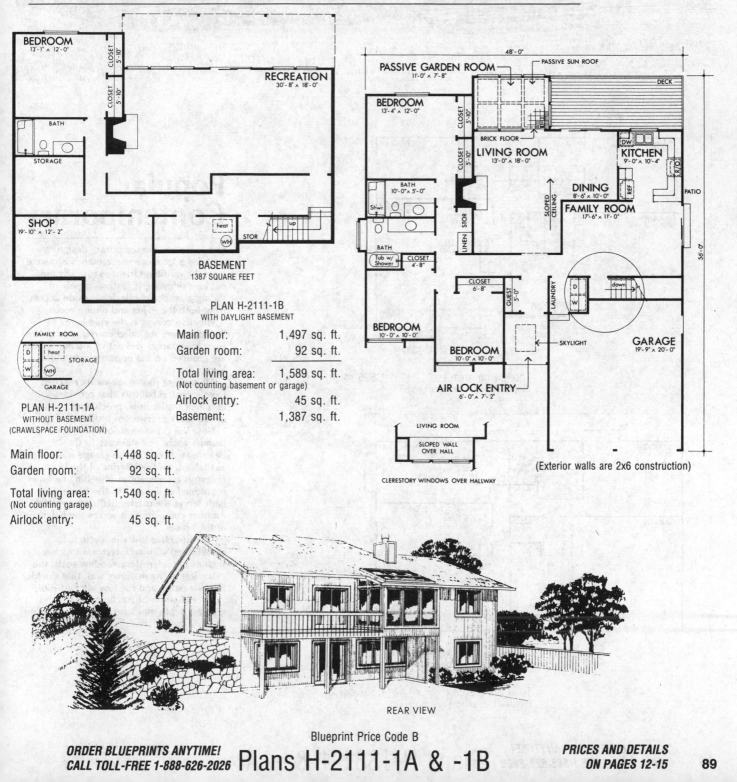

REAR VIEW

Blueprint Price Code B

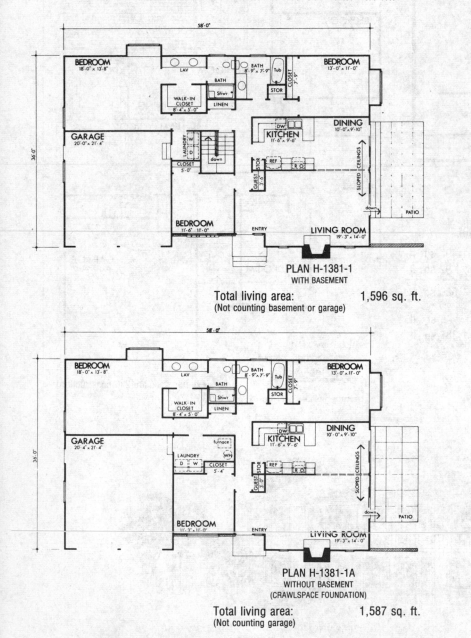

PLAN H-1381-1
WITH BASEMENT

Total living area: 1,596 sq. ft.
(Not counting basement or garage)

PLAN H-1381-1A
WITHOUT BASEMENT
(CRAWLSPACE FOUNDATION)

Total living area: 1,587 sq. ft.
(Not counting garage)

Popular Contemporary

This low-slung contemporary design contains a lot more space than is apparent from the outside. Oriented towards the outdoor sideyard, it features a pair of sliding glass doors offering outside access from both the living and dining room.

Effective zoning is the rule here: Bedrooms are secluded on one side to the rear; living areas and active kitchen space are grouped on the opposite side of the home.

All of these rooms are easily reached from a central hallway that provides excellent traffic flow, precluding unnecessary cross-room traffic.

Note the convenient location of the laundry room and staircase to the basement. Access to the garage is also available from the interior of the home. A generous assortment of plumbing facilities is grouped at the rear of the home. One bath serves the master bedroom privately. Another complete unit serves the balance of the house.

The attractive low silhouette is embellished with architectural touches such as the interesting window seats, the extension of the masonry wall that shields the side patio, and the low pitched roof.

Overall width of the home is 58' and greatest depth measures 36'. Exterior walls are 2x6 construction.

Blueprint Price Code B

ORDER BLUEPRINTS ANYTIME!
CALL TOLL-FREE 1-888-626-2026

Plans H-1381-1 & -1A

PRICES AND DETAILS
ON PAGES 12-15

90

Distinctive and Elegant

- A distinctive look is captured in the exterior of this elegant one-story. Half-round transoms grace the three glass doors that open to the columned, covered front porch.

- The spacious living room at the center of the homer commands attention, with its 15-ft. ceiling and inviting fireplace. A glass door flanked by windows opens to a skylighted porch, which is also accessible from the secondary bedroom at the back of the home.

- The unique dining room overlooks the two backyard porches and boasts an elegant octagonal design, shaped by columns and cased openings.

- A 14-ft. sloped, skylighted ceiling adds drama to the gourmet kitchen, which also showcases an angled cooktop bar and a windowed sink. Laundry facilities and storage space are nearby.

- The luxurious master suite is secluded at the rear of the home, with private access to the porch. The sumptuous master bath features an oval spa tub, a separate shower, dual vanities and a huge walk-in closet.

Plan E-1628

Bedrooms: 3	Baths: 2
Living Area:	
Main floor	1,655 sq. ft.
Total Living Area:	**1,655 sq. ft.**
Garage and storage	549 sq. ft.
Exterior Wall Framing:	2x6

Foundation Options:

Crawlspace

Slab

(All plans can be built with your choice of foundation and framing. A generic conversion diagram is available. See order form.)

BLUEPRINT PRICE CODE: **B**

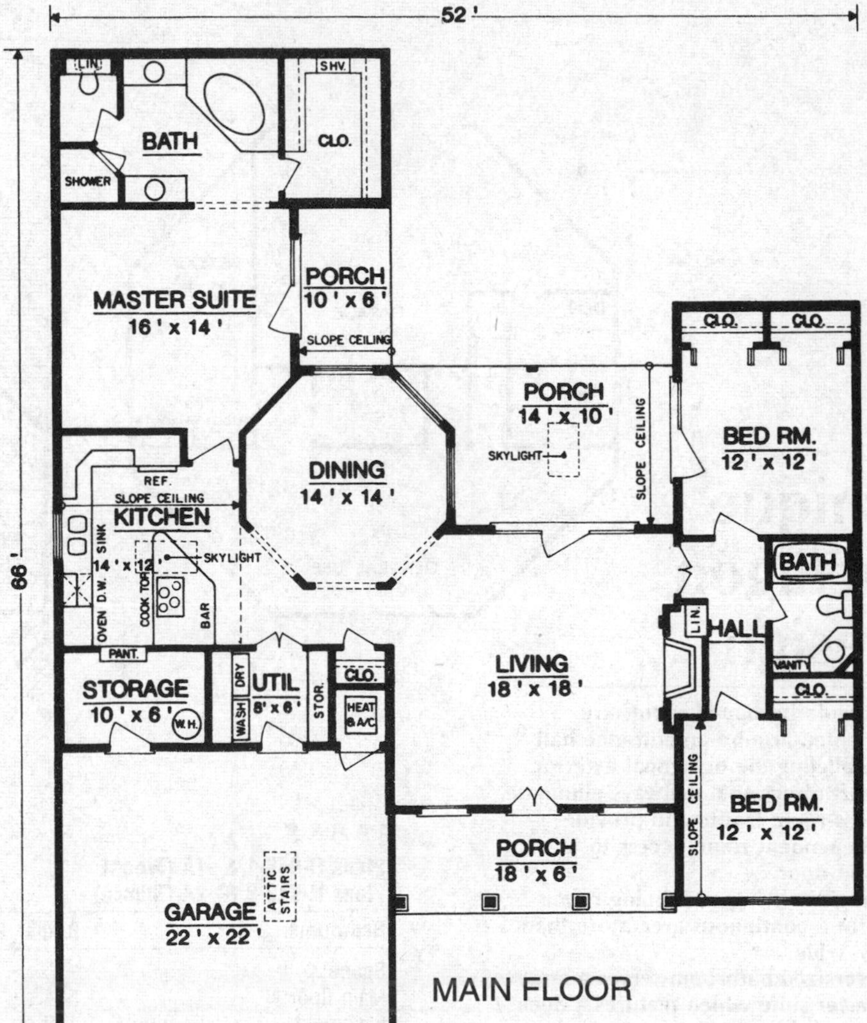

MAIN FLOOR

(Floor plan labels:)

BATH · LIN. · SHV. · CLO. · SHOWER · MASTER SUITE 16' x 14' · PORCH 10' x 6' · SLOPE CEILING · PORCH 14' x 10' · SKYLIGHT · SLOPE CEILING · CLO. · CLO. · BED RM. 12' x 12' · REF. · SLOPE CEILING · KITCHEN 14' x 12' · SKYLIGHT · DINING 14' x 14' · OVEN · D.W. · SINK · COOK TOP · BAR · PANT. · BATH · LIN. · HALL · VANITY · CLO. · LIVING 18' x 18' · SLOPE CEILING · STORAGE 10' x 6' · W.H. · WASH · DRY · UTIL 8' x 6' · STOR. · CLO. · HEAT & A/C · BED RM. 12' x 12' · GARAGE 22' x 22' · ATTIC STAIRS · PORCH 18' x 6'

52'

66'

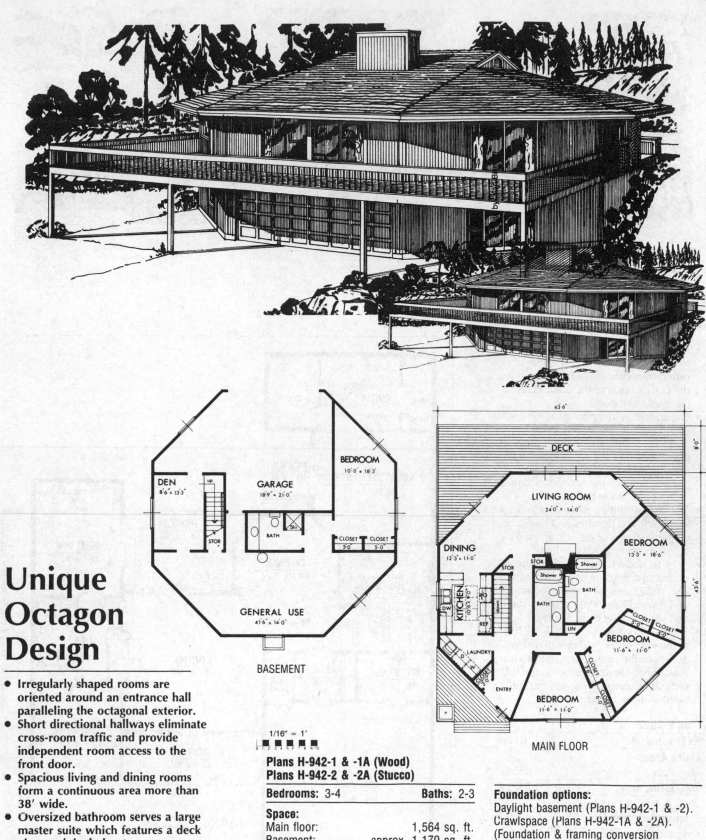

Unique Octagon Design

- Irregularly shaped rooms are oriented around an entrance hall paralleling the octagonal exterior.
- Short directional hallways eliminate cross-room traffic and provide independent room access to the front door.
- Spacious living and dining rooms form a continuous area more than 38' wide.
- Oversized bathroom serves a large master suite which features a deck view and dual closets.
- This plan is also available with a stucco exterior (Plans H-942-2, with daylight basement, and H-942-2A, without basement).

DEN 8'-6" x 13'-3"

up

STOR

GARAGE 18'-9" x 21'-0"

BATH

Shr

BEDROOM 10'-0" x 18'-3"

CLOSET 5'-0"

CLOSET 5'-0"

GENERAL USE 41'-6" x 14'-0"

BASEMENT

1/16" = 1'

DECK 43'-6" — 8'-0"

LIVING ROOM 24'-0" x 14'-0"

DINING 12'-3" x 11'-0"

STOR

Shower

Shower

Shower

BATH

BATH

KITCHEN 10'-6" x 9'-0"

DW

REF

down

LIN

BEDROOM 13'-3" x 18'-6"

CLOSET 5'-0"

CLOSET 5'-0"

BEDROOM 11'-6" x 11'-0"

CLOSET

LAUNDRY

W

D

CLOSET 3'-0"

ENTRY

CLOSET

BEDROOM 11'-6" x 11'-0"

43'-6"

MAIN FLOOR

Plans H-942-1 & -1A (Wood)
Plans H-942-2 & -2A (Stucco)

Bedrooms: 3-4	Baths: 2-3

Space:	
Main floor:	1,564 sq. ft.
Basement:	approx. 1,170 sq. ft.

Total with basement:	2,734 sq. ft.
Garage:	394 sq. ft.

Exterior Wall Framing:	2x6

Foundation options:
Daylight basement (Plans H-942-1 & -2).
Crawlspace (Plans H-942-1A & -2A).
(Foundation & framing conversion diagram available — see order form.)

Blueprint Price Code:

Without basement:	B
With basement:	D

Plans H-942-1/1A & -2/2A

PRICES AND DETAILS
ON PAGES 12-15

Porch Offers Three Entries

- Showy window treatments, stately columns and three sets of French doors give this Plantation-style home an inviting exterior.
- High 12-ft. ceilings in the living room, dining room and kitchen add volume to the economically-sized home.
- A corner fireplace and a view to the back porch are found in the living room. The porch is accessed from a door in the dining room.
- The adjoining kitchen features an angled snack bar that easily serves the dining room and the casual eating area.
- The secluded master suite offers a cathedral ceiling, a walk-in closet and a luxurious private bath with a spa tub and a separate shower.
- Across the home, two additional bedrooms share a second full bath.

Plan E-1602

Bedrooms: 3	Baths: 2
Living Area:	
Main floor	1,672 sq. ft.
Total Living Area:	**1,672 sq. ft.**
Standard basement	1,672 sq. ft.
Garage	484 sq. ft.
Exterior Wall Framing:	2x6

Foundation Options:
Standard basement
Crawlspace
Slab
(All plans can be built with your choice of foundation and framing. A generic conversion diagram is available. See order form.)

BLUEPRINT PRICE CODE: B

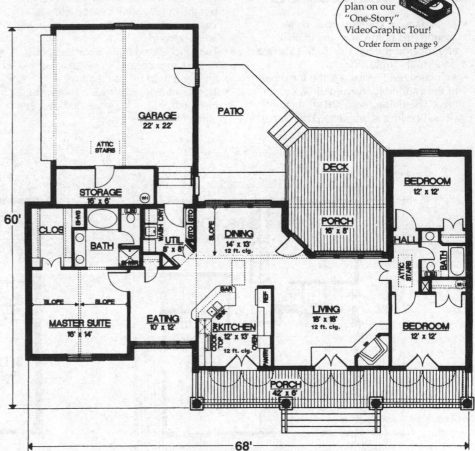

See this plan on our "One-Story" VideoGraphic Tour! Order form on page 9

MAIN FLOOR

Wraparound Deck Featured

- An expansive covered deck wraps around this home from the main entrance on the left side to the kitchen door on the right side.
- An oversized fireplace is the focal point of the vaulted living and dining room area. The living room's 10-ft.-high sloped ceiling is brightened by corner windows, while the dining area has sliding glass doors to access the adjoining deck.
- The kitchen is tucked into one corner, but the open counter space allows visual contact with the adjoining living areas beyond.
- Two good-sized main-floor bedrooms, each with sufficient closet space, are convenient to the hall bath.
- The basement level adds a roomy third bedroom, plus a huge general-use area and a tuck-under garage.

Plan H-806-2	
Bedrooms: 3	**Baths: 1**
Living Area:	
Main floor	952 sq. ft.
Daylight basement	673 sq. ft.
Total Living Area:	**1,625 sq. ft.**
Tuck-under garage	279 sq. ft.
Exterior Wall Framing:	2x6
Foundation Options:	
Daylight basement	

(All plans can be built with your choice of foundation and framing. A generic conversion diagram is available. See order form.)

BLUEPRINT PRICE CODE:	**B**

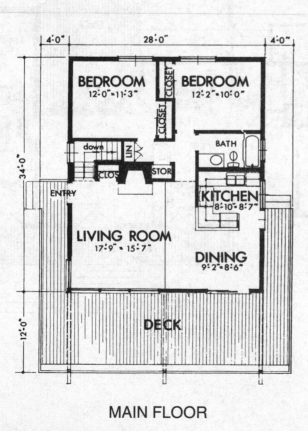

MAIN FLOOR

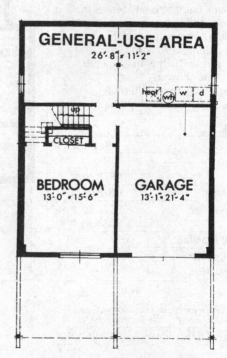

DAYLIGHT BASEMENT

Plan H-806-2

Angled Solar Design

- This passive-solar design with a six-sided core is angled to capture as much sunlight as possible.
- Finished in natural vertical cedar planks and stone veneer, this contemporary three-bedroom requires a minimum of maintenance.
- Double doors at the entry open into the spacious living and dining areas.

- The formal area features a 14-ft. domed ceiling with skylights, a freestanding fireplace and three sets of sliding glass doors. The central sliding doors lead to a glass-enclosed sun room.
- The bright eat-in kitchen merges with the den, where sliding glass doors lead to one of three backyard terraces.
- The master bedroom, in the quiet sleeping wing, boasts ample closets, a private terrace and a luxurious bath, complete with a whirlpool tub.
- The two secondary bedrooms share a convenient hall bath.

Plan K-534-L

Bedrooms: 3	**Baths:** 2

Living Area:

Main floor	1,647 sq. ft.
Total Living Area:	**1,647 sq. ft.**
Standard basement	1,505 sq. ft.
Garage	400 sq. ft.
Exterior Wall Framing:	2x4 or 2x6

Foundation Options:

Standard basement
Slab
(All plans can be built with your choice of foundation and framing. A generic conversion diagram is available. See order form.)

BLUEPRINT PRICE CODE:	B

See this plan on our "Best-Sellers" VideoGraphic Tour!
Order form on page 9

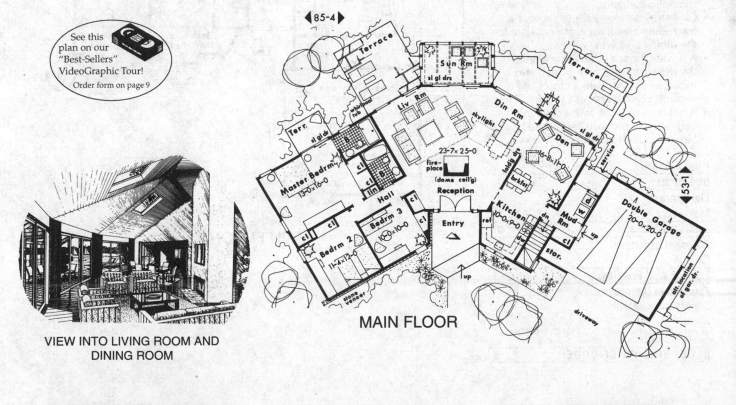

VIEW INTO LIVING ROOM AND DINING ROOM

MAIN FLOOR

Sensible and Sun-Drenched!

- This brilliant design combines lots of open, vaulted space with an abundance of windows to maximize its exquisite sun-drenched feel.
- The well-equipped kitchen features a handy snack bar, plus easy access to the dinette and the formal dining room, both of which are highlighted by warmly elegant, curved glass walls.
- Laundry facilities are conveniently located in the handy mudroom just off the kitchen.
- Your favorite room may well be the vaulted family room, with its cozy fireplace, adjoining terrace and romantic skylight.
- Clerestory windows above provide an interesting and dramatic use of light for the dining and living rooms.
- A private terrace is a unique feature of the deluxe master suite, which also includes a large walk-in closet and a secluded bath boasting a whirlpool tub.
- A full bath services two secondary bedrooms, which are brightened by large, beautiful boxed-out windows.

Plan K-818-D

Bedrooms: 3	Baths: 2½
Living Area:	
Main floor	1,674 sq. ft.
Total Living Area:	**1,674 sq. ft.**
Standard basement	1,627 sq. ft.
Garage	486 sq. ft.
Exterior Wall Framing:	2x4 or 2x6

Foundation Options:

Standard basement

Slab

(All plans can be built with your choice of foundation and framing. A generic conversion diagram is available. See order form.)

BLUEPRINT PRICE CODE: B

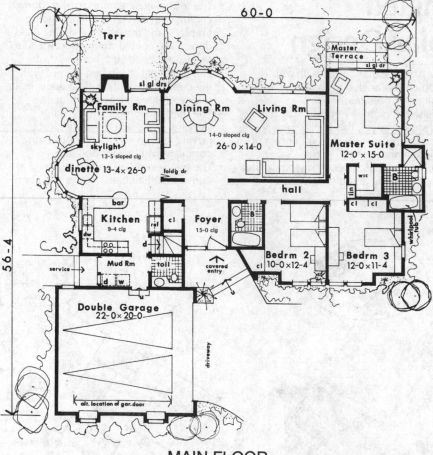

MAIN FLOOR

Plan K-818-D

PRICES AND DETAILS
ON PAGES 12-15

Intriguing Spaces for Your Special Location

Primarily envisioned as a home away from home, a retreat from the maddening crowd, this basically simple bungalow would be ideally located in some secluded mountain clearing. If it overlooks a lake or other spectacular view, it is well equipped with windows to take full advantage of the view. Exterior plywood in a variety of textures and styles not only provides a pleasant appearance when stained but also helps increase the building's rigidity. Natural cedar shakes, the more rugged the better, blend the pyramidal roof design into wooded surroundings. Various preservative treatments are available to add years to the life of a shake roof in a forested atmosphere.

By placing the living room a few steps below the rest of the main floor, a sense of warmth and security is achieved. This feeling is enhanced by the fireplace rising unobstructed from the hearth to the vaulted ceiling above. Clerestory windows far above highlight the interior as well as illuminating the balcony loft room.

The open design and spacious living areas allow plenty of room for entertaining.

The well-appointed kitchen is equipped to delight the most devoted "chef". A large laundry and utility space is located next to the kitchen and an attached double garage with automatic door opener eliminates the inconvenience of detached entry and exit. Multiple decks promote outdoor living and viewing on all sides.

First floor:	1,385 sq. ft.
Loft:	230 sq. ft.
Total living area:	1,615 sq. ft.
(Not counting basement or garage)	

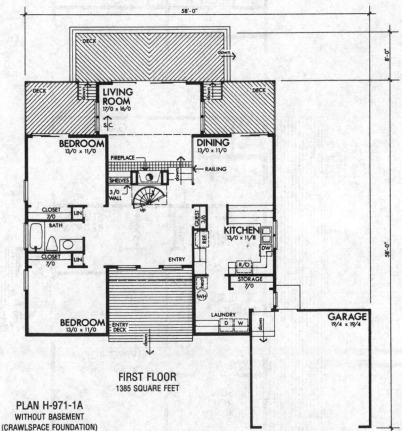

LOFT
230 SQUARE FEET

FIRST FLOOR
1385 SQUARE FEET

PLAN H-971-1A
WITHOUT BASEMENT
(CRAWLSPACE FOUNDATION)

Blueprint Price Code B
Plan H-971-1A

PRICES AND DETAILS
ON PAGES 12-15

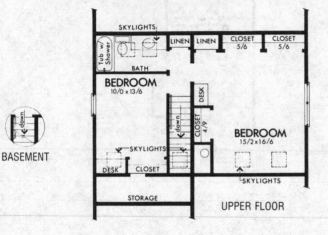

BASEMENT

Upper floor labels:
- SKYLIGHTS
- Tub w/ Shower
- LINEN
- LINEN
- CLOSET 5/6
- CLOSET 5/6
- BATH
- BEDROOM 10/0 x 13/6
- DESK
- CLOSET 4/9
- down
- BEDROOM 15/2 x 16/6
- SKYLIGHTS
- DESK
- CLOSET
- SKYLIGHTS
- STORAGE

UPPER FLOOR

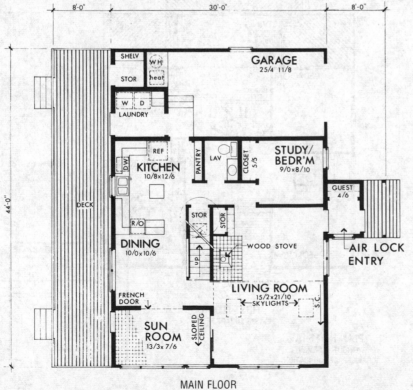

Main floor labels:
- 8'-0" 30'-0" 8'-0"
- 44'-0"
- SHELV
- W H
- STOR
- heat
- GARAGE 25/4 11/8
- W D
- LAUNDRY
- REF
- DW
- KITCHEN 10/8 x 12/6
- PANTRY
- LAV
- CLOSET 5/5
- STUDY/ BEDR'M 9/0 x 8/10
- GUEST 4/6
- DECK
- R/O
- STOR
- STOR
- DINING 10/0 x 10/6
- UP
- WOOD STOVE
- AIR LOCK ENTRY
- FRENCH DOOR
- SLOPED CEILING
- LIVING ROOM 15/2 x 21/10 SKYLIGHTS
- S.C.
- SUN ROOM 13/3 x 7/6

MAIN FLOOR

A Home for All Seasons

- Battened and barnlike, this rustic facade conceals a treasure of contemporary living.
- The airlock entry allows access without loss of heat, while the passive sun room collects heat. Other efficiencies include skylights and a woodstove.
- The step-saving kitchen offers a central work island and a pantry, plus easy access to the convenient main-floor laundry room.
- The study or extra bedroom could also be used as a den or home office.
- Two spacious bedrooms are located on the upper level, both with skylights, a built-in desk, and abundant closet space.

Plans H-970-2 & -2A

Bedrooms: 2-3	Baths: 1½
Living Area:	
Upper floor	563 sq. ft.
Main floor	1,009 sq. ft.
Total Living Area:	**1,572 sq. ft.**
Standard basement	768 sq. ft.
Garage	288 sq. ft.
Exterior Wall Framing:	2x6
Foundation Options:	Plan #
Standard basement	H-970-2
Crawlspace	H-970-2A

(Typical foundation & framing conversion diagram available—see order form.)

BLUEPRINT PRICE CODE:	B

Delightful Styling

- This quaint home's delightful styling is obvious, with its triple roof dormers and full-width covered front porch.
- Inside, 9-ft. ceilings grace the main floor, as the living room, dining room and kitchen merge to maximize space.
- The living room features a fireplace and three pairs of French doors. The dining room has rear access to a covered porch, which connects the house to the garage. The kitchen's wet bar is centrally located to serve all three rooms.
- The main-floor master suite has two pairs of French doors leading to the front porch. The master bath includes a raised marble tub, a dual-sink vanity, a walk-in closet and a sloped ceiling with a sunny skylight.
- The two bedrooms upstairs share a second full bath. Each bedroom features a quaint dormer to let the light shine in.

Plan E-1709

Bedrooms: 3	Baths: 2½
Living Area:	
Upper floor	540 sq. ft.
Main floor	1,160 sq. ft.
Total Living Area:	**1,700 sq. ft.**
Standard basement	1,160 sq. ft.
Garage	484 sq. ft.
Exterior Wall Framing:	2x6

Foundation Options:
Standard basement
Crawlspace
Slab
(All plans can be built with your choice of foundation and framing. A generic conversion diagram is available. See order form.)

BLUEPRINT PRICE CODE:	B

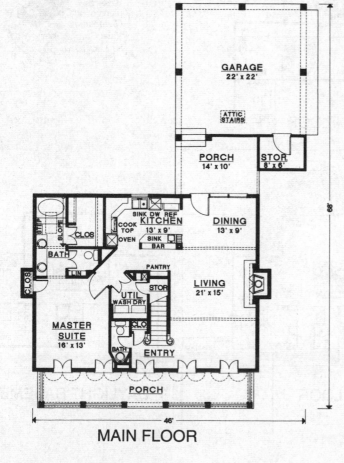

MAIN FLOOR

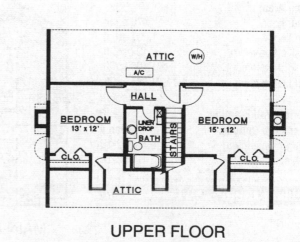

UPPER FLOOR

Deck and Spa!

- Designed for relaxation as well as for active indoor/outdoor living, this popular home offers a gigantic deck and an irresistible spa room.
- A covered porch welcomes guests into the entry hall, which flows past the central, open-railed stairway to the spectacular Great Room.
- Sliding glass doors on each side of the Great Room extend the living space to the huge V-shaped deck. The 22-ft. sloped ceiling and a woodstove add to the stunning effect.
- The master suite features a cozy window seat, a walk-in closet and private access to a full bath.
- The passive-solar spa room can be reached from the master suite as well as the backyard deck.
- The upper floor hosts two additional bedrooms, a full bath and a balcony hall that overlooks the Great Room.

REAR VIEW

Plans H-952-1A & -1B

Bedrooms: 3+	Baths: 2-3
Living Area:	
Upper floor	470 sq. ft.
Main floor	1,207 sq. ft.
Passive spa room	102 sq. ft.
Daylight basement	1,105 sq. ft.
Total Living Area:	**1,779/2,884 sq. ft.**
Garage	496 sq. ft.
Exterior Wall Framing:	2x6
Foundation Options:	**Plan #**
Daylight basement	H-952-1B
Crawlspace	H-952-1A

(All plans can be built with your choice of foundation and framing. A generic conversion diagram is available. See order form.)

BLUEPRINT PRICE CODE:	**B/D**

See this plan on our "Two-Story" VideoGraphic Tour!
Order form on page 9

UPPER FLOOR

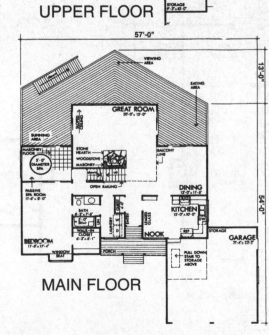

MAIN FLOOR

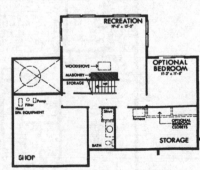

DAYLIGHT BASEMENT

Country Highlights

- A roomy front porch, narrow lap siding and paned windows give this two-story home a warm country feel.
- A sidelighted French door leads to the two-story foyer, brightened by a large half-round window above.
- Just off the foyer, the living room is warmed by a stone-hearthed fireplace and equipped with a wet bar. Sliding glass doors in the adjoining dining room and the nearby Great Room access the rear terrace.
- The large kitchen, just steps from the Great Room and the mudroom, includes a sunny breakfast nook with a broad bay window overlooking the front porch.
- The upper floor boasts a tray-ceilinged master suite with a luxurious bath, featuring a whirlpool tub, a dual-sink vanity and a separate shower.
- A balcony hall leads to two more bedrooms that share a full bath.

Plan AHP-9394

Bedrooms: 3+	Baths: 2½
Living Area:	
Upper floor	602 sq. ft.
Main floor	1,099 sq. ft.
Total Living Area:	**1,701 sq. ft.**
Standard basement	1,099 sq. ft.
Garage and storage	510 sq. ft.
Exterior Wall Framing:	2x4 or 2x6

Foundation Options:
Standard basement
Crawlspace
Slab
(All plans can be built with your choice of foundation and framing. A generic conversion diagram is available. See order form.)

BLUEPRINT PRICE CODE:	B

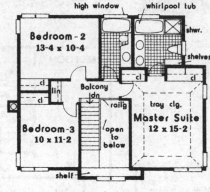

UPPER FLOOR

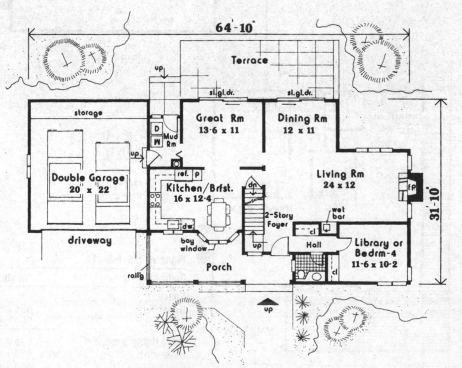

MAIN FLOOR

ORDER BLUEPRINTS ANYTIME!
CALL TOLL-FREE 1-888-626-2026

Plan AHP-9394

PRICES AND DETAILS
ON PAGES 12-15

101

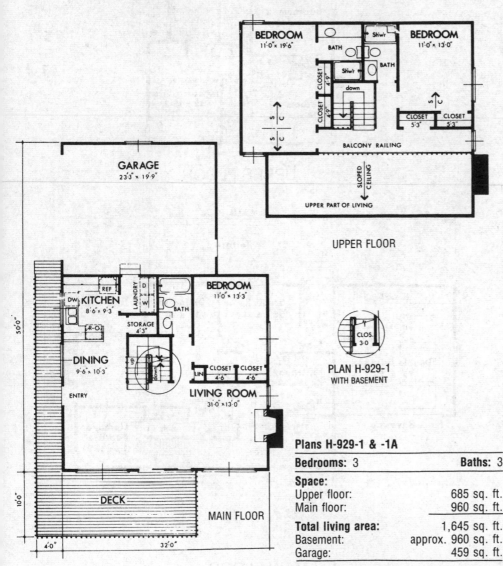

UPPER FLOOR

GARAGE
23'3" x 19'9"

KITCHEN
8'6" x 9'3"

REF
DW
F

LAUNDRY
D
W

BATH

STORAGE
4'3"

BEDROOM
11'0" x 13'3"

DINING
9'6" x 10'3"

ENTRY

CLOSET
4'6"

CLOSET
4'6"

LIN

LIVING ROOM
31'0" x 13'0"

DECK

MAIN FLOOR

50'0"

10'0"

4'0"

32'0"

BEDROOM
11'0" x 19'6"

BATH

Sh'w'r

BEDROOM
11'0" x 13'0"

Sh'w'r

BATH

CLOSET
4'9"

CLOSET
4'9"

down

CLOSET
5'3"

CLOSET
5'3"

S C

S C

S C

BALCONY RAILING

SLOPED CEILING

UPPER PART OF LIVING

CLOS.
3'0"

PLAN H-929-1
WITH BASEMENT

Contemporary Retreat

- Main floor plan revolves around an open, centrally located stairway.
- Spaciousness prevails throughout entire home with open kitchen and combination dining/living room.
- Living room features a great-sized fireplace and access to two-sided deck.
- Separate baths accommodate each bedroom.
- Upstairs hallway reveals an open balcony railing to oversee activities below.

Plans H-929-1 & -1A

Bedrooms: 3	Baths: 3
Space:	
Upper floor:	685 sq. ft.
Main floor:	960 sq. ft.
Total living area:	**1,645 sq. ft.**
Basement:	approx. 960 sq. ft.
Garage:	459 sq. ft.

Exterior Wall Framing:	2x6

Foundation options:
Daylight basement (Plan H-929-1).
Crawlspace (Plan H-929-1A).
(Foundation & framing conversion diagram available — see order form.)

Blueprint Price Code: B

REAR VIEW

FRONT VIEW

Bright Ideas!

- Four clerestory windows, a boxed-out window and wing walls sheltering the entry porch give this home definition.
- Inside, an open room arrangement coupled with vaulted ceilings, abundant windows and a sensational sun room make this home a definite bright spot.
- The living room features a 22-ft.-high vaulted ceiling, a warm woodstove and a glass-filled wall that offers views into the sun room. A patio door in the sun room opens to a large backyard deck.
- The adjoining dining room flows into the kitchen, which offers a versatile snack bar. A handy laundry room is just steps away, near the garage.
- Upstairs, the intimate bedroom suite includes a 14-ft.-high vaulted ceiling, a view to the living room, a walk-in closet and a private bath.
- The optional daylight basement boasts a spacious recreation room with a second woodstove, plus a fourth bedroom and a third bath. A shaded patio occupies the area under the deck.

Plans H-877-5A & -5B

Bedrooms: 3+	Baths: 2-3
Living Area:	
Upper floor	382 sq. ft.
Main floor	1,200 sq. ft.
Sun room	162 sq. ft.
Daylight basement	1,200 sq. ft.
Total Living Area:	**1,744/2,944 sq. ft.**
Garage	457 sq. ft.
Exterior Wall Framing:	2x6
Foundation Options:	**Plan #**
Daylight basement	H-877-5B
Crawlspace	H-877-5A

(All plans can be built with your choice of foundation and framing. A generic conversion diagram is available. See order form.)

BLUEPRINT PRICE CODE: **B/D**

UPPER FLOOR

DAYLIGHT BASEMENT

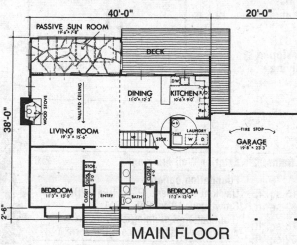

MAIN FLOOR

See this plan on our "Best-Sellers" VideoGraphic Tour!
Order form on page 9

BASEMENT STAIRWAY LOCATION

ORDER BLUEPRINTS ANYTIME!
CALL TOLL-FREE 1-888-626-2026

Plans H-877-5A & -5B

PRICES AND DETAILS
ON PAGES 12-15

103

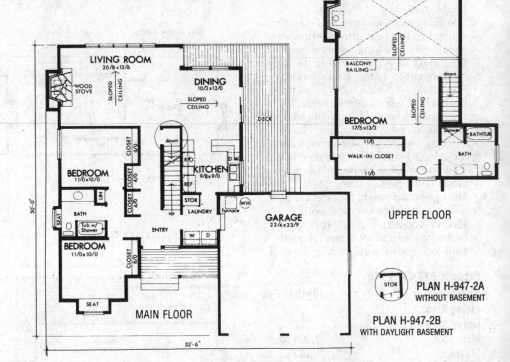

Compact Three-Bedroom Home

- A stylish blend of traditional and contemporary architecture emanates from this compact, three-bedroom home.
- Two bedrooms and an adjoining bath occupy one corner of the main level, segregated from the living areas by a central hallway.
- Large living and dining area has sloped ceilings, wood stove, and access to side deck.
- Master suite occupies entire 516 sq. ft. second floor, features sloped ceilings, and overlooks the living room below.

LIVING ROOM 20/8 x 13/6

DINING 10/3 x 12/0

SLOPED CEILING

WOOD STOVE

CLOSET 6/0

BEDROOM 11/0 x 10/0

CLOSET 4/0

CLOSET 4/0

BATH

LIN

SEAT

Tub w/ Shower

BEDROOM 11/0 x 10/0

CLOSET 6/0

SEAT

ENTRY

KITCHEN 9/8 x 9/0

REF

R/O

D.W.

STOR

LAUNDRY

down

up

WH

furnace

W D

DECK

GARAGE 22/4 x 23/9

MAIN FLOOR

52'-6"

50'-0"

UPPER FLOOR

SLOPED CEILING

BALCONY RAILING

BEDROOM 17/5 x 13/3

SLOPED CEILING

WALK-IN CLOSET

11/0

11/0

11/0

down

SHOWER

BATHTUB

BATH

STOR

PLAN H-947-2A WITHOUT BASEMENT

PLAN H-947-2B WITH DAYLIGHT BASEMENT

Plans H-947-2A & -2B			
Bedrooms: 3		**Baths:** 2	

Space:	
Upper floor:	516 sq. ft.
Main floor:	1,162 sq. ft.
Total living area:	**1,678 sq. ft.**
Basement:	approx. 1,162 sq. ft.
Garage:	530 sq. ft.

Exterior Wall Framing: 2x6

Foundation options:
Daylight basement (Plan H-947-2B).
Crawlspace (Plan H-947-2A).
(Foundation & framing conversion diagram available — see order form.)

Blueprint Price Code: B

Easy-Living Spaces

- A pair of half-round windows introduce this stylish two-story home, where open, easy living is the theme.
- Decorative columns set off the dining room, which boasts a sloped ceiling.
- Off the gallery and between the dining room and the living room is an angled serving bar, which is great for social functions or for meals on the go.
- A 16-ft. sloped ceiling and a nice fireplace accent the living room, which is open to the upper floor. A patio door accesses the covered back porch.
- A pantry, a windowed sink and a laundry closet are featured in the efficiently designed kitchen.
- A step from the entry, the master suite has an 11-ft. sloped ceiling and private access to the main-floor bath, which is also accessible from the hall. A pocket door closes off the first section of the bath to allow for separate sink areas. Two walk-in closets are also available.
- Another full bath serves the two secondary bedrooms on the upper floor.

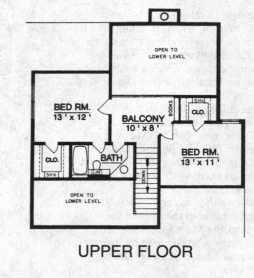

UPPER FLOOR

Plan E-1708

Bedrooms: 3	Baths: 2
Living Area:	
Upper floor	512 sq. ft.
Main floor	1,205 sq. ft.
Total Living Area:	**1,717 sq. ft.**
Garage and storage	556 sq. ft.
Exterior Wall Framing:	2x6

Foundation Options:

Crawlspace
Slab

(All plans can be built with your choice of foundation and framing. A generic conversion diagram is available. See order form.)

BLUEPRINT PRICE CODE: B

MAIN FLOOR

ORDER BLUEPRINTS ANYTIME!
CALL TOLL-FREE 1-888-626-2026

Plan E-1708

PRICES AND DETAILS
ON PAGES 12-15

105

Appealing, Angled Ranch

- This unique, angled ranch boasts a striking interior, which is highlighted by a dramatic domed ceiling at its center.
- The gabled entryway opens to a spacious pentagonal living area. A handsome fireplace, lots of glass and an adjoining backyard terrace are showcased, in addition to the 14-ft.-high domed ceiling.
- The dining room can be extended into the nearby den by opening the folding doors. The den features a 14-ft. sloped ceiling, an exciting solar bay and terrace access.
- A casual eating area and a nice-sized kitchen expand to the front of the home, ending at a windowed sink.
- The nearby mudroom area includes laundry facilities and an optional powder room.
- The sleeping wing offers four bedrooms, including an oversized master suite with a private terrace and a skylighted bath with dual sinks and a whirlpool tub. The secondary bedrooms share another full bath.

Plan K-669-N

Bedrooms: 4	Baths: 2-2½
Living Area:	
Main floor	1,728 sq. ft.
Total Living Area:	**1,728 sq. ft.**
Standard basement	1,545 sq. ft.
Garage and storage	468 sq. ft.
Exterior Wall Framing:	2x4 or 2x6

Foundation Options:
Standard basement
Slab
(All plans can be built with your choice of foundation and framing. A generic conversion diagram is available. See order form.)

BLUEPRINT PRICE CODE:	B

VIEW INTO DINING ROOM AND LIVING ROOM

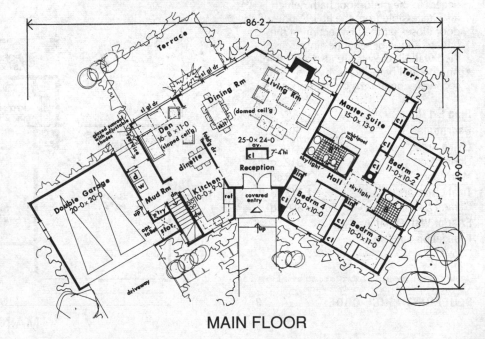

MAIN FLOOR

Dynamic Design

- This dynamic five-sided design is perfect for scenic sites. The front (or street) side of the home is shielded by a two-car garage, while the back of the home hosts a glass-filled living area surrounded by a spectacular deck.
- The unique shape of the home allows for an unusually open and spacious interior design.
- The living/dining room is further expanded by a 20-ft.-high vaulted ceiling. The centrally located fireplace provides a focal point while distributing heat efficiently.
- The space-saving galley-style kitchen is connected to the living/dining area by a snack bar.
- A large main-floor bedroom has two closets and easy access to a full bath.
- The upper floor is highlighted by a breathtaking balcony overlook. Also, two bedrooms share a nice-sized bath.
- The optional daylight basement includes a huge recreation room.

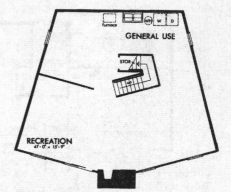

UPPER FLOOR

DAYLIGHT BASEMENT

Plans H-855-1 & -1A

Bedrooms: 3	Baths: 2
Living Area:	
Upper floor	625 sq. ft.
Main floor	1,108 sq. ft.
Daylight basement	1,108 sq. ft.
Total Living Area:	**1,733/2,841 sq. ft.**
Garage	346 sq. ft.
Exterior Wall Framing:	2x6
Foundation Options:	**Plan #**
Daylight basement	H-855-1
Crawlspace	H-855-1A

(All plans can be built with your choice of foundation and framing. A generic conversion diagram is available. See order form.)

BLUEPRINT PRICE CODE:	**B/D**

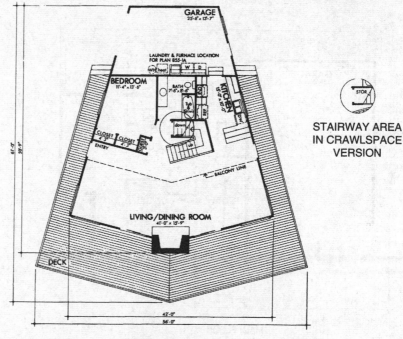

STAIRWAY AREA IN CRAWLSPACE VERSION

MAIN FLOOR

Compact Design with Energy-Saving Features

UPPER FLOOR

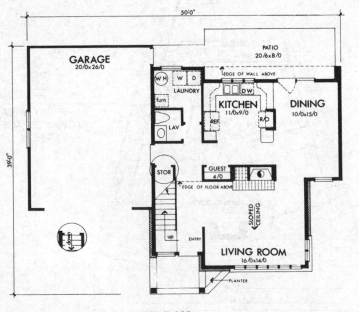

MAIN FLOOR

- This stylish family home is wrapped in an attractive exterior of wood siding and brick veneer accents
- Covered entry leads into commodious living room with heat-circulating fireplace and sloped ceilings.
- Dining room opens to a patio via French doors and lies opposite an efficient U-shaped kitchen.
- Ample closet space, master bedroom, and two additional bedrooms comprise the second level.

Plans H-3741-1 & -1A

Bedrooms: 3	Baths: 2½
Space:	
Upper floor:	900 sq. ft.
Main floor:	853 sq. ft.
Total living area:	1,753 sq. ft.
Basement:	approx. 853 sq. ft.
Garage:	520 sq. ft.
Exterior Wall Framing:	2x6

Foundation options:
Standard basement (Plan H-3741-1).
Crawlspace (Plan H-3741-1A).
(Foundation & framing conversion diagram available — see order form.)

Blueprint Price Code:	B

108

ORDER BLUEPRINTS ANYTIME!
CALL TOLL-FREE 1-888-626-2026

Plans H-3741-1 & -1A

PRICES AND DETAILS
ON PAGES 12-15

New-Fashioned Farmhouse

- Traditional styling and a highly contemporary floor plan distinguish this new-fashioned farmhouse.
- The home is embraced by a covered porch, which is accessible from the foyer and the family room.
- The floor plan is zoned for formal and casual living. The casual living spaces are oriented to the rear and integrated for family interaction. The family room's inviting fireplace can be seen from the adjoining kitchen, which features a handy snack bar and a bayed breakfast nook.
- Upstairs are three bedrooms. The larger master bedroom has a vaulted ceiling that soars to approximately 12 feet. Two walk-in closets and a private, vaulted bath with an oval tub, a separate shower and dual sinks are also included. The secondary bedrooms share another full bath.

Plan S-62893

Bedrooms: 3	Baths: 2½
Living Area:	
Upper floor	774 sq. ft.
Main floor	963 sq. ft.
Total Living Area:	**1,737 sq. ft.**
Standard basement	930 sq. ft.
Garage	520 sq. ft.
Exterior Wall Framing:	2x6

Foundation Options:
Standard basement
Crawlspace
Slab
(All plans can be built with your choice of foundation and framing. A generic conversion diagram is available. See order form.)

BLUEPRINT PRICE CODE: B

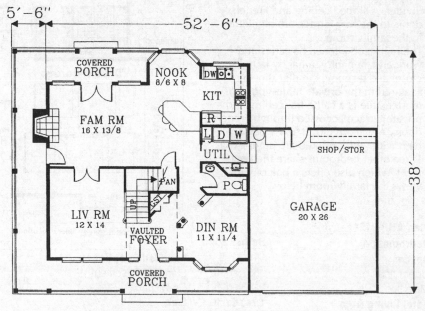

UPPER FLOOR

MAIN FLOOR

ORDER BLUEPRINTS ANYTIME!
CALL TOLL-FREE 1-888-626-2026

Plan S-62893

PRICES AND DETAILS
ON PAGES 12-15

109

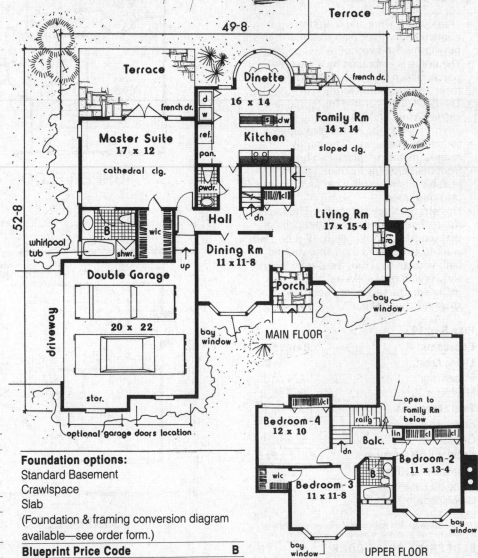

Colonial Has Modern Features

- This stately Colonial is as distinguished on the inside as it is on the outside.
- The dramatic entrance reveals a spacious living room with a big fireplace and a front bay window and an adjoining family room separated only by a decorative see-through wood divider. A sloped ceiling and French doors to the rear terrace are highlights in the family room.
- The high-tech kitchen has an island work area, a pantry, a handy laundry closet and a sunny, circular dinette.
- Featured in the private main-floor master suite is a cathedral ceiling and a private terrace accessed through French doors. A walk-in closet and a personal bath with whirlpool tub are other extras.
- Three other bedrooms share the upper level, which also offers a balcony that views the family room below.

Plan AHP-9121

Bedrooms: 4	Baths: 2 ½
Space:	
Upper floor	557 sq. ft.
Main floor	1,183 sq. ft.
Total Living Area	**1,740 sq. ft.**
Basement	1,183 sq. ft.
Garage	440 sq. ft.
Exterior Wall Framing	2x4 or 2x6

Foundation options:

Standard Basement
Crawlspace
Slab
(Foundation & framing conversion diagram available—see order form.)

Blueprint Price Code   **B**

Plan AHP-9121

PRICES AND DETAILS
ON PAGES 12-15

Open and Airy Design

- The open and airy design of this compact, affordable home makes the most of its space.
- Inside, the entry's 23½-ft. vaulted ceiling soars to the upper floor. Two decorative wood rails set off the entry from the living room. A corner fireplace topped by a wood mantel anchors the room, and French doors lead to the backyard.
- The good-sized dining room extends to the kitchen, where a handy island maximizes workspace, and a bright window adds light. Plenty of room is available for cooking and dining.
- Across the home, the secluded master bedroom is a great adult retreat. The private master bath boasts two separate vanities and a walk-in closet with convenient built-in shelves.
- At the top of the open staircase, a railed sitting area with a 16-ft. vaulted ceiling is ideal for a computer nook.
- Two spacious bedrooms are serviced by a centrally located hall bath.
- Plans for a detached two-car garage are also included in the blueprints.

Plan LS-94046-E

Bedrooms: 3	Baths: 2
Living Area:	
Upper floor	561 sq. ft.
Main floor	1,190 sq. ft.
Total Living Area:	**1,751 sq. ft.**
Standard basement	1,145 sq. ft.
Exterior Wall Framing:	2x6

Foundation Options:

Standard basement
(All plans can be built with your choice of foundation and framing. A generic conversion diagram is available. See order form.)

BLUEPRINT PRICE CODE: B

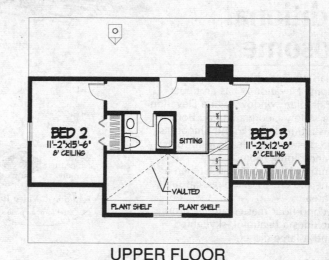

UPPER FLOOR

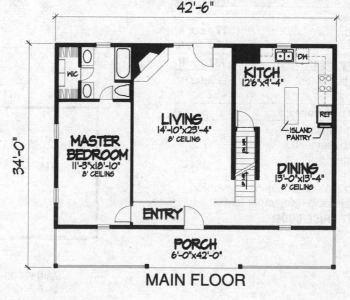

MAIN FLOOR

ORDER BLUEPRINTS ANYTIME!
CALL TOLL-FREE 1-888-626-2026

Plan LS-94046-E

*PRICES AND DETAILS
ON PAGES 12-15*

111

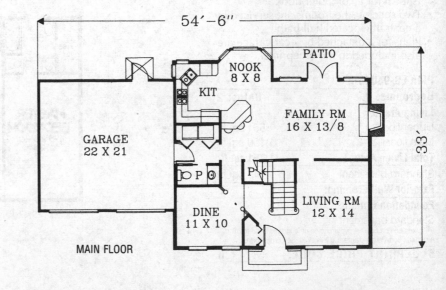

Elevation B

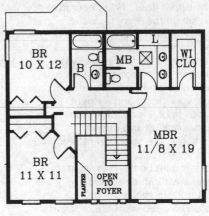

Elevation A

Traditional Twosome

- This plan offers a choice of two elevations. Elevation A has an upper-level Palladian window, while Elevation B has a stately Georgian entry. Both versions are included in the blueprints.
- A vaulted entry foyer leads to formal living and dining rooms.
- The family room, nook and kitchen are combined to create one huge casual living area.
- The second-floor master suite is roomy and includes a beautiful, skylighted bath and a large closet.

See this plan on our "Country & Traditional" Video Tour!
Order form on page 9

Plan S-22189

Bedrooms: 3	Baths: 2½
Living Area:	
Upper floor	774 sq. ft.
Main floor	963 sq. ft.
Total Living Area:	**1,737 sq. ft.**
Standard basement	963 sq. ft.
Garage	462 sq. ft.
Exterior Wall Framing:	2x6

Foundation Options:
Standard basement
Crawlspace
Slab
(Typical foundation & framing conversion diagram available—see order form.)

BLUEPRINT PRICE CODE: B

UPPER FLOOR

BR 10 X 12
B
MB
L
WI CLO
BR 11 X 11
PLANTER
OPEN TO FOYER
MBR 11/8 X 19

MAIN FLOOR

54'-6"
33'
GARAGE 22 X 21
NOOK 8 X 8
KIT
PATIO
FAMILY RM 16 X 13/8
P
P
DINE 11 X 10
LIVING RM 12 X 14

Plan S-22189

PRICES AND DETAILS
ON PAGES 12-15

Clean, Stylish Lines

- The sweeping roofline and arched windows give this home plenty of "presence", even though it is fairly modest in size.
- Besides being stylish, the plan is also sturdy and energy-efficient, with 2x6 walls, R-19 perimeter insulation and R-38 in the ceilings.
- The sheltered entry leads to an effective foyer which in turn leads visitors to the dining area or living room. These two spaces flow together to create a huge space for entertaining.
- The roomy kitchen includes abundant cabinet and counter space. A utility room is in the garage entry area.
- A large downstairs bedroom adjoins a full bath and includes a large walk-in closet. This would make a great guest or in-law suite.
- Upstairs, another large bedroom features a private bath and walk-in closet.
- A versatile loft overlooks the living room below, and provides room for children to play or for adults to keep a library, sewing room, studio or study.

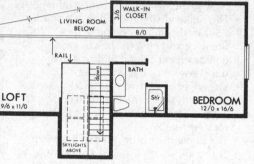

UPPER FLOOR

Plans H-1448-1 & -1A	
Bedrooms: 2-3	**Baths:** 2
Space:	
Upper floor	487 sq. ft.
Main floor	1,278 sq. ft.
Total Living Area	**1,765 sq. ft.**
Basement	1,278 sq. ft.
Garage	409 sq. ft.
Exterior Wall Framing	2x6
Foundation options:	Plan #
Standard Basement	H-1448-1
Crawlspace	H-1448-1A
(Foundation & framing conversion diagram available—see order form.)	
Blueprint Price Code	B

BASEMENT

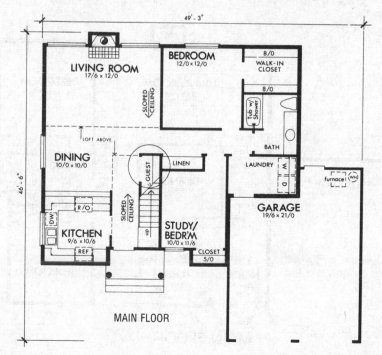

MAIN FLOOR

Combining Past and Present

- This home combines the best from the past and the present. The shed roof is reminiscent of a New England saltbox, while the gabled dormers and half-circle windows recall the Victorian era.
- Inside, the cozy kitchen features an island cooktop and a breakfast counter. A built-in pantry and a china closet are centrally located between the dining room and the kitchen.

- The sunny nook is popular for everyday meals. The formal dining room offers a view to the living room over a railing.
- The sunken living room boasts a soaring 25-ft.-high vaulted ceiling, a nice fireplace and built-in shelves for an entertainment center. Sliding glass doors open to a backyard deck.
- The larger of the two main-floor bedrooms provides additional deck access. The full bath is conveniently located nearby.
- The upper floor is devoted to the master bedroom, which features a hydro-spa, a separate shower and a walk-in closet.

Plan H-1453-1A

Bedrooms: 3	**Baths:** 2

Living Area:

Upper floor	386 sq. ft.
Main floor	1,385 sq. ft.
Total Living Area:	**1,771 sq. ft.**
Garage	438 sq. ft.
Exterior Wall Framing:	2x6

Foundation Options:

Crawlspace
(All plans can be built with your choice of foundation and framing. A generic conversion diagram is available. See order form.)

BLUEPRINT PRICE CODE:	**B**

MAIN FLOOR

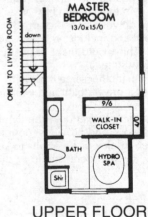

UPPER FLOOR

Updated Creole

- This Louisiana-style raised cottage features a tin roof, shuttered windows and three pairs of French doors, all of which add to the comfort and nostalgic appeal of this Creole classic.
- The French doors enter from the cool and relaxing front porch to the formal living areas and a front bedroom.
- The central living room, which features a 12-ft. ceiling, merges with the dining room and the kitchen's eating area. A fireplace warms the whole space while more French doors access a porch.
- The efficient kitchen offers a 12-ft. flat ceiling, an angled snack bar and a bayed nook with a 12-ft. sloped ceiling.
- A secluded master suite showcases a private bath, fit for the most demanding tastes. Across the home, the secondary bedrooms include abundant closet space and share a full bath.
- This full-featured, energy-efficient design also includes a large utility room and extra storage space in the garage.

Plan E-1823

Bedrooms: 3	Baths: 2
Living Area:	
Main floor	1,800 sq. ft.
Total Living Area:	**1,800 sq. ft.**
Garage	550 sq. ft.
Exterior Wall Framing:	2x6

Foundation Options:
Crawlspace
Slab
(All plans can be built with your choice of foundation and framing. A generic conversion diagram is available. See order form.)

BLUEPRINT PRICE CODE: B

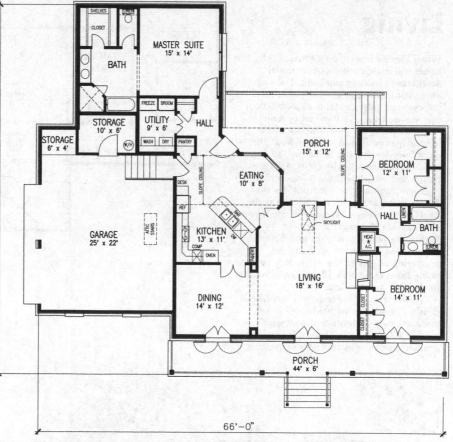

MAIN FLOOR

ORDER BLUEPRINTS ANYTIME!
CALL TOLL-FREE 1-888-626-2026

Plan E-1823

PRICES AND DETAILS
ON PAGES 12-15

115

Solar Berm Offers Innovative Living

When viewed from the front road side, this home will match other conventional dwellings in its neighborhood. The approach to the garage is at street level and the covered entry protects a double door that serves a 12'-3" x 9'-6" entry hall.

At this point the plan introduces an innovative concept in construction. The main floor level drops 6' below the entry hall and is connected by eight staircase treads and separated by a 3' open railing.

Open planning that incorporates the family living area with the kitchen is the heart of this home. Extensions on either side provide abundant spaces for bedrooms, laundry, storage and baths.

Surrounded on three sides by the tempering affects of the earth, this bermed home takes maximum advantage of nature for heating and cooling.

The numerous double-paned sun-faced windows are oriented to shower the masonry massed floors and wall with passive solar warmth. Openable clerestories provide cooling and control overheating.

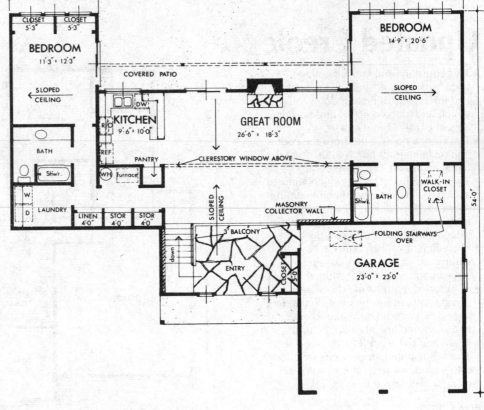

PLAN H-938-1A
WITHOUT BASEMENT
(SLAB-ON-GRADE FOUNDATION)

Total living area: 1,789 sq. ft.
(Not counting garage)

(EXTERIOR WALLS FRAMED
IN 2X6 STUDS)

Blueprint Price Code B

Plan H-938-1A

PRICES AND DETAILS
ON PAGES 12-15

Cozy Covered Porches

- Twin dormers give this raised one-story design the appearance of a two-story. Two covered porches and a deck supplement the main living areas with plenty of outdoor entertaining space.
- The large central living room features a dramatic fireplace, a 12-ft. ceiling with a skylight and access to both porch areas.
- Double doors open to a bayed eating area, which overlooks the adjoining deck and includes a sloped ceiling that rises to 12 ft. in the kitchen. An angled snack bar and a pantry are also featured.
- The elegant master suite is tucked to one side of the home and also overlooks the backyard and deck. Laundry facilities and garage access are nearby.
- Across the home, two additional bedrooms share another full bath.

Plan E-1826

Bedrooms: 3	Baths: 2

Living Area:

Main floor	1,800 sq. ft.
Total Living Area:	**1,800 sq. ft.**
Garage	550 sq. ft.
Storage	84 sq. ft.
Exterior Wall Framing:	2x6

Foundation Options:

Crawlspace
Slab

(All plans can be built with your choice of foundation and framing. A generic conversion diagram is available. See order form.)

BLUEPRINT PRICE CODE: B

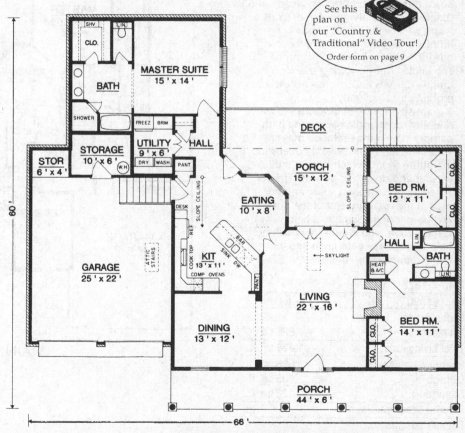

MAIN FLOOR

See this plan on our "Country & Traditional" Video Tour! Order form on page 9

ORDER BLUEPRINTS ANYTIME!
CALL TOLL-FREE 1-888-626-2026

Plan E-1826

PRICES AND DETAILS
ON PAGES 12-15

117

High Interest!

- Angles, high ceilings and an excellent use of space add interest and volume to the living areas of this efficient four-bedroom home.
- Beyond the beautiful stucco facade, the spacious central living room extends a warm welcome with its handsome fireplace; a French door whisks you outside to the covered back porch.
- The kitchen and breakfast room's unique designs ensure easy access and mobility for the family.
- A giant-sized walk-in closet, a separate dressing room and an adjoining bath pamper you in the secluded master suite. The bath conveniently opens to the utility room, which houses the washer and dryer and an extra freezer.
- Three more bedrooms share another bath at the opposite end of the home.
- To the rear of the garage, a handy storage room and a built-in workbench help to organize your lawn and maintenance equipment.

Plan E-1828

Bedrooms: 4	Baths: 2
Living Area:	
Main floor	1,828 sq. ft.
Total Living Area:	**1,828 sq. ft.**
Standard basement	1,828 sq. ft.
Garage	605 sq. ft.
Storage	120 sq. ft.
Exterior Wall Framing:	2x6

Foundation Options:

Standard basement

Crawlspace

Slab

(All plans can be built with your choice of foundation and framing. A generic conversion diagram is available. See order form.)

BLUEPRINT PRICE CODE:	B

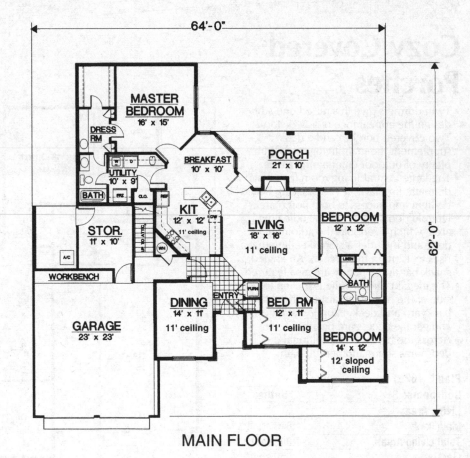

MAIN FLOOR

Eye-Catching One-Story

- This eye-catching design sports cedar siding, multiple gables and a stylish planter that frames a bayed nook.
- The covered entry opens to a roomy foyer, where double doors lead to a quiet den or bedroom.
- Straight ahead, a corner fireplace in the Great Room radiates warmth to the surrounding rooms. The dramatic rear window wall culminates at French doors. A 14½-ft. vaulted ceiling and a wet bar are other embellishments.
- The deluxe kitchen includes a pantry, a built-in desk and a boxed-out window above the sink. The delightful nook features an 11½-ft. vaulted ceiling.
- A skylighted hall leads to the relaxing master bedroom, complete with a sitting area and private access to the outdoors. The master bath offers a garden tub, a separate shower and a toilet closet.
- The remaining bedroom has easy access to another compartmentalized bath.

Plan S-42093

Bedrooms: 2+	Baths: 2
Living Area:	
Main floor	1,830 sq. ft.
Total Living Area:	**1,830 sq. ft.**
Standard basement	1,765 sq. ft.
Garage	433 sq. ft.
Exterior Wall Framing:	2x6

Foundation Options:

Standard basement
Crawlspace
Slab

(All plans can be built with your choice of foundation and framing. A generic conversion diagram is available. See order form.)

BLUEPRINT PRICE CODE: **B**

MAIN FLOOR

SIT

MBR
19/6 X 14
INC SITTING AREA

WI CLO

M BATH

TUB

BR
12/4 X 11

VAULTED
GREAT RM
23 X 23/6
INC DIN

DIN

BAR

KIT

DW

R

STOR

FOYER

PAN

GST

VAULTED
NOOK
10 X 12

UTIL

BATH

DEN/BR
12/4 X 10

ENTRY

PLANTER

GARAGE
22 X 19/8

65´

46´

BASEMENT STAIRWAY LOCATION

DOWN

FOYER

STOR

DEN/BR
12/4 X 10

Economical Split-Entry

- This split-entry home's rectangular shape and straight roofline make it simple and economical to build.
- The sidelighted entry is brightened by a large transom window. A railed stairway leads up to the primary living areas and a second stairway leads to the recreation spaces and garage below.
- The living and dining rooms combine for a spacious entertaining area, featuring a fabulous fireplace.
- The efficient kitchen includes a windowed sink and a handy pantry.

The bright breakfast nook gives access to a backyard deck through sliding glass doors.
- Three bedrooms and two baths occupy the sleeping wing. The secluded master bedroom boasts a big walk-in closet and a private bath with an oversized, sit-down shower.
- The two front bedrooms share the main bath and a good-sized linen closet.
- Downstairs, a second fireplace warms the large recreation room, which combines with a game room to provide plenty of space for hobbies and relaxation.
- A sizable laundry/utility room, a storage closet and a two-car, tuck-under garage round out the basement level.

Plan H-1332-5	
Bedrooms: 3	**Baths:** 2
Living Area:	
Main floor	1,262 sq. ft.
Daylight basement	576 sq. ft.
Total Living Area:	**1,838 sq. ft.**
Tuck-under garage	576 sq. ft.
Exterior Wall Framing:	2x6
Foundation Options:	

Daylight basement
(All plans can be built with your choice of foundation and framing. A generic conversion diagram is available. See order form.)

BLUEPRINT PRICE CODE:	B

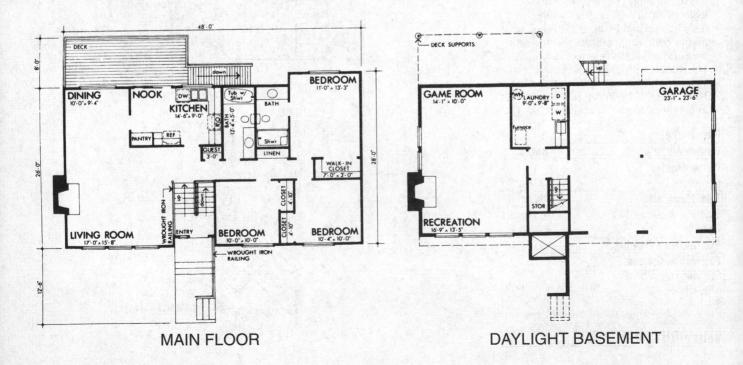

MAIN FLOOR

DAYLIGHT BASEMENT

Plan H-1332-5

PRICES AND DETAILS
ON PAGES 12-15

Delightful Great Room

- An expansive Great Room with a 10-ft. vaulted ceiling, a warm corner fireplace and an angled wet bar highlights this tastefully appointed home.

- On the exterior, decorative plants thrive in the lush wraparound planter that leads to the sheltered entry. The foyer is brightened by a sidelight and a skylight.

- To the left, the kitchen offers an island cooktop with lots room for food preparation and serving. The bayed breakfast nook is enhanced by bright windows and a 12½-ft. vaulted ceiling.

- Formal dining is hosted in the space adjoining the Great Room. Graced by a lovely bay window, the room also offers French doors to a covered patio.

- In the sleeping wing of the home, the master bedroom features a sitting area and a walk-in closet. The private master bath boasts a relaxing Jacuzzi tub.

- Two secondary bedrooms share a full bath nearby. Laundry facilities are also convenient.

Plan S-52394

Bedrooms: 3	Baths: 2
Living Area:	
Main floor	1,841 sq. ft.
Total Living Area:	**1,841 sq. ft.**
Standard basement	1,789 sq. ft.
Garage	432 sq. ft.
Exterior Wall Framing:	2x6

Foundation Options:

Standard basement
Crawlspace
Slab

(All plans can be built with your choice of foundation and framing. A generic conversion diagram is available. See order form.)

BLUEPRINT PRICE CODE:	B

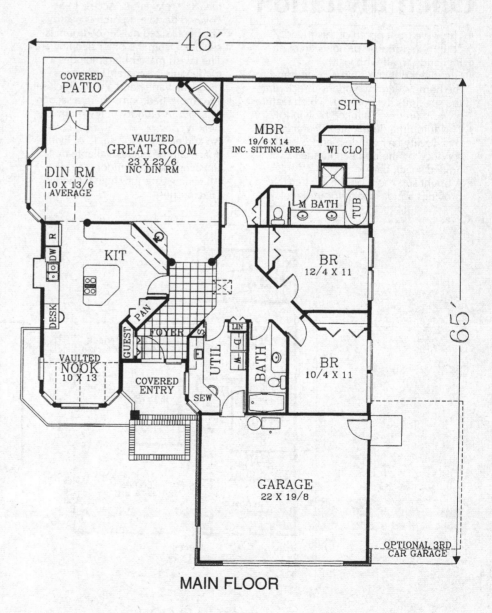

MAIN FLOOR

Open Invitation

- The wide front porch of this friendly country farmhouse presents an open invitation to all who visit.
- Highlighted by a round-topped transom, the home's entrance opens directly into the spacious living room, which features a warm fireplace flanked by windows.
- The adjoining dining area is enhanced by a lovely bay window and is easily serviced by the updated kitchen's angled snack bar.
- A bright sun room off the kitchen provides a great space for informal

meals or relaxation. Access to a covered backyard porch is nearby.
- The good-sized master bedroom is secluded from the other sleeping areas. The lavish master bath includes a garden tub, a separate shower, a dual-sink vanity and a walk-in closet.
- Two more bedrooms share a second full bath. A laundry/utility room is nearby.
- An additional 1,007 sq. ft. of living space can be made available by finishing the upper floor.
- All ceilings are 9 ft. high for added spaciousness.

Plan J-91078

Bedrooms: 3	Baths: 2
Living Area:	
Main floor	1,846 sq. ft.
Total Living Area:	**1,846 sq. ft.**
Future upper floor	1,007 sq. ft.
Standard basement	1,846 sq. ft.
Garage	484 sq. ft.
Exterior Wall Framing:	2x6

Foundation Options:
Standard basement
Crawlspace
Slab
(All plans can be built with your choice of foundation and framing. A generic conversion diagram is available. See order form.)

BLUEPRINT PRICE CODE:	B

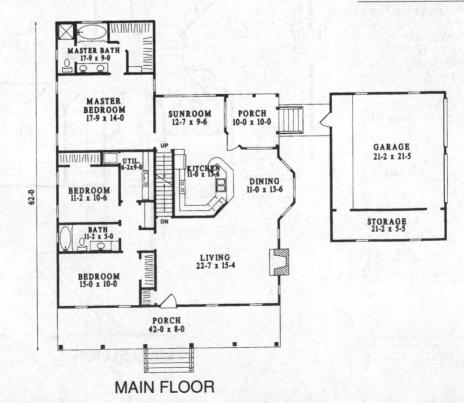

MAIN FLOOR

Plan J-91078

PRICES AND DETAILS
ON PAGES 12-15

Gables Abound

- With columns and bright windows up front, this affordable home features stylish gables on all four sides.
- The sidelighted entry flows to the formal dining room at right and back to the central Great Room.
- A 16-ft., 8-in. vaulted ceiling enhances the Great Room, which includes a soothing fireplace, a built-in media center and a bayed area with French doors to a backyard deck.
- The island kitchen offers an angled sink, a built-in planning desk and a walk-in pantry. The adjoining breakfast room, with a 12-ft. vaulted ceiling, provides built-in shelves and sliding glass doors to the deck. Also nearby is a laundry room with plenty of counter space.
- Across the home, the master suite has a 14-ft. vaulted ceiling and private access to the deck. The master bath boasts a large walk-in closet, a dual-sink vanity, a garden tub and a separate shower.
- On the upper floor, two secondary bedrooms with 11-ft. vaulted ceilings share another full bath.

Plan B-95015

Bedrooms: 3	Baths: 2½
Living Area:	
Upper floor	407 sq. ft.
Main floor	1,440 sq. ft.
Total Living Area:	**1,847 sq. ft.**
Basement	1,242 sq. ft.
Garage	420 sq. ft.
Exterior Wall Framing:	2x6

Foundation Options:
Daylight basement
Standard basement
(All plans can be built with your choice of foundation and framing. A generic conversion diagram is available. See order form.)

BLUEPRINT PRICE CODE:	B

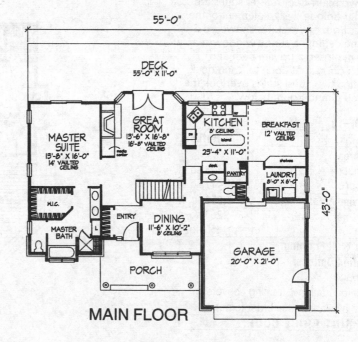

UPPER FLOOR

MAIN FLOOR

ORDER BLUEPRINTS ANYTIME!
CALL TOLL-FREE 1-888-626-2026

Plan B-95015

**PRICES AND DETAILS
ON PAGES 12-15**

123

Unique Inside and Out

- This delightful design is as striking on the inside as it is on the outside.
- The focal point of the home is the huge Grand Room, which features a vaulted ceiling, plant shelves and lots of glass, including a clerestory window. French doors flanking the fireplace lead to the covered porch and the two adjoining sun decks.
- The centrally located kitchen offers easy access from any room in the house, and a full bath, a laundry area and the garage entrance are nearby.
- The two main-floor master suites are another unique design element of the home. Both of the suites showcase a volume ceiling, a sunny window seat, a walk-in closet, a private bath and French doors that open to a sun deck.
- Upstairs, two guest suites overlook the vaulted Grand Room below.

Plan EOF-13	
Bedrooms: 4	**Baths: 3**
Living Area:	
Upper floor	443 sq. ft.
Main floor	1,411 sq. ft.
Total Living Area:	**1,854 sq. ft.**
Garage	264 sq. ft.
Storage	50 sq. ft.
Exterior Wall Framing:	2x6
Foundation Options:	
Crawlspace	
(Typical foundation & framing conversion diagram available—see order form.)	
BLUEPRINT PRICE CODE:	**B**

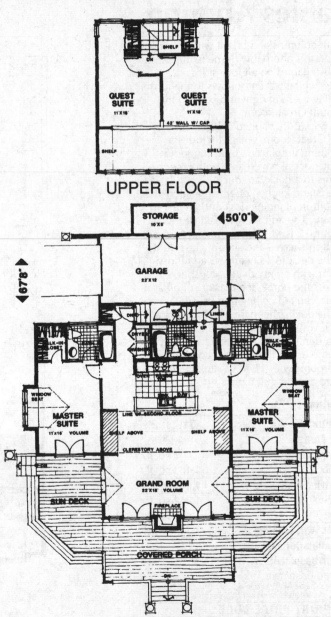

UPPER FLOOR

MAIN FLOOR

ORDER BLUEPRINTS ANYTIME!
CALL TOLL-FREE 1-888-626-2026

Plan EOF-13

PRICES AND DETAILS
ON PAGES 12-15

Attainable Luxury

- This traditional ranch home offers a large, central living room with a 12-ft. ceiling, a corner fireplace and an adjoining patio.
- The U-shaped kitchen easily services both the formal dining room and the bayed eating area.
- The luxurious master suite features a large bath with separate vanities and dressing areas.
- Two secondary bedrooms share a second full bath.
- A covered carport boasts a decorative brick wall and attic space above. Two additional storage areas provide plenty of room for gardening supplies and sports equipment.

Plan E-1812

Bedrooms: 3	Baths: 2
Living Area:	
Main floor	1,860 sq. ft.
Total Living Area:	**1,860 sq. ft.**
Carport	484 sq. ft.
Storage	132 sq. ft.
Exterior Wall Framing:	2x6

Foundation Options:

Crawlspace

Slab

(All plans can be built with your choice of foundation and framing. A generic conversion diagram is available. See order form.)

BLUEPRINT PRICE CODE: B

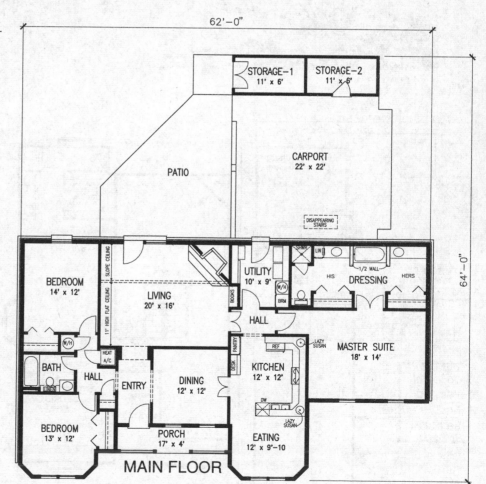

MAIN FLOOR

ORDER BLUEPRINTS ANYTIME!
CALL TOLL-FREE 1-888-626-2026

Plan E-1812

PRICES AND DETAILS
ON PAGES 12-15

125

FRONT VIEW

Queen Anne with Contemporary Interior

This gracious home offers numerous features for convenience and charm:
- 1,864 sq. ft. of living area.
- 2 bedrooms, plus den.
- Traditional exterior style.
- 30' wide at first floor, 32' wide at second floor.
- Versatile kitchen with range/oven/eating bar combination.
- Practical spice cabinet, pantry and nook.
- Sunken living room with vaulted ceiling, fireplace, French doors, wet bar and built-in shelves.
- Dramatic open staircase.
- Interesting entry open to bridge above.
- 2½ baths.
- Cozy loft open to living area.
- Spacious and elegant master bedroom with bay window, walk-in closet, separate shower, double-sink vanity and window overlooking living/loft area.
- Energy-efficient specifications throughout, including 2x6 wall framing.

PATIO

30'-0"

DINING
12/0 x 11/0

down

KITCHEN
13/0 x 13/0
REF

R/O
DW

LIVING RM
17/0 x 15/0

SHELVES
LAV
up
down
PANTRY
LIN

LAUNDRY
W
D

NOOK

50'-0"

GUEST
3/0

CLOSET
5/6

GARAGE
13/0 x 21/6

ENTRY
heat

BEDROOM
9/0 x 8/6

PLAN H-1458-1A
WITHOUT BASEMENT
(CRAWLSPACE FOUNDATION)

PLAN H-1458-1
WITH BASEMENT

FIRST FLOOR
983 SQUARE FEET
315 SQUARE FEET - GARAGE

BATH
Sh'r

WALK-IN CLOSET
7/0 x 6/6

MASTER BEDR'M
13/0 x 19/0

OPEN TO LIVING ROOM

down

BRIDGE

LIN

BATH
Tub w/Shower

OPEN TO ENTRY

LOFT
8/0 x 18/0

BEDROOM
10/6 x 10/6

CLOSET
7/0

SECOND FLOOR
881 SQUARE FEET

First floor:	983 sq. ft.
Second floor:	881 sq. ft.
Total living area: (Not counting basement or garage)	1,864 sq. ft.

Blueprint Price Code B

Plans H-1458-1 & 1A

PRICES AND DETAILS
ON PAGES 12-15

Impressive Master Suite

- This attractive one-story home features an impressive master suite located apart from the secondary bedrooms.
- A lovely front porch opens to the entry, which flows to the formal dining room, the rear-oriented living room and the secondary bedroom wing.
- The living room boasts a large corner fireplace, a ceiling that slopes to 11 ft. and access to a backyard patio.
- A U-shaped kitchen services the dining room and its own eating area. It also boasts a built-in desk, a handy pantry closet and access to the nearby laundry room and carport.
- The wide master bedroom hosts a lavish master bath with a spa tub, a separate shower and his-and-hers dressing areas.
- Across the home, the two secondary bedrooms share another full bath.

Plan E-1818

Bedrooms: 3	**Baths:** 2

Living Area:	
Main floor	1,868 sq. ft.
Total Living Area:	**1,868 sq. ft.**
Carport	484 sq. ft.
Storage	132 sq. ft.
Exterior Wall Framing:	2x6

Foundation Options:

Crawlspace
Slab

(All plans can be built with your choice of foundation and framing. A generic conversion diagram is available. See order form.)

BLUEPRINT PRICE CODE: B

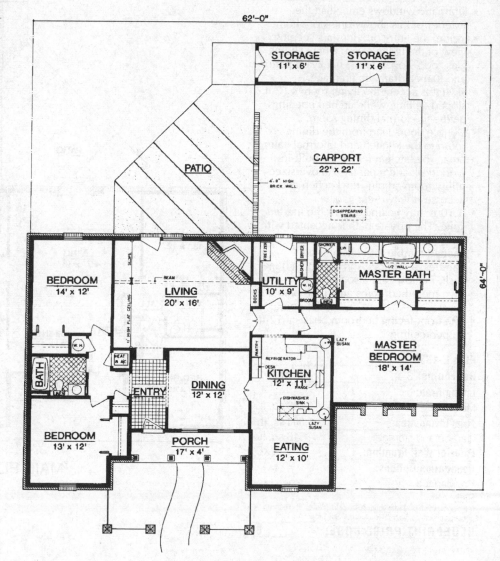

MAIN FLOOR

Plan E-1818

Showy One-Story

- Dramatic windows embellish the exterior of this showy one-story home.
- Inside, the entry provides a sweeping view of the living room, where sliding glass doors open to the backyard patio and flank a dramatic fireplace.
- Skylights accent the living room's 12-ft. sloped ceiling, while arched openings define the formal dining room.
- Double doors lead from the dining room to the kitchen and informal eating area. The kitchen features a built-in work desk and a pantry. An oversized utility room adjoins the kitchen and accesses the two-car garage.
- A 10-ft. tray ceiling adorns the master suite. The private bath is accented with a skylight above the fabulous fan-shaped marble tub. His-and-hers vanities, a separate shower and a huge walk-in closet are also featured.
- Two more bedrooms and a full bath are located at the other end of the home.
- The front-facing bedroom boasts a 12-ft. sloped ceiling.

Plan E-1830

Bedrooms: 3	Baths: 2
Living Area:	
Main floor	1,868 sq. ft.
Total Living Area:	**1,868 sq. ft.**
Garage and storage	616 sq. ft.
Exterior Wall Framing:	2x6

Foundation Options:
Crawlspace
Slab
(All plans can be built with your choice of foundation and framing. A generic conversion diagram is available. See order form.)

BLUEPRINT PRICE CODE: B

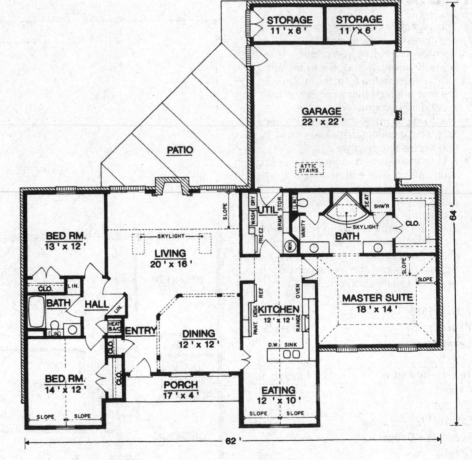

MAIN FLOOR

Rest Easy

- If you're out of town, or just making your way through a particularly hard day, you'll rest easy knowing this peaceful retreat awaits your return.
- The living and dining rooms and the kitchen share an 11-ft. vaulted ceiling.
- When romance tops the agenda, sit in front of the living room's corner fireplace and cuddle. In the bayed dining room, friends and loved ones will enjoy fun-filled feasts.
- A pass-through between the kitchen and the dining room will come in handy the next time you serve a heavy casserole or roast. The sunny nook boasts a 9½-ft. vaulted ceiling.
- Outside, a wraparound deck serves as a fun gathering spot. On the Fourth of July or Memorial Day, friends will flock to your house for brats and chips.
- In the master suite, private access to the deck offers an appealing getaway. Other features include an 11-ft. vaulted ceiling and a walk-in closet.
- The family room downstairs includes ample space for the kids to build king-sized forts and Lego worlds.

Plan SUN-2120

Bedrooms: 3	**Baths:** 2½
Living Area:	
Main floor	1,150 sq. ft.
Partial daylight basement	730 sq. ft.
Total Living Area:	**1,880 sq. ft.**
Garage	440 sq. ft.
Exterior Wall Framing:	2x6

Foundation Options:

Partial daylight basement
(All plans can be built with your choice of foundation and framing. A generic conversion diagram is available. See order form.)

BLUEPRINT PRICE CODE: B

REAR VIEW

MAIN FLOOR

DECK

VAULTED DINING 12/10X10/2

VAULTED LIVING RM. 16/4X15/4

FIREPLACE

SINK D.W.

RANGE

REFER.

2 CAR GARAGE 19/6 X 21/0

W.I. CLOSET 10/0X5/0

VAULTED KITCHEN 12/8X10/0

DN

PANTRY

NOOK

PWDR.

CLOSET

VAULTED MSTR. BEDRM. 14/10 X 14/0

ENTRY

DOWN

DRIVE

39'-0"

55'-6"

DAYLIGHT BASEMENT

BEDRM 2 12/0X10/4

FAMILY RM. 16/8X13/2

W D

TUB

BEDRM 3 12/0X10/0

LAUNDRY

BATH

LIN.

lau

CRAWL SPACE

ORDER BLUEPRINTS ANYTIME!
CALL TOLL-FREE 1-888-626-2026

Plan SUN-2120

PRICES AND DETAILS
ON PAGES 12-15

129

A Real Original

- This home's round window, elegant entry and transom windows create an eye-catching, original look.
- Inside, high ceilings and tremendous views let the eyes wander. The foyer provides an exciting look at an expansive deck and inviting spa through the living room's tall windows. The windows frame a handsome fireplace, while a 10-ft. ceiling adds volume and interest.
- To the right of the foyer is a cozy den or home office with its own fireplace, 10-ft. ceiling and dramatic windows.
- The spacious kitchen/breakfast area features an oversized snack bar island and opens to a large screen porch. Within easy reach are the laundry room and the entrance to the garage.
- The bright formal dining room overlooks the deck and boasts a ceiling that vaults up to 10 feet.
- The secluded master suite looks out to the deck as well, with access through a patio door. The private bath features a dynamite corner spa tub, a separate shower and a large walk-in closet.
- A second bedroom and bath complete the main floor.

Plan B-90065

Bedrooms: 2+	Baths: 2
Living Area:	
Main floor	1,889 sq. ft.
Total Living Area:	**1,889 sq. ft.**
Screen porch	136 sq. ft.
Standard basement	1,889 sq. ft.
Garage	406 sq. ft.
Exterior Wall Framing:	2x6

Foundation Options:

Standard basement

(All plans can be built with your choice of foundation and framing. A generic conversion diagram is available. See order form.)

BLUEPRINT PRICE CODE: B

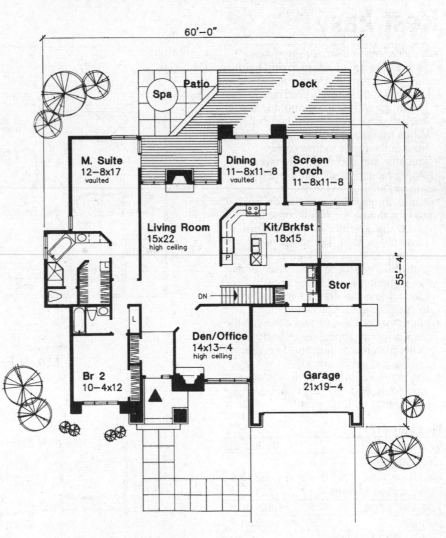

MAIN FLOOR

Friendly Farmhouse

- Reminiscent of a turn-of-the-century farmhouse, this warm, friendly home is characterized by an authentic front porch with fine post-and-rail detailing.
- The open entry provides a sweeping view of the dining room and the adjoining living room. Three columns function as an elegant divider between the two rooms.
- The living room features a 12-ft.-high sloped ceiling with exposed beams, an inviting fireplace, built-in bookshelves and windows overlooking a patio.
- A nice-sized eating area opens to the airy kitchen, which offers a snack bar, a pantry and a lazy Susan. Double doors conceal a utility room with extra storage space.
- Another set of double doors opens to the sleeping wing, where all three bedrooms boast walk-in closets. The master suite has a private bath with a dual-sink vanity. The secondary bedrooms share another full bath.

Plan E-1813

Bedrooms: 3	Baths: 2
Living Area:	
Main floor	1,892 sq. ft.
Total Living Area:	**1,892 sq. ft.**
Carport	440 sq. ft.
Storage	120 sq. ft.
Exterior Wall Framing:	2x6

Foundation Options:

Crawlspace
Slab
(All plans can be built with your choice of foundation and framing. A generic conversion diagram is available. See order form.)

BLUEPRINT PRICE CODE: B

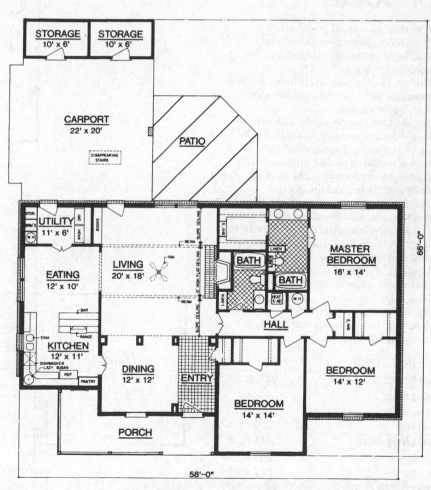

MAIN FLOOR

ORDER BLUEPRINTS ANYTIME!
CALL TOLL-FREE 1-888-626-2026

Plan E-1813

PRICES AND DETAILS
ON PAGES 12-15

131

Farmhouse for Today

- An inviting covered porch and decorative dormer windows lend traditional warmth and charm to this attractive design.
- The up-to-date interior includes ample space for entertaining as well as for daily family activities.
- The elegant foyer is flanked on one side by the formal, sunken living room and on the other by a sunken family room with a fireplace and an entertainment center. Each room features an 8½-ft. tray ceiling and views of the porch.
- The dining room flows from the living room to increase the entertaining space.
- The kitchen/nook/laundry area forms a large expanse for casual family living and domestic chores.
- Upstairs, the grand master suite includes a large closet and a private bath with a garden tub, a designer shower and a private deck.
- A second full bath serves the two secondary bedrooms.

Plan U-87-203

Bedrooms: 3	Baths: 2½
Living Area:	
Upper floor	857 sq. ft.
Main floor	1,064 sq. ft.
Total Living Area:	**1,921 sq. ft.**
Standard basement	1,064 sq. ft.
Garage	552 sq. ft.
Exterior Wall Framing:	2x4 or 2x6

Foundation Options:

Standard basement

Crawlspace

Slab

(All plans can be built with your choice of foundation and framing. A generic conversion diagram is available. See order form.)

BLUEPRINT PRICE CODE: **B**

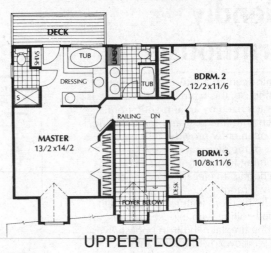

UPPER FLOOR

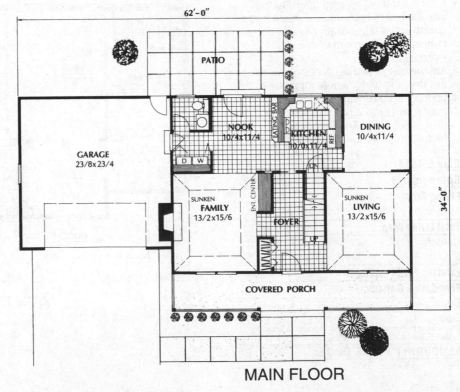

MAIN FLOOR

Plan U-87-203

PRICES AND DETAILS
ON PAGES 12-15

Wonderful Walk-Out

- A scenic or sloping lot can be accommodated nicely with this wonderful walk-out design. The optional daylight basement can be finished now if funds allow, or later as the family grows.
- The main floor includes a dramatic vaulted Great Room with windows on three sides and a two-story masonry woodstove on the other.
- The main-floor master suite features a vaulted ceiling, a window seat, a walk-in closet and a private skylighted bath.

Plans H-94003-A & -B

Bedrooms: 3+	Baths: 2½-3½
Living Area:	
Upper floor	560 sq. ft.
Main floor	1,340 sq. ft.
Daylight basement	1,340 sq. ft.
Total Living Area:	**1,900/3,240 sq. ft.**
Garage	496 sq. ft.
Exterior Wall Framing:	2x6
Foundation Options:	**Plan #**
Daylight basement	H-94003-B
Crawlspace	H-94003-A

(All plans can be built with your choice of foundation and framing. A generic conversion diagram is available. See order form.)

BLUEPRINT PRICE CODE:	B/E

REAR VIEW

DAYLIGHT BASEMENT

UPPER FLOOR

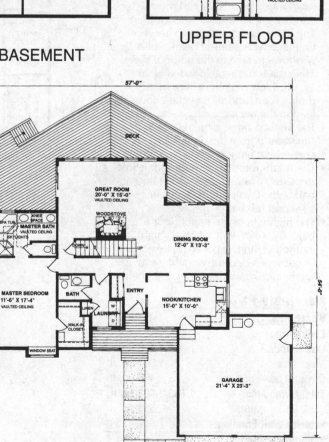

MAIN FLOOR

ORDER BLUEPRINTS ANYTIME!
CALL TOLL-FREE 1-888-626-2026

Plans H-94003-A & -B

PRICES AND DETAILS
ON PAGES 12-15

133

Decked-Out Chalet

- This gorgeous chalet is partially surrounded by a large and roomy deck that is great for indoor/outdoor living.
- The living and dining area shows off a fireplace with a raised hearth, plus large windows to take in the outdoor views. The area is further expanded by a 17½-ft.-high vaulted ceiling in the dining room and sliding glass doors that lead to the deck.
- The kitchen offers a breakfast bar that separates it from the dining area. A convenient laundry room is nearby.
- The main-floor master bedroom is just steps away from a linen closet and a hall bath. Two upstairs bedrooms share a second full bath.
- The highlight of the upper floor is a balcony room with a 12½-ft.-high vaulted ceiling, exposed beams and tall windows. A decorative railing provides an overlook into the dining area below.

Plans H-919-1 & -1A

Bedrooms: 3	Baths: 2
Living Area:	
Upper floor	869 sq. ft.
Main floor	1,064 sq. ft.
Daylight basement	475 sq. ft.
Total Living Area:	**1,933/2,408 sq. ft.**
Tuck-under garage	501 sq. ft.
Exterior Wall Framing:	**2x6**
Foundation Options:	**Plan #**
Daylight basement	H-919-1
Crawlspace	H-919-1A

(All plans can be built with your choice of foundation and framing. A generic conversion diagram is available. See order form.)

BLUEPRINT PRICE CODE: B/C

UPPER FLOOR

DAYLIGHT BASEMENT

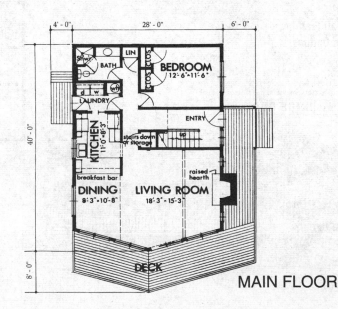

MAIN FLOOR

Plans H-919-1 & -1A
PRICES AND DETAILS ON PAGES 12-15

Elegance Inside and Out

- The raised front porch of this home is finely detailed with wood columns, railings, moldings, and French doors with half-round transoms.
- The living room, dining room and entry have 12-ft.-high ceilings. Skylights illuminate the living room, which offers a fireplace and access to a roomy deck.
- The efficient kitchen permits easy service to both the dining room and the casual eating area.
- The master suite features a raised tray ceiling and an enormous skylighted bath with a walk-in closet, dual vanities and a large quarter-circle spa tub surrounded by a mirror wall.
- On the left, two secondary bedrooms are insulated from the more active areas of the home by an efficient hallway, and also share another full bath.

Plan E-1909

Bedrooms: 3	Baths: 2
Living Area:	
Main floor	1,936 sq. ft.
Total Living Area:	**1,936 sq. ft.**
Garage	484 sq. ft.
Storage	132 sq. ft.
Exterior Wall Framing:	2x6

Foundation Options:

Crawlspace
Slab
(All plans can be built with your choice of foundation and framing. A generic conversion diagram is available. See order form.)

BLUEPRINT PRICE CODE: **B**

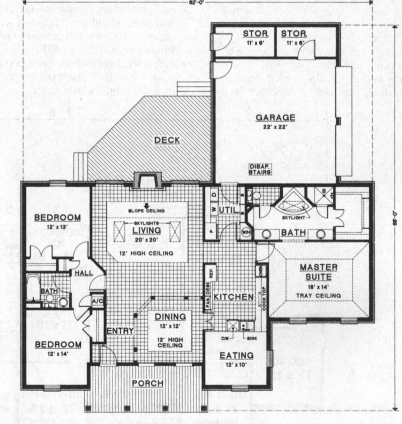

MAIN FLOOR

ORDER BLUEPRINTS ANYTIME!
CALL TOLL-FREE 1-888-626-2026

Plan E-1909

PRICES AND DETAILS
ON PAGES 12-15

135

Amenities Add Up

- The amenities add up throughout this well-planned one-story home, creating an inviting refuge from the world.
- Inside, the foyer leads directly into the Great Room, which will function as your home's heart and soul. Whether you're gathering around the television to catch up on current events, or throwing a holiday bash for a crowd, this room will serve you well.
- In the kitchen nearby, a neat snack bar seats four, providing a fun place for the kids to enjoy chocolate chip cookies and milk after school. For boisterous family dinners, the sunny morning room is the perfect spot.
- When the occasion calls for more formality, try the lovely dining room. A folding door to the kitchen can be shut for an even more dignified setting.
- Secluded from events in the home's common living areas, the master bedroom offers much-deserved peace and quiet. Highlights include a walk-in closet and a bath with a whirlpool tub. What a treat at day's end!
- Across the home, three more bedrooms share a hall bath. Each of the rooms includes ample closet space.

Plan AHP-9601	
Bedrooms: 4	**Baths:** 2½
Living Area:	
Main floor	1,939 sq. ft.
Total Living Area:	**1,939 sq. ft.**
Standard basement	1,404 sq. ft.
Garage and storage	493 sq. ft.
Exterior Wall Framing:	2x4 or 2x6

Foundation Options:
Standard basement
Crawlspace
Slab
(All plans can be built with your choice of foundation and framing. A generic conversion diagram is available. See order form.)

BLUEPRINT PRICE CODE: B

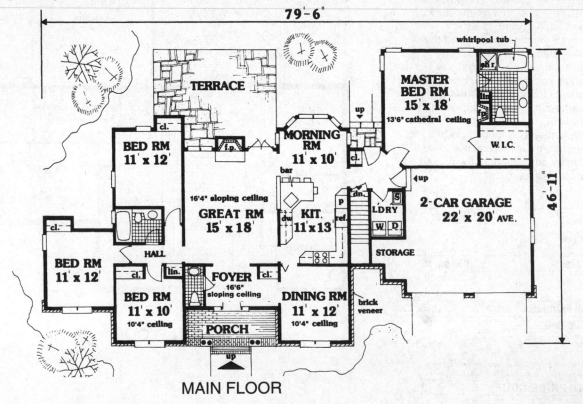

MAIN FLOOR

Plan AHP-9601

Updated Tudor

- Updated Tudor styling gives this home an extra-appealing exterior. Inside, the bright and open living spaces are embellished with a host of wonderfully contemporary details.
- An inviting brick arch frames the front door, which opens directly into the living room. Here, a 14-ft. sloped ceiling, a fireplace and a view to the covered rear porch provide an impressive welcome.
- The octagonal dining area is absolutely stunning—the perfect complement for the skylighted kitchen, which boasts an angled cooktop/snack bar and a 12-ft. sloped ceiling. Double doors in the kitchen lead to a roomy utility area and the cleverly disguised side-entry garage.
- No details were left out in the sumptuous master suite, which features access to a private porch with a 14-ft. sloped ceiling and skylights. The luxurious bath offers a platform tub, a sit-down shower, his-and-hers vanities and lots of storage and closet space.
- Two more bedrooms are situated at the opposite side of the home and share a hall bath. One bedroom features a window seat, while the other has direct access to the central covered porch.

Plan E-1912

Bedrooms: 3	Baths: 2
Living Area:	
Main floor	1,946 sq. ft.
Total Living Area:	**1,946 sq. ft.**
Garage and storage	562 sq. ft.
Exterior Wall Framing:	2x6

Foundation Options:

Crawlspace
Slab
(All plans can be built with your choice of foundation and framing. A generic conversion diagram is available. See order form.)

BLUEPRINT PRICE CODE: C

MAIN FLOOR

American Home Plans

Space-Saving Traditional

- Although this home has just under 2,000 sq. ft. of living area, it abounds with bonus features.
- The formal living room with fireplace is divided from the family room by the stairway. The family room's fireplace is framed by a built-in media center and windows overlooking the backyard. A wet bar is between the family room and the kitchen.
- An angled counter links the kitchen to the family room and the dinette. Sliding glass doors in the dinette open to a terrace. A pocket door closes off the kitchen from the formal dining room at the front of the home.
- A large laundry room serves as a buffer between the rear service entrance, the garage entrance and the living areas. The adjacent two-car garage incorporates space for both storage and a workshop.
- The upper level includes a luxurious master suite with a tray ceiling, a cozy window seat, a large walk-in closet and a private bath with whirlpool tub.

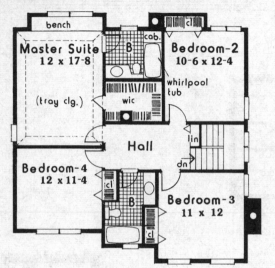

UPPER FLOOR

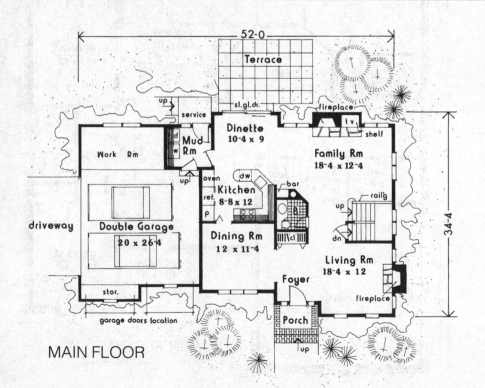

MAIN FLOOR

Plan AHP-9110	
Bedrooms: 4	**Baths:** 2 ½
Space:	
Upper floor	925 sq. ft.
Main floor	1,023 sq. ft.
Total Living Area	**1,948 sq. ft.**
Basement	910 sq. ft.
Garage, Work Room and Storage	533 sq. ft.
Exterior Wall Framing	2x4 or 2x6
Foundation options:	
Standard Basement	
Crawlspace	
Slab	
(Foundation & framing conversion diagram available—see order form.)	
Blueprint Price Code	B

Plan AHP-9110

PRICES AND DETAILS
ON PAGES 12-15

Meant to Be

- One glimpse of the beautiful front view will tempt you, and a good look at the stunning rear view will convince you, that this home was meant to be yours!
- The vaulted, skylighted entry ushers you to the Great Room, which vaults up to 10 feet and features an inspiring fireplace. Sliding glass doors provide speedy access to an incredible wraparound deck.
- Equipped for any sudden culinary inspirations, the well-planned kitchen features its own pantry. You'll also appreciate its close proximity to the

garage when it's time to unload those heavy grocery bags.
- The master suite will take your breath away, with its walk-in closet and a secluded bath with dual sinks and a spa tub. Exquisite French doors create easy access to the deck.
- Imagine magical nights on the deck. With the kids at Grandma's house, put on some soft music and use the deck as your own private dance floor!
- A vast unfinished area in the daylight basement promises excitement. Turn it into a game room for the ultimate in entertainment! A fourth bedroom and a full bath complete the space.

Plan SUN-1310-C	
Bedrooms: 4	**Baths:** 3½
Living Area:	
Main floor	1,636 sq. ft.
Daylight basement (finished)	315 sq. ft.
Total Living Area:	**1,951 sq. ft.**
Daylight basement (unfinished)	730 sq. ft.
Garage	759 sq. ft.
Exterior Wall Framing:	2x6

Foundation Options:
Daylight basement
Crawlspace
Slab
(All plans can be built with your choice of foundation and framing. A generic conversion diagram is available. See order form.)

BLUEPRINT PRICE CODE:	B

MAIN FLOOR

70'-0"
45'-0"

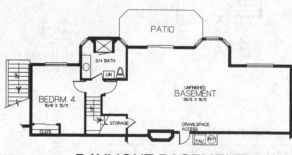

DAYLIGHT BASEMENT

REAR VIEW

ORDER BLUEPRINTS ANYTIME!
CALL TOLL-FREE 1-888-626-2026

Plan SUN-1310-C

PRICES AND DETAILS
ON PAGES 12-15

139

FRONT VIEW

Tradition with Modern Touch

- Dining room and master bedroom offer access to rear patio.
- Entryway approaches large living room with sloped ceilings and built-in fireplace, both exposed to second-level loft.
- Roomy kitchen has corner pantry and convenient nearby laundry facilities.
- First floor master bedroom includes generous walk-in closet and "his 'n hers" vanities.

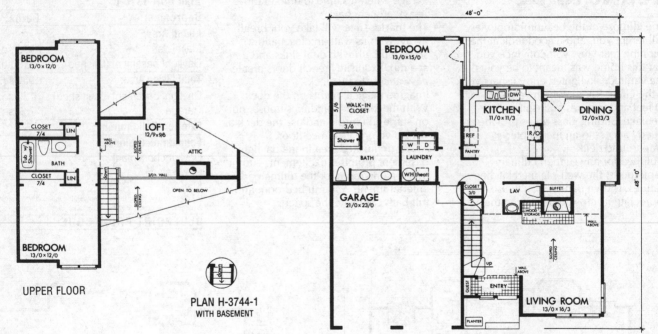

UPPER FLOOR

PLAN H-3744-1
WITH BASEMENT

MAIN FLOOR

Plans H-3744-1 & -1A

Bedrooms: 3	**Baths:** 2½

Space:	
Upper floor:	660 sq. ft.
Main floor:	1,300 sq. ft.
Total living area:	**1,960 sq. ft.**
Basement:	approx. 1,300 sq. ft.
Garage:	483 sq. ft.
Exterior Wall Framing:	2x6

Foundation options:
Standard basement (Plan H-3744-1).
Crawlspace (Plan H-3744-1A).
(Foundation & framing conversion diagram available — see order form.)

Blueprint Price Code:	B

REAR VIEW

Plans H-3744-1 & -1A

PRICES AND DETAILS
ON PAGES 12-15

Light-Filled Interior

- A stylish contemporary exterior and an open, light-filled interior define this two-level home.
- The covered entry leads to a central gallery. The huge living room and dining room combine to generate a spacious ambience that is enhanced by a 15½-ft. cathedral ceiling and a warm fireplace with tall flanking windows.
- Oriented to the rear and overlooking a terrace and backyard landscaping are the informal spaces. The family room, the sunny semi-circular dinette and the modern kitchen share a snack bar.
- The main-floor master suite boasts a 13-ft. sloped ceiling, a private terrace, a dressing area and a personal bath with a whirlpool tub.
- Two to three extra bedrooms with 11-ft. ceilings share a skylighted bath on the upper floor.

Plan K-683-D

Bedrooms: 3+	Baths: 2½+
Living Area:	
Upper floor	491 sq. ft.
Main floor	1,475 sq. ft.
Total Living Area:	**1,966 sq. ft.**
Standard basement	1,425 sq. ft.
Garage and storage	487 sq. ft.
Exterior Wall Framing:	2x4 or 2x6

Foundation Options:
Standard basement
Slab
(All plans can be built with your choice of foundation and framing. A generic conversion diagram is available. See order form.)

BLUEPRINT PRICE CODE: **B**

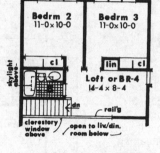

UPPER FLOOR

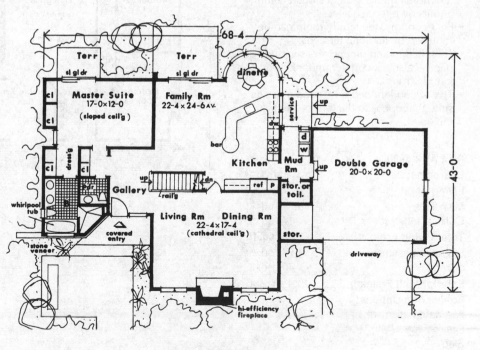

MAIN FLOOR

ORDER BLUEPRINTS ANYTIME!
CALL TOLL-FREE 1-888-626-2026

Plan K-683-D

PRICES AND DETAILS
ON PAGES 12-15

141

Grand Ranch with Colonial Style

- Comfortable family living is the focal point of this three-bedroom ranch.
- At the center of the home is a big living room with a dramatic cathedral ceiling, skylights and French doors that open to a covered terrace.
- The cozy adjoining family room offers a functional media wall, a sloped ceiling and its own terrace access.
- For economy, the family room can be replaced by an open terrace.
- The kitchen and dinette areas include a pantry, a snack counter and a nearby laundry room.
- Two secondary bedrooms and a master suite that opens to the terrace are also included.

Plan AHP-6090

Bedrooms: 3	Baths: 2
Living Area:	
Main floor	1,798 sq. ft.
Optional family room	173 sq. ft.
Total Living Area:	**1,971 sq. ft.**
Standard basement	1,775 sq. ft.
Garage	400 sq. ft.
Exterior Wall Framing:	2x4 or 2x6

Foundation Options:
Standard basement
Crawlspace
Slab
(Typical foundation & framing conversion diagram available—see order form.)

BLUEPRINT PRICE CODE:	B

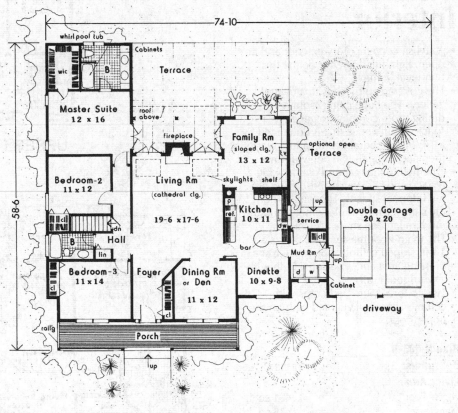

MAIN FLOOR

Old Homestead

Almost everyone has a soft place in his heart for a certain home in his childhood. A home like this one, with understated farmhouse styling and wrap-around porch, may be the image of "Home" that your children remember.

Two versions of the first floor plan provide a choice between a country kitchen and a more formal dining room.

All versions feature 2x6 exterior wall framing.

Upper floor:	626 sq. ft.
Main floor:	1,359 sq. ft.
Total living area:	1,985 sq. ft.

(Not counting basement or garage)
(Non-basement versions designed with crawlspace)

Garage:	528 sq. ft.

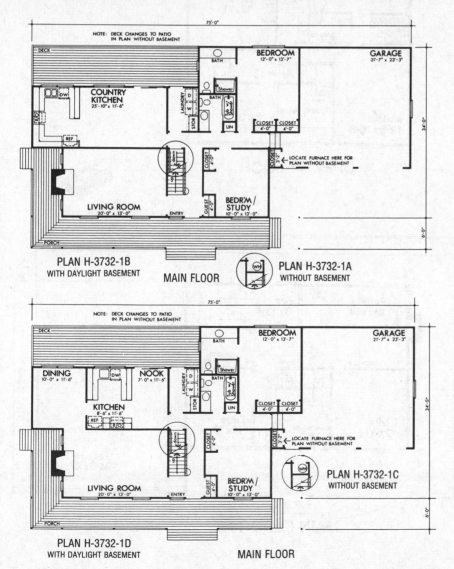

PLAN H-3732-1B
WITH DAYLIGHT BASEMENT

PLAN H-3732-1A
WITHOUT BASEMENT

MAIN FLOOR

PLAN H-3732-1D
WITH DAYLIGHT BASEMENT

PLAN H-3732-1C
WITHOUT BASEMENT

MAIN FLOOR

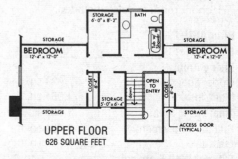

UPPER FLOOR
626 SQUARE FEET

ORDER BLUEPRINTS ANYTIME!
CALL TOLL-FREE 1-888-626-2026

Blueprint Price Code B
Plans H-3732-1A,-1B,-1C & -1D

PRICES AND DETAILS
ON PAGES 12-15

143

Relax on the Front Porch

- With its wraparound covered porch, this quaint two-story home makes summer evenings a breeze.
- Inside, a beautiful open stairway welcomes guests into the vaulted foyer, which connects the formal areas. The front-facing living and dining rooms have views of the covered front porch.
- French doors open from the living room to the family room, where a fireplace and corner windows warm and brighten this spacious activity area.
- The breakfast nook, set off by a half-wall, hosts a handy work desk and opens to the back porch.
- The country kitchen offers an oversized island, a pantry closet and illuminating windows flanking the corner sink.
- The upper-floor master suite boasts two walk-in closets and a private bath with a tub and a separate shower. Two more bedrooms, another full bath and a laundry room are also included.

Plan AGH-1997

Bedrooms: 3	Baths: 2½
Living Area:	
Upper floor	933 sq. ft.
Main floor	1,064 sq. ft.
Total Living Area:	**1,997 sq. ft.**
Standard basement	1,064 sq. ft.
Garage	662 sq. ft.
Exterior Wall Framing:	2x6

Foundation Options:

Standard basement

(All plans can be built with your choice of foundation and framing. A generic conversion diagram is available. See order form.)

BLUEPRINT PRICE CODE:	B

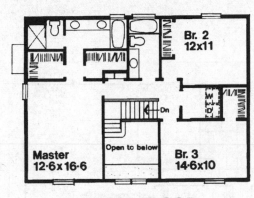

UPPER FLOOR

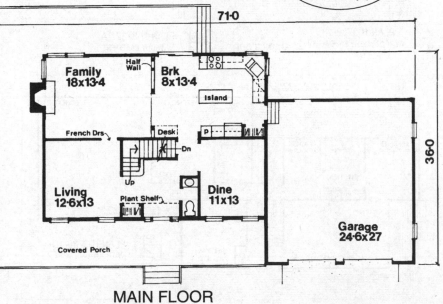

MAIN FLOOR

Plan AGH-1997

PRICES AND DETAILS ON PAGES 12-15

Rustic Charmer

- A rustic stone exterior and an inviting covered porch beckon you to look closely at this charming design. Its floor plan generously maximizes space and offers many unexpected luxuries.
- The living room, brightened by a lovely bay window, includes a cozy corner fireplace that will glow nicely on chilly autumn evenings. A pass-through to the kitchen simplifies gala occasions.
- The formal dining room overlooks the front porch and flows to the kitchen and the rear of the home.

- Plenty of counter space in the kitchen ensures comfortable meal preparations. French doors to an outdoor terrace add flair to casual meals in the dinette.
- Nearby, a convenient mudroom/laundry room allows ample room for chores and provides easy access to the garage.
- Off the dinette, the master suite pampers its occupants with privacy. Numbered among its perks are a huge walk-in closet and a whirlpool bath with dual sinks and a separate shower.
- Across the home, two more bedrooms share a full bath.

Plan HFL-1920-AV	
Bedrooms: 3	**Baths: 2**
Living Area:	
Main floor	1,466 sq. ft.
Total Living Area:	**1,466 sq. ft.**
Standard basement	1,466 sq. ft.
Garage and storage	477 sq. ft.
Exterior Wall Framing:	2x6
Foundation Options:	

Standard basement
Slab
(All plans can be built with your choice of foundation and framing. A generic conversion diagram is available. See order form.)

BLUEPRINT PRICE CODE:	A

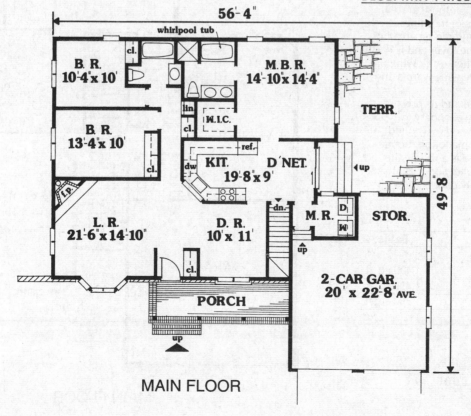

MAIN FLOOR

ORDER BLUEPRINTS ANYTIME!
CALL TOLL-FREE 1-888-626-2026

Plan HFL-1920-AV

PRICES AND DETAILS
ON PAGES 12-15

145

A Lesson In Cooperation

- This home offers wonderfully versatile spaces that allow cooperation between your family values and your desire to entertain.
- The vaulted family room flows into a bayed breakfast nook, creating an expansive area perfectly suited for informal meals and gatherings.
- The U-shaped kitchen is open to the family room and features a convenient snack island—great for those grab-a-Pop-Tart-before-school mornings.
- The vaulted living and dining area lies just to the right of the foyer and is easily serviced by the kitchen. A glowing fire in the handsome fireplace warms any formal occasion.
- The master bedroom and its private bath, as well as the secondary bedrooms, are crowned by vaulted ceilings, adding drama to the rooms. The master bath boasts a roomy tile shower, a private toilet and a dual-sink vanity, ensuring easy cooperation on busy mornings.

Plan S-11495

Bedrooms: 3	Baths: 2
Living Area:	
Main floor	1,490 sq. ft.
Total Living Area:	**1,490 sq. ft.**
Garage	386 sq. ft.
Exterior Wall Framing:	2x6

Foundation Options:

Crawlspace
(All plans can be built with your choice of foundation and framing. A generic conversion diagram is available. See order form.)

BLUEPRINT PRICE CODE: A

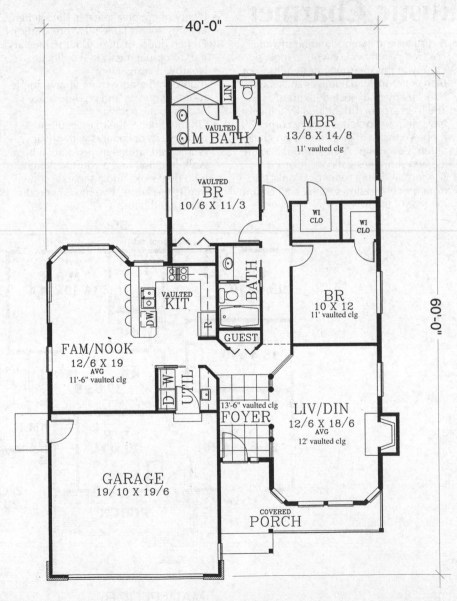

MAIN FLOOR

Plan S-11495

PRICES AND DETAILS ON PAGES 12-15

Gabled Wonder

- A multi-level gabled roof and a large living room are featured in this 1-1/2-story country home.
- The covered front porch and projected entry lead into the spacious living room, an area large enough to accommodate any family activity. A corner fireplace enhances the room's appeal as a center for gathering.
- A bayed dining room open to the living room creates an ideal setting for mealtime conversation.
- Each day's events can be planned from the dinette area, and the U-shaped kitchen is roomy enough for all the cooks in your home.
- The first floor master suite offers plenty of amenities for today's couple–a large walk-in closet and a master bath with a dual-sink vanity and a whirlpool tub.
- Two bedrooms and a full bath highlight the upstairs of the home.
- A large rear deck and a split-entry garage with ample storage accent this gabled wonder.

Plan HFL-1930-GA

Bedrooms: 3	Baths: 2½
Living Area:	
Upper floor	441 sq. ft.
Main floor	1,110 sq. ft.
Total Living Area:	**1,551 sq. ft.**
Standard basement	1,118 sq. ft.
Garage	482 sq. ft.
Exterior Wall Framing:	2x6

Foundation Options:

Standard basement

Slab

(All plans can be built with your choice of foundation and framing. A generic conversion diagram is available. See order form.)

BLUEPRINT PRICE CODE:	B

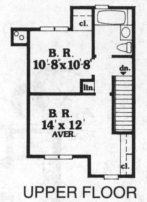

UPPER FLOOR

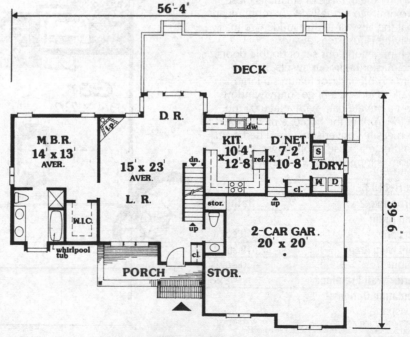

MAIN FLOOR

ORDER BLUEPRINTS ANYTIME!
CALL TOLL-FREE 1-888-626-2026

Plan HFL-1930-GA

PRICES AND DETAILS
ON PAGES 12-15

147

Effective and Efficient

- This darling one-story stucco home provides an effective and efficient lifestyle for its fortunate owners.
- The sizable Great Room dominates the floor plan. Its commanding fireplace creates a warm, cozy ambience during social events or quiet family evenings.
- Nearby, you'll find a dining nook that features access to a charming back patio—the perfect spot for barbecuing or star-gazing on a summer night.
- With a spacious pantry and plenty of cabinet space, the kitchen stands ready for any meal, large or small. Its close proximity to virtually every room means that the answer to any sudden culinary craving is just steps away!
- Behind a gorgeous set of double doors, the master bedroom awaits. Its remarkable interior features a large walk-in closet, a huge sunny window and a private bath with a Jacuzzi tub.
- In the front of the home, a nicely sized den easily converts to a third bedroom.
- To create a sense of openness, every room is topped by a 9-ft. ceiling.

Plan R-1103

Bedrooms: 2+	Baths: 2
Living Area:	
Main floor	1,619 sq. ft.
Total Living Area:	**1,619 sq. ft.**
Garage	430 sq. ft.
Exterior Wall Framing:	2x6
Foundation Options:	

Crawlspace
(All plans can be built with your choice of foundation and framing. A generic conversion diagram is available. See order form.)

BLUEPRINT PRICE CODE:	B

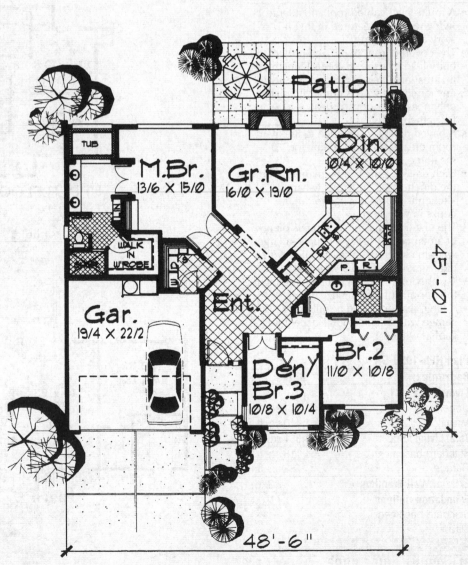

MAIN FLOOR

ORDER BLUEPRINTS ANYTIME! CALL TOLL-FREE 1-888-626-2026   Plan R-1103   *PRICES AND DETAILS ON PAGES 12-15*

Easy Brilliance

- You'll find a sophisticated aura and an easy brilliance in this traditionally styled two-story home.
- Passersby will be impressed by the gorgeous covered porch on the right side of the home. It's not only good-looking, but also provides an ideal spot to while away a warm spring day.
- Inside, you'll be quickly drawn to the spacious living room, which features a lovely fireplace and access to the covered porch.
- The enormous kitchen, with a large family dining area next to it, is a natural place to discuss daily events while preparing and serving meals.
- The master bedroom boasts a sizable walk-in closet and features a whirlpool tub in the private bath. A corner location gives it a sense of seclusion from the rest of the home.
- Upstairs, you'll find two additional bedrooms, both of which are nicely sized. A full split bath is conveniently located just a few steps away.

Plan YS-5603

Bedrooms: 3	Baths: 2½
Living Area:	
Upper floor	500 sq. ft.
Main floor	1,177 sq. ft.
Total Living Area:	**1,677 sq. ft.**
Standard basement	1,117 sq. ft.
Garage	464 sq. ft.
Exterior Wall Framing:	2x6

Foundation Options:

Standard basement

(All plans can be built with your choice of foundation and framing. A generic conversion diagram is available. See order form.)

BLUEPRINT PRICE CODE: B

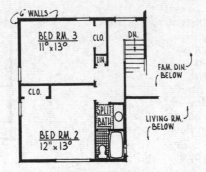

UPPER FLOOR

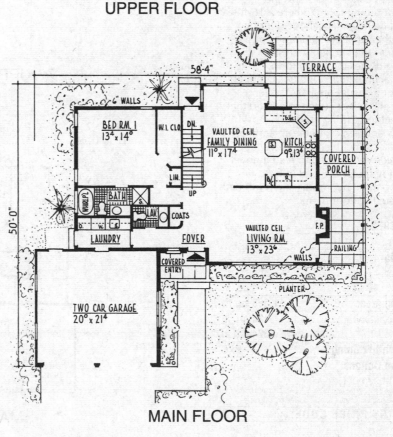

MAIN FLOOR

ORDER BLUEPRINTS ANYTIME!
CALL TOLL-FREE 1-888-626-2026

Plan YS-5603

PRICES AND DETAILS
ON PAGES 12-15

149

Cute Cottage

- This home's rustic stone exterior gives it a charming, peaceful look, reminiscent of a cottage in a European village.
- Inside, a 17-ft. vaulted ceiling in the living room brings a bit of up-to-date comfort and style to the home. The greatest work of art can't hold a candle to the beauty of the picture window on the front wall. On winter nights, build a fire in the fireplace and enjoy the view from your own living room.
- Two handsome columns topped by a plant shelf usher guests into the adjacent dining room, where a 16-ft. vaulted ceiling soars above. During meals, the serving counter and pass-through to the kitchen save steps carrying dishes back and forth.
- The adjacent kitchen includes enough room for a casual breakfast table. Sliding glass doors open to a patio that is perfect for grilling outdoors.
- At day's end, sink into the serenity of the master suite. Here, a quiet sitting area gives you a place to read a novel and enjoy the peace and quiet.
- Upstairs, three bedrooms and a full bath complete the floor plan.

Plan B-92023

Bedrooms: 4	Baths: 2½
Living Area:	
Upper floor	564 sq. ft.
Main floor	1,134 sq. ft.
Total Living Area:	**1,698 sq. ft.**
Standard basement	1,134 sq. ft.
Garage	374 sq. ft.
Exterior Wall Framing:	2x6

Foundation Options:

Standard basement

(All plans can be built with your choice of foundation and framing. A generic conversion diagram is available. See order form.)

BLUEPRINT PRICE CODE:	**B**

UPPER FLOOR

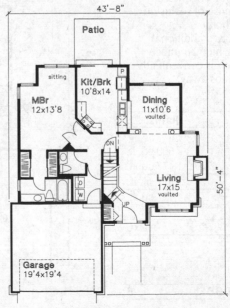

MAIN FLOOR

ORDER BLUEPRINTS ANYTIME! CALL TOLL-FREE 1-888-626-2026

Plan B-92023

PRICES AND DETAILS ON PAGES 12-15

Angling for Compliments

- This home's unique angled shape and attractive gabled roofline will draw compliments from family and friends.
- Designed with entertaining in mind, the floor plan creates central, open living areas. Obtuse angles add interest and increase the feeling of spaciousness.
- The foyer opens into the formal dining room, which separates the living room and the family room.
- Situated to the rear of the home, the casual family room offers sliding glass doors to the backyard.
- Every morning is a good one in the breakfast nook, which shares a serving counter with the kitchen.
- A windowed sink brightens the efficient kitchen, which offers ample counter space. A nearby mudroom includes laundry facilities, a half bath and easy access to the garage.
- Across the home, two bedrooms share a full bath while maintaining a sense of privacy. The master bedroom boasts his-and-hers closets.

Plan LS-95808-BJ

Bedrooms: 2	Baths: 1½
Living Area:	
Main floor	1,701 sq. ft.
Total Living Area:	**1,701 sq. ft.**
Standard basement	1,695 sq. ft.
Garage	514 sq. ft.
Exterior Wall Framing:	2x6

Foundation Options:

Standard basement

(All plans can be built with your choice of foundation and framing. A generic conversion diagram is available. See order form.)

BLUEPRINT PRICE CODE:	B

Floor Plan

62'-4"

57'-4"

BRKFST
8'-0"x8'-0"
8' CEILING

KITCHEN
11'-0"x13'-8"
8' CEILING

MUD ROOM

REF

FAMILY
13'-0"x12'-0"
8' CEILING

GARAGE
18'-0"x20'-0"

BEDRM
16'-6"x12'-8"
8' CEILING

DN

DINING
12'-0"x16'-0"
8' CEILING

DN

LIVING
16'-0"x16'-0"
8' CEILING

MAIN FLOOR

MASTER BEDROOM
15'-0"x15'-6"
8' CEILING

ORDER BLUEPRINTS ANYTIME!
CALL TOLL-FREE 1-888-626-2026

Plan LS-95808-BJ

PRICES AND DETAILS
ON PAGES 12-15

151

Visual Splendor

- The smooth transitions inside and eye-catching forms outside make this contemporary design an object of visual pleasure.
- From the covered porch, a grand two-story entry presents you with a multitude of options.
- The octagonal dining area on one side features a coffered ceiling, while the sunken living room flanking the other side boasts a 14½-ft. vaulted ceiling and a soaring fireplace.
- Form and function combine in the Great Room, where the sliding doors provide access to the back patio. The adjoining kitchen, with a built-in desk and a walk-in pantry, make this area a place where the family can relax and play in style.
- A beautiful, U-shaped staircase, open to both the Great Room and the living room, takes you to the balcony and upstairs bedrooms.
- Entrance to the master suite through double doors reveals the natural light pouring through the front window and skylight in the master bath.

Plan SUN-2515

Bedrooms: 3	Baths: 2½
Living Area:	
Upper floor	750 sq. ft.
Main floor	1,066 sq. ft.
Total Living Area:	**1,816 sq. ft.**
Garage	495 sq. ft.
Exterior Wall Framing:	2x6

Foundation Options:

Crawlspace
(All plans can be built with your choice of foundation and framing. A generic conversion diagram is available. See order form.)

BLUEPRINT PRICE CODE: B

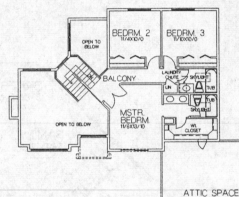

UPPER FLOOR

REAR VIEW

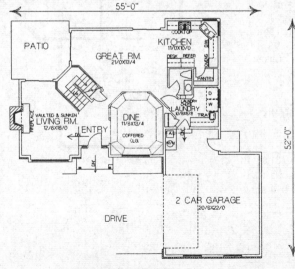

MAIN FLOOR

Gentle Greatness

- An inviting porch extends an easy welcome to guests, while a trio of front-facing gables gives passersby a pleasing hint of the gentle greatness that lies within this exciting design.
- The enormous Great Room is the undeniable heart of this family home. Its mood-setting fireplace and a charming deck in back make it a stylish spot to begin building your dreams.
- The well-designed kitchen, with its large island and sizable pantry, makes preparing and storing meals a breeze. Situated between the breakfast nook and the formal dining room, it's poised for any culinary urge.
- You'll find a delightful master bedroom on the upper floor. Its large walk-in closet and private bath will provide soothing relaxation when you need it.
- Two additional bedrooms offer space for guests or a growing family.

Plan CAR-9518

Bedrooms: 3	Baths: 2½
Living Area:	
Upper floor	878 sq. ft.
Main floor	1,002 sq. ft.
Total Living Area:	**1,880 sq. ft.**
Standard basement	1,002 sq. ft.
Garage	400 sq. ft.
Exterior Wall Framing:	2x6

Foundation Options:
Standard basement
Crawlspace
Slab
(All plans can be built with your choice of foundation and framing. A generic conversion diagram is available. See order form.)

BLUEPRINT PRICE CODE: B

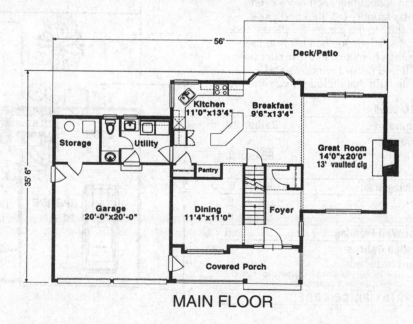

UPPER FLOOR

MAIN FLOOR

ORDER BLUEPRINTS ANYTIME!
CALL TOLL-FREE 1-888-626-2026

Plan CAR-9518

**PRICES AND DETAILS
ON PAGES 12-15**

153

Life of Leisure

- In this appealing country home, you're free to kick back and pursue a life of leisure and comfort. Indoor and outdoor relaxation is tops on the list!

- A railed front porch reminiscent of simpler times wraps around the side of the home. Picture your little ones scampering down its length, intent on catching the family puppy.

- Inside, pocket doors can separate the joined living and family rooms, creating a cozy ambience in each.

- Sliding glass doors open from the casual dining area to a fabulous backyard deck that is perfect for a family picnic!

- Parents will appreciate the openness of the walk-through kitchen, which gives them plenty of room to serve meals while ruling the roost. A built-in desk aids in scheduling each day's events. Nearby laundry facilities and close proximity to the garage are pluses, too.

- Upstairs, a balcony hall leads to the sleeping chambers. In the master suite you'll find radiant windows and a private bath that includes two vanities.

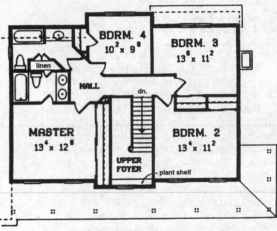

UPPER FLOOR

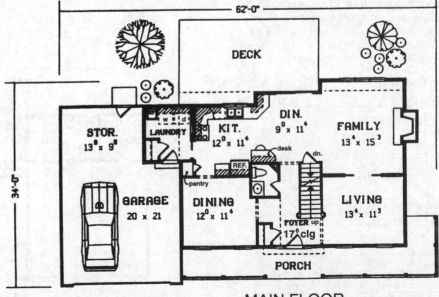

MAIN FLOOR

Plan GL-1966

Bedrooms: 4	Baths: 2½
Living Area:	
Upper floor	934 sq. ft.
Main floor	1,032 sq. ft.
Total Living Area:	**1,966 sq. ft.**
Standard basement	1,032 sq. ft.
Garage	532 sq. ft.
Exterior Wall Framing:	2x6

Foundation Options:

Standard basement
(All plans can be built with your choice of foundation and framing. A generic conversion diagram is available. See order form.)

BLUEPRINT PRICE CODE: B

Plan GL-1966

PRICES AND DETAILS
ON PAGES 12-15

Come On In!

- Handsome exterior columns frame this home's two-story entry, which serves as an elegant place to greet visitors, offering views of the Great Room as well as the tasteful formal dining room.

- With a fire roaring in the fireplace, comfort is assured in the large Great Room. Transom windows along the rear wall offer splendid views of backyard life, and the open staircase creates a picture-perfect setting.

- Two stately columns define the formal dining room, which also features a bright bay window.

- An informal dinette is large enough to seat the whole family comfortably. The adjoining kitchen boasts a walk-in pantry and an island work station.

- Upstairs, a generous walk-in closet and a lavish master bath with a whirlpool tub and a dual-sink vanity welcome the homeowners to the master suite.

- Two additional bedrooms are generously sized, with wall-length closets. The rooms share a full bath.

Plan LS-95880-PP

Bedrooms: 3	Baths: 2½
Living Area:	
Upper floor	860 sq. ft.
Main floor	1,169 sq. ft.
Total Living Area:	**2,029 sq. ft.**
Daylight basement	1,155 sq. ft.
Garage	780 sq. ft.
Exterior Wall Framing:	2x6

Foundation Options:
Daylight basement

(All plans can be built with your choice of foundation and framing. A generic conversion diagram is available. See order form.)

BLUEPRINT PRICE CODE:	C

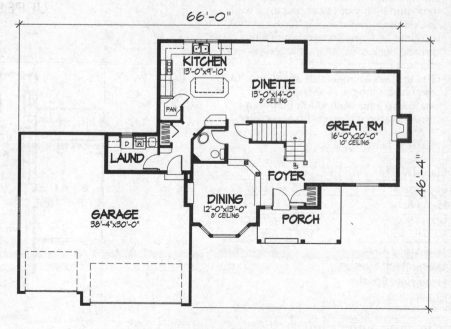

UPPER FLOOR

MAIN FLOOR

ORDER BLUEPRINTS ANYTIME!
CALL TOLL-FREE 1-888-626-2026

Plan LS-95880-PP

PRICES AND DETAILS
ON PAGES 12-15

155

All Decked Out

- A spacious deck spans the front of this symmetrical chalet, creating the perfect atmosphere for a relaxing twilight chat or a family barbecue.

- The open living and dining area, with a 10-ft., 6-in. vaulted ceiling, welcomes guests into a comfortable setting and provides ample space for recreation. A built-in entertainment center anchors the area, with large windows letting natural light fill the room.

- The U-shaped kitchen accents the open concept of the living area, allowing for casual conversations while the day's meals are prepared. A snack bar serves as an alternate eating space.

- Each of the three bedrooms boasts a full bath and plenty of closet space, as well as a sliding glass door for access to the outside. The upstairs bedroom enjoys a private deck overlooking the lower deck and the front yard.

- The upstairs loft offers an abundance of options for the creative home owner, including a possible fourth bedroom, mirroring the design of the other three.

- A half-bath and the laundry area frame the rear entry of the home.

Plan NW-914

Bedrooms: 3+	Baths: 3½
Living Area:	
Upper floor	858 sq. ft.
Main floor	1,196 sq. ft.
Total Living Area:	**2,054 sq. ft.**
Exterior Wall Framing:	2x6

Foundation Options:

Crawlspace
(All plans can be built with your choice of foundation and framing. A generic conversion diagram is available. See order form.)

BLUEPRINT PRICE CODE: C

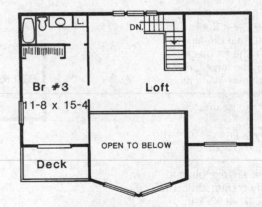

UPPER FLOOR

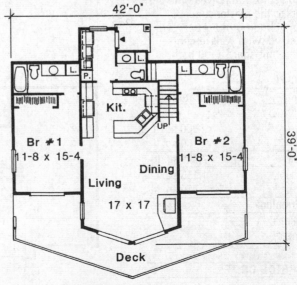

MAIN FLOOR

Memory Maker

- A glorious wraparound porch welcomes family and friends alike to this charming country home, creating an atmosphere where memories can be made.
- Inside, the spacious family room offers access to the best of both worlds—a fireplace to warm your soul and a kitchen to satisfy your appetite.
- Entertainment is a breeze in the formal living area, which frames the foyer on one side. Pocket doors opening into the family room give additional space for the occasional overflow of guests.
- Cooking is a snap when the family is hovering about the island kitchen, waiting for the next meal. Access to the dining room allows smooth service for more formal occasions.
- Upstairs, four bedrooms provide ample space for today's family. The master bedroom features an elegant tray ceiling and a bathroom with a large shower.
- An alternate bath layout is included for the second floor, creating additional space for the second bedroom.

Plan GL-2017-2	
Bedrooms: 4	**Baths:** 2½
Living Area:	
Upper floor	988 sq. ft.
Main floor	1,029 sq. ft.
Total Living Area:	**2,017 sq. ft.**
Standard basement	942 sq. ft.
Garage	462 sq. ft.
Exterior Wall Framing:	2x6
Foundation Options:	
Standard basement	

(All plans can be built with your choice of foundation and framing. A generic conversion diagram is available. See order form.)

BLUEPRINT PRICE CODE: C

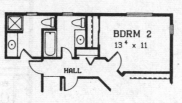

ALTERNATE BATH

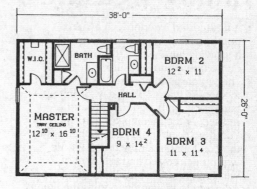

UPPER FLOOR

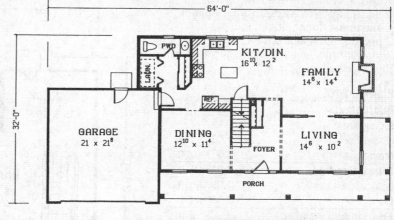

MAIN FLOOR

ORDER BLUEPRINTS ANYTIME!
CALL TOLL-FREE 1-888-626-2026

Plan GL-2017-2

PRICES AND DETAILS
ON PAGES 12-15

157

Family Treasure

- A time-tested exterior with a cozy porch, and an interior that's perfect for a growing family, turn this two-story home into a pure treasure.
- The wraparound porch is an ideal spot to spend a warm spring day. String up a hammock, grab a good book and rediscover the meaning of relaxation.
- You'll no doubt hold large gatherings in the comfortable family room, whose warming fireplace and triple set of windows create a beautiful setting.
- Adjacent to the family room is the living room, a perfect place for guests to spill into when a few friends become a houseful.
- Formal meals get special treatment in the bay-windowed dining room. It's just steps from the U-shaped kitchen, which also serves the dinette. The bayed dinette features access to a back patio.
- The upper floor holds all four bedrooms, including the stunning master suite, which boasts a flawless private bath.

Plan GL-2026

Bedrooms: 4	Baths: 2½
Living Area:	
Upper floor	965 sq. ft.
Main floor	1,061 sq. ft.
Total Living Area:	**2,026 sq. ft.**
Standard basement	1,038 sq. ft.
Garage	610 sq. ft.
Exterior Wall Framing:	2x6

Foundation Options:

Standard basement

(All plans can be built with your choice of foundation and framing. A generic conversion diagram is available. See order form.)

BLUEPRINT PRICE CODE:	C

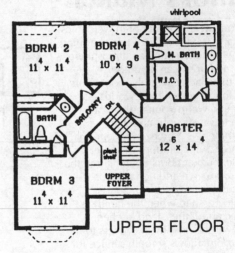

UPPER FLOOR

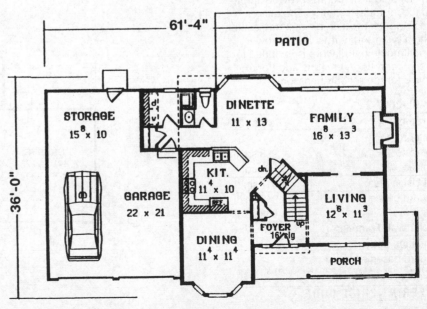

MAIN FLOOR

Plan GL-2026

PRICES AND DETAILS
ON PAGES 12-15

Skylight Lover

- Natural light from numerous skylights brightens the open design of this lovely one-story home.
- A bright, 15-ft., 6-in. vaulted entry leads into the main living area–a spacious Great Room and a dining room topped by a coffered ceiling, divided by a fireplace. A 17-ft. vault in the Great Room adds volume, and French doors access a covered patio, providing ample room for outdoor entertaining.
- The sunny bayed breakfast nook and a skylight make the vaulted island kitchen shine in the morning.
- Popular amenities in the master bath, such as a dual-sink vanity, a whirlpool tub and a walk-in closet, give the master suite character. A 9-ft. coffered ceiling and French doors leading to the backyard deck add distinction.
- Two secondary bedrooms share a full bath. The front bedroom features a built-in desk.
- A covered rear patio and an expansive deck provide endless possibilities for outdoor fun.
- A generous storage space at the back of the garage is perfect for the weekend project enthusiast.

Plan SUN-1630

Bedrooms: 3	Baths: 2½
Living Area:	
Main floor	2,103 sq. ft.
Total Living Area:	**2,103 sq. ft.**
Garage and storage	1,263 sq. ft.
Exterior Wall Framing:	2x6

Foundation Options:

Crawlspace

(All plans can be built with your choice of foundation and framing. A generic conversion diagram is available. See order form.)

BLUEPRINT PRICE CODE: C

Floor Plan

62'-0"

73'-0"

COVERED PATIO

SKYLIGHT

DOWN

NOOK
13/3 X 8/0

VAULTED
KITCHEN
12/2 X 12/3

FRENCH DRS

VAULTED CEIL

SKYLIGHT

VAULTED
GREAT RM
16/10 X 22/4

RANGE

SKYLIGHT

VAULTED CEIL

PANTRY

DESK

REFER

DW

FRENCH DRS

SPA

M BATH

W.I.C.

COFFERED
MASTER
BEDRM
12/8 X 19/8

FIREPLACE

COFFERED
DINING
9/0 X 12/6

FAU

A/C UNDER

W/H OVER

SHELVES

STORAGE

BEDRM 3
13/2 X 10/6

LINEN

CLOSET

SHELVES

PANTRY

LAUNDRY
6/4 X 5/2

W D

CLOSET

CLOSET

SHELVES

VAULTED
ENTRY
6/4 X 8/8

SKYLIGHT

CLOSET

BEDRM 2
13/2 X 12/6

COVERED
PORCH

3 CAR GARAGE
32/0 X 49/3

DESK

DRIVE

MAIN FLOOR

ORDER BLUEPRINTS ANYTIME!
CALL TOLL-FREE 1-888-626-2026

Plan SUN-1630

PRICES AND DETAILS
ON PAGES 12-15
159

Independence Day

- This two-story Colonial design is perfect for the family that has outgrown its starter home and seeks the freedom and happiness that extra space can provide.
- A sidelighted, two-story foyer is flanked by elegant spaces. Serve high tea in the living room, which is graced by decorative columns. Even a standard like apple pie takes on extra flavor in the graciousness of the dining room.
- The island kitchen extends into a unique prowed bay, providing extra space. A chic French door opens to an optional backyard deck or patio.
- A cheery fireplace warms the family room, which offers plenty of room for a TV, a piano or whatever it is that makes your time together most special.
- The second-floor sleeping spaces feature room enough to quarter all your troops. Double doors access a vaulted master suite that boasts a walk-in closet and a private bath loaded with amenities.

Plan JWA-4904-A

Bedrooms: 4	Baths: 2½
Living Area:	
Upper floor	1,090 sq. ft.
Main floor	1,188 sq. ft.
Total Living Area:	**2,278 sq. ft.**
Standard basement	1,236 sq. ft.
Garage	528 sq. ft.
Exterior Wall Framing:	2x6

Foundation Options:

Standard basement
(All plans can be built with your choice of foundation and framing. A generic conversion diagram is available. See order form.)

BLUEPRINT PRICE CODE: C

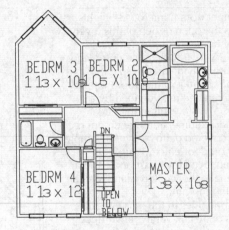

UPPER FLOOR

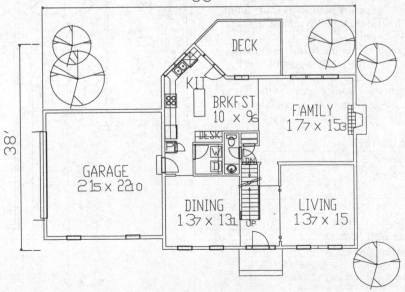

MAIN FLOOR

Plan JWA-4904-A

PRICES AND DETAILS
ON PAGES 12-15

The One!

- The sweet promises made by the bold brick and stucco exterior of this classy two-story home are nicely kept by the smart interior. In short, this is the one!
- From the foyer, you're just steps away from almost any room on the main floor. To the left is a quiet study suitable for finishing the extra work you brought home—but there's no law that says you can't use it to give the kids' latest video game a test run.
- On the other side of the foyer lies the formal dining room, a secluded spot ideal for entertaining friends on what will become memorable occasions.
- The Gathering Room's bay window, handsome fireplace and 10-ft.-high ceiling lend an open coziness to a space large enough to handle all your biggest holiday events.
- Unless otherwise noted, all main-floor rooms have spacious 9-ft. ceilings.
- Upstairs, the master bedroom boasts a deluxe private bath and a lengthy walk-in closet. Two additional bedrooms have individual access to a full bath.

Plan LS-95903-MC

Bedrooms: 3+	Baths: 2½
Living Area:	
Upper floor	1,200 sq. ft.
Main floor	1,570 sq. ft.
Total Living Area:	**2,770 sq. ft.**
Standard basement	1,570 sq. ft.
Garage	919 sq. ft.
Exterior Wall Framing:	2x6
Foundation Options:	

Standard basement
(All plans can be built with your choice of foundation and framing. A generic conversion diagram is available. See order form.)

BLUEPRINT PRICE CODE:	D

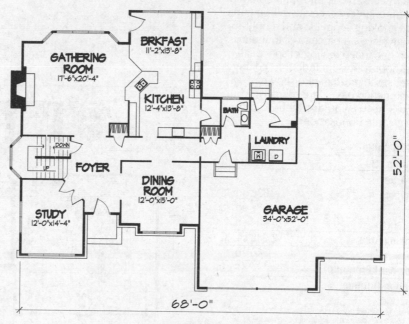

UPPER FLOOR

MAIN FLOOR

ORDER BLUEPRINTS ANYTIME!
CALL TOLL-FREE 1-888-626-2026

Plan LS-95903-MC

PRICES AND DETAILS
ON PAGES 12-15

161

Very Victorian

- This home's pretty wraparound porch and striking turret lend it a pleasant Victorian flavor. Surrounded by oak trees, it will display the dignity and presence of a much older home.

- During a springtime garden party, guests can mingle on the porch, visiting and savoring the gentle breezes. If the air turns chilly or you prefer a sit-down dinner, move the gathering inside to the dining room and the welcoming parlor.

- At the rear of the home, the family room accommodates the day-to-day activities that turn a house into a home. When reading a bedtime story to the kids, this space ensures your peace of mind.

- The kitchen promises an efficient working area to prepare culinary masterpieces. Here, an island cooktop frees up counter space, a walk-in pantry stores cooking supplies, and a built-in desk gives you a place to plan menus.

- For an enhanced feeling of space, all main-floor rooms include 9-ft. ceilings.

- Upstairs, the master suite showcases a sun-drenched bay. Depending on your family's needs, you decide how to use the versatile bonus room.

Plan CDG-2094

Bedrooms: 3+	Baths: 2½
Living Area:	
Upper floor	838 sq. ft.
Main floor	1,087 sq. ft.
Bonus room	424 sq. ft.
Total Living Area:	**2,349 sq. ft.**
Garage	560 sq. ft.
Exterior Wall Framing:	2x6

Foundation Options:

Crawlspace

(All plans can be built with your choice of foundation and framing. A generic conversion diagram is available. See order form.)

BLUEPRINT PRICE CODE: C

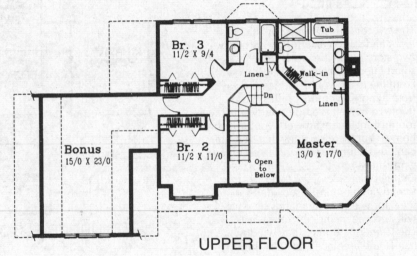

UPPER FLOOR

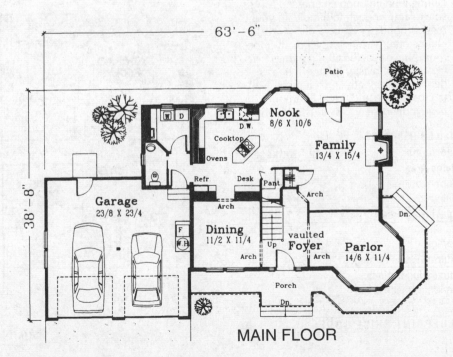

MAIN FLOOR

Plan CDG-2094

PRICES AND DETAILS
ON PAGES 12-15

Family Design

- This Mediterranean-style home boasts smart, comfortable living areas designed with the family in mind.
- To the right of the foyer, a vaulted den offers a great space for a quiet getaway or a convenient home office.
- To the foyer's left, the sunken living room provides a fashionable location for formal parties. Its large bay is lined with arched windows, and a vaulted ceiling magnifies the room's airiness.

- The L-shaped kitchen will tantalize any cook. Its open design allows for socializing with those gathered in the family room. A gentle alcove offers the ideal spot for a breakfast table.
- The family room is crowned with a vaulted ceiling, and a fireplace casts light and warmth over the faces of family and friends gathered there.
- The master bedroom enjoys a three-sided fireplace, straddling the spa tub and the sleeping area, giving off an irresistably romantic glow.

Plan LS-95804-BJ

Bedrooms: 3+	**Baths:** 2½

Living Area:	
Main floor	2,508 sq. ft.
Total Living Area:	**2,508 sq. ft.**
Garage	688 sq. ft.
Exterior Wall Framing:	2x6

Foundation Options:

Slab
(All plans can be built with your choice of foundation and framing. A generic conversion diagram is available. See order form.)

BLUEPRINT PRICE CODE: D

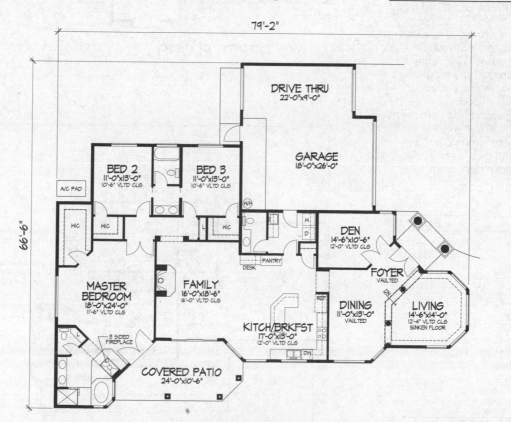

MAIN FLOOR

ORDER BLUEPRINTS ANYTIME!
CALL TOLL-FREE 1-888-626-2026

Plan LS-95804-BJ

**PRICES AND DETAILS
ON PAGES 12-15**

163

Inviting Smiles

- Corner quoins, keystones and a unique roofline trim the exterior of this home and invite smiling gazes from passersby. A wraparound porch makes a welcoming impression on visitors.

- Flanking the sparkling, skylighted foyer, two spaces are well-suited for entertaining: to the left, the tray-ceilinged dining room offers a boxed-out window, while to the right, the expansive Great Room is cheered by a roaring fireplace.

- The master suite, secluded at one end of the upper level, boasts a wonderful private bath with a dual-sink vanity for practicality and an oval spa for pleasure.

- Not to be outdone, the secondary bedrooms each flaunt their own personality. The second bedroom sports a front-facing, boxed-out window seat, while the third bedroom features a vaulted ceiling and nice-sized nooks, perfect for a wooden desk or an over-stuffed chair.

Plan G-20217

Bedrooms: 3	Baths: 2½
Living Area:	
Upper floor	1,388 sq. ft.
Main floor	1,183 sq. ft.
Total Living Area:	**2,571 sq. ft.**
Standard basement	1,183 sq. ft.
Garage and storage	607 sq. ft.
Exterior Wall Framing:	2x6

Foundation Options:

Standard basement

Crawlspace

Slab

(All plans can be built with your choice of foundation and framing. A generic conversion diagram is available. See order form.)

BLUEPRINT PRICE CODE:	D

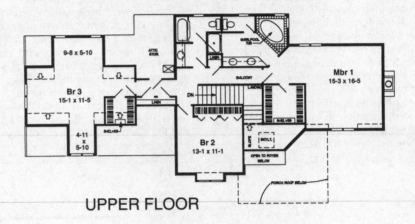

UPPER FLOOR

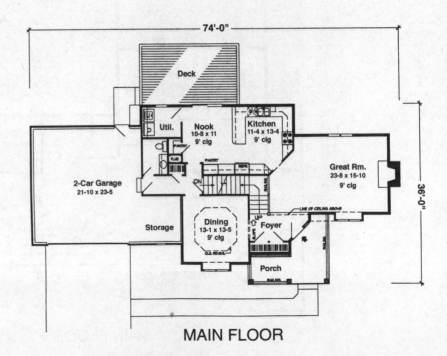

MAIN FLOOR

Plan G-20217

PRICES AND DETAILS
ON PAGES 12-15

Bold and Sunny

- This bold two-story design offers an outstanding floor plan and a brilliant use of windows and outdoor areas to help bring in the sunshine!
- A large, wraparound covered deck in front and an equally spacious sun deck in back give you plenty of room to host a grand summertime barbecue.
- Inside, the foyer welcomes guests with a dramatic 16-ft., 10-in. ceiling. From there, you'll be drawn to the huge family room, which boasts access to both outdoor areas via French doors. The family room's fireplace provides

warmth when the nights get chilly, and mood when the night is young.
- You'll find a second fireplace in the living room, which features a bay window and a 10-ft., 3-in. tray ceiling.
- Nestled between the nook and the formal dining room, the island kitchen stands ready for any occasion.
- A quiet study, which converts easily to a bedroom, completes the main floor.
- The upper floor contains the commanding master suite, which includes a large walk-in closet and a private bath with a whirlpool tub.
- A full-sized bath with a dual-sink vanity serves the remaining three bedrooms.

Plan IDG-2023	
Bedrooms: 4+	**Baths: 2½**
Living Area:	
Upper floor	1,179 sq. ft.
Main floor	1,464 sq. ft.
Total Living Area:	**2,643 sq. ft.**
Daylight basement	1,282 sq. ft.
Garage	506 sq. ft.
Exterior Wall Framing:	2x6
Foundation Options:	

Daylight basement
(All plans can be built with your choice of foundation and framing. A generic conversion diagram is available. See order form.)

BLUEPRINT PRICE CODE:	**D**

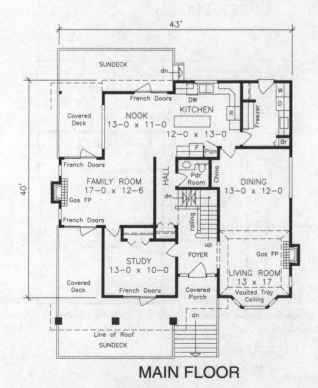

MAIN FLOOR

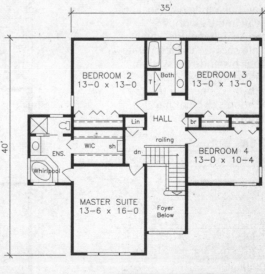

UPPER FLOOR

ORDER BLUEPRINTS ANYTIME!
CALL TOLL-FREE 1-888-626-2026

Plan IDG-2023

PRICES AND DETAILS
ON PAGES 12-15

165

Glory Days

- Regal lines and classic door embellishments accent this home's traditional Colonial styling.
- A stunning two-story foyer introduces the interior, which pays close attention to all your family's needs.
- Situated at the front of the home, on either side of the foyer, the formal living room and dining room lend an impression of elegance to any affair.
- A cozy fireplace in the family room exudes ambience for casual gatherings. Here, a sliding-glass door opens to an outdoor deck or patio.
- The adjoining breakfast room flows into the galley-style kitchen, which accesses a handy laundry/utility area.
- The master suite provides the perfect retreat at the end of a long day. Soak your cares away in the glorious whirlpool bath, which includes dual sinks, a separate shower and a separate toilet. Enormous his-and-hers walk-in closets further ensure your comfort.
- A balcony hallway connects three additional bedrooms, which share another full bath.

Plan JWA-5003-3A

Bedrooms: 4	Baths: 2½
Living Area:	
Upper floor	1,504 sq. ft.
Main floor	1,232 sq. ft.
Total Living Area:	**2,736 sq. ft.**
Standard basement	1,253 sq. ft.
Garage	514 sq. ft.
Exterior Wall Framing:	2x6

Foundation Options:

Standard basement

(All plans can be built with your choice of foundation and framing. A generic conversion diagram is available. See order form.)

BLUEPRINT PRICE CODE:	D

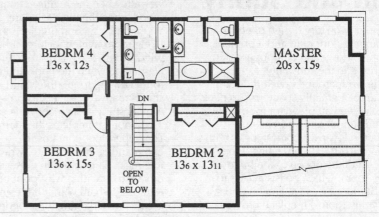

UPPER FLOOR

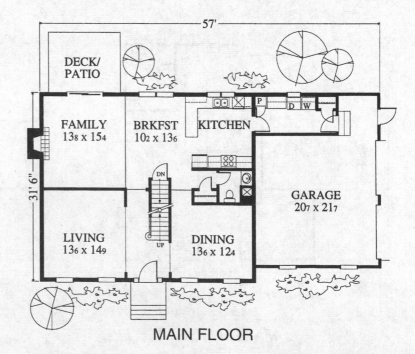

MAIN FLOOR

Pleasures of Secrecy

- Private, secluded spaces fill out this home, which envelops them in a lovely brick facade.
- The master suite offers a private bath with a delicious garden spa, which overlooks the private terrace—the ideal place to enjoy your morning cup of coffee while listening to birdsong flow through a thicket of lilac.
- A small room, set off in a remote corner of the home, offers the perfect space for a quiet office or hobby room. A secondary bedroom, situated at the front of the home, may be used as an additional office space, making this home a fitting choice for the working couple.
- Above the island kitchen, a secret room provides a space limited in its function only by the owner's imagination.
- The luxury of the common living areas is not to be minimized by the private ones—the tray-ceilinged dining room and central living room provide a nice arrangement for entertaining, while the family room and bayed breakfast nook are ideal spaces for cozier gatherings.

Plan YS-5606	
Bedrooms: 3+	**Baths:** 2½
Living Area:	
Upper floor	252 sq. ft.
Main floor	2,599 sq. ft.
Total Living Area:	**2,851 sq. ft.**
Standard basement	2,047 sq. ft.
Garage	476 sq. ft.
Exterior Wall Framing:	2x6

Foundation Options:

Standard basement
(All plans can be built with your choice of foundation and framing. A generic conversion diagram is available. See order form.)

BLUEPRINT PRICE CODE: D

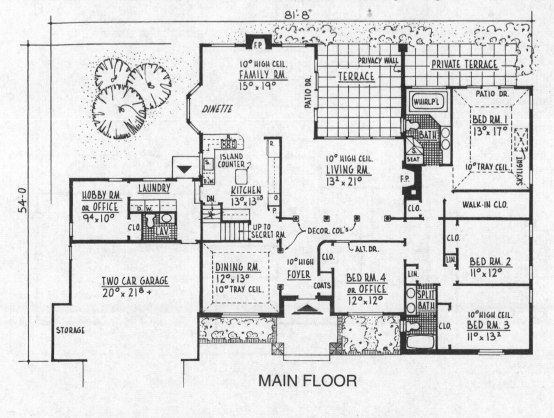

MAIN FLOOR

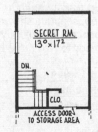

UPPER FLOOR

ORDER BLUEPRINTS ANYTIME!
CALL TOLL-FREE 1-888-626-2026

Plan YS-5606

PRICES AND DETAILS
ON PAGES 12-15

167

Good Night, John Boy!

- Friendly, nostalgic living is easily attainable in this Walton-style farmhouse. Modern features make life more comfortable than it once was.
- The wraparound porch is a great place to visit with Grandpa. Inside, a 17½-ft.-high foyer welcomes Daddy home with the Christmas gifts.
- A fireplace warms the bay-windowed living room. Memorable feasts fill up the spacious dining room with yummy aromas and precious loved ones.
- You needn't be a learned chef to appreciate the roomy kitchen, complete with an island cooktop, a walk-in pantry, double ovens and a menu desk.
- The breakfast nook and family room combine for lots of casual living space.
- Unless otherwise noted, all main-floor rooms have 8½-ft. ceilings.
- Upstairs, the master suite is thoroughly up-to-date, with its corner whirlpool tub, separate shower, walk-in closet and peaceful sitting bay. A balcony hall leads to two more bedrooms.

Plan TS-9641

Bedrooms: 3+	Baths: 2½
Living Area:	
Upper floor	1,154 sq. ft.
Main floor	1,508 sq. ft.
Total Living Area:	**2,662 sq. ft.**
Garage	991 sq. ft.
Exterior Wall Framing:	2x6

Foundation Options:

Crawlspace
(All plans can be built with your choice of foundation and framing. A generic conversion diagram is available. See order form.)

BLUEPRINT PRICE CODE: D

UPPER FLOOR

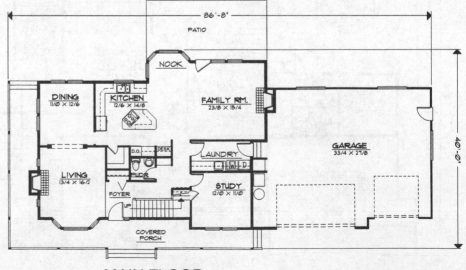

MAIN FLOOR

Plan TS-9641

PRICES AND DETAILS
ON PAGES 12-15

Light the Way

- A beautiful arched transom tops the double-door entry of this home, lighting the way to the hidden gems within its confines.
- Comfort beckons your family to the sunken Great Room, where the fireplace warms you and the transom windows brighten the day. A 19-ft. ceiling accentuates the space.
- The kitchen is a cook's dream, featuring an island cooktop, ample pantry space, an adjoining breakfast nook and a pass-through to the formal dining room.
- Relax with a cup of java and your favorite novel in the den, which also has a private deck.
- The master bedroom showcases an incredible bathroom, an oasis in the night for the restless or weary. A large walk-in closet completes the package.
- Upstairs, an open area outside the bedrooms creates additional space for kids at work or play.
- First floor ceiling heights are 9 ft., and second floor ceiling heights are 8 ft.

Plan LRD-11108

Bedrooms: 3+	Baths: 2½
Living Area:	
Upper floor	760 sq. ft.
Main floor	2,323 sq. ft.
Total Living Area:	**3,083 sq. ft.**
Standard basement	2,323 sq. ft.
Garage	704 sq. ft.
Exterior Wall Framing:	2x6

Foundation Options:

Standard basement

Crawlspace

(All plans can be built with your choice of foundation and framing. A generic conversion diagram is available. See order form.)

BLUEPRINT PRICE CODE:	E

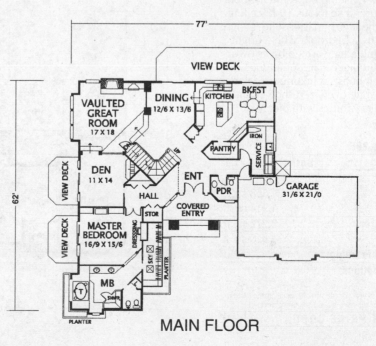

UPPER FLOOR

MAIN FLOOR

ORDER BLUEPRINTS ANYTIME!
CALL TOLL-FREE 1-888-626-2026

Plan LRD-11108

PRICES AND DETAILS
ON PAGES 12-15

169

Grand Scale

- Old World elegance on a grand scale is yours in this lovely two-story design.
- The foyer opens to a formal living room, where an arrangement of arched windows creates a sun-drenched bay. French doors lead to a rear patio that embraces the back of the home.
- Boxed columns define the formal dining room, the perfect spot for distinctive entertaining. A wet bar stands nearby.
- The open kitchen features an island cooktop with plenty of work space for the family gourmet. The kitchen and a tiled breakfast area melt into the vaulted family room, where the ceiling soars to a lofty height of 15 ft., 9 inches. A fireplace warms this wonderful area.
- Unless otherwise noted, each first-floor room features a spacious 10-ft. ceiling.
- Upstairs, the lavish master suite is anchored by a bedroom with a bright bayed sitting area warmed by its own romantic fireplace. The sumptuous master bath boasts a luxurious soaking tub, a separate oversized shower and his-and-hers vanities with plenty of counter space.

Plan HDS-99-295

Bedrooms: 4	Baths: 2 full, 2 half
Living Area:	
Upper floor	1,358 sq. ft.
Main floor	1,914 sq. ft.
Total Living Area:	**3,272 sq. ft.**
Garage	610 sq. ft.
Exterior Wall Framing:	2x6

Foundation Options:

Slab
(All plans can be built with your choice of foundation and framing. A generic conversion diagram is available. See order form.)

BLUEPRINT PRICE CODE:	E

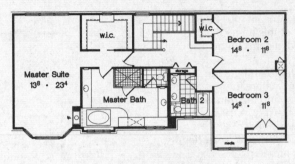

UPPER FLOOR

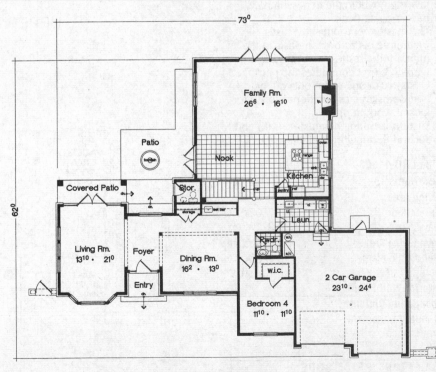

MAIN FLOOR

ORDER BLUEPRINTS ANYTIME!
CALL TOLL-FREE 1-888-626-2026

Plan HDS-99-295

PRICES AND DETAILS
ON PAGES 12-15

Power House

- This vibrant home packs quite a wallop with its features and amenities.
- A soaring, 18-ft.-high sidelighted entry introduces the formal rooms.
- To the right, bowed glass brightens the living room, which boasts a stunning fireplace for romantic "night lights." A 13-ft. vaulted ceiling tops the space.
- Straight ahead from the foyer, the sunken family room flaunts another fireplace and built-in bookshelves under a 9-ft., 8-in. ceiling. Access to the huge backyard patio is just a step away.
- A roomy kitchen with an oversized island is joined to a breakfast nook.
- Unless otherwise noted, all main-floor rooms have 9-ft. ceilings.
- Upstairs, 11-ft. ceilings top the master bedroom and its luxurious bath. A peninsula fireplace and a bayed sitting room combine to treat you like the landed gentry. You even have private access to the laundry room/office!
- Three more bedrooms and a second full bath complete the upper floor. The front bedroom boasts a 12-ft. vaulted ceiling.

Plan B-91036

Bedrooms: 4+	Baths: 2½
Living Area:	
Upper floor	1,735 sq. ft.
Main floor	1,619 sq. ft.
Total Living Area:	**3,354 sq. ft.**
Standard basement	1,619 sq. ft.
Garage	863 sq. ft.
Exterior Wall Framing:	2x6

Foundation Options:

Standard basement

(All plans can be built with your choice of foundation and framing. A generic conversion diagram is available. See order form.)

BLUEPRINT PRICE CODE: E

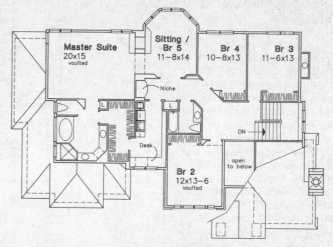

UPPER FLOOR

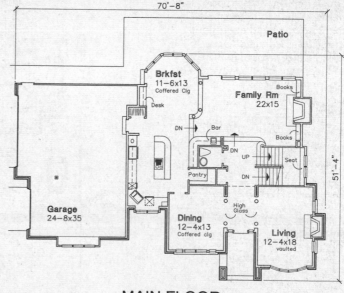

MAIN FLOOR

ORDER BLUEPRINTS ANYTIME!
CALL TOLL-FREE 1-888-626-2026

Plan B-91036

PRICES AND DETAILS
ON PAGES 12-15

171

On the Prairie

- With its low-slung roofline, natural stonework and detailed windows, this design recalls the stylish prairie homes built early in the twentieth century.
- Inside, a 16½-ft. vaulted ceiling in the entry greets visitors. On the right, the living room extends into the dining room, where a 9-ft. tray ceiling adds a look of distinction. This pleasing layout makes entertaining a snap.
- Across the entry, a peaceful study accommodates work-at-home days. Built-in cabinets keep papers and files close at hand and in order.
- The family room awaits casual activities. The fireplace is flanked by built-in cabinets that hold media equipment, while a 15-ft., 4-in. vaulted ceiling soars overhead. The area opens to the island kitchen for pleasant evening chats.
- Across the home, the master suite promises quiet nights. The bath boasts a Jacuzzi, perfect after a long bike ride.
- Unless otherwise noted, all main-floor rooms include 9-ft. ceilings.
- Upstairs, a large bonus room may be adapted to meet your needs. How about a playroom for the kids?

Plan R-2173-G

Bedrooms: 3+	Baths: 2½
Living Area:	
Upper floor	658 sq. ft.
Main floor	2,312 sq. ft.
Bonus room	462 sq. ft.
Total Living Area:	**3,432 sq. ft.**
Garage	653 sq. ft.
Exterior Wall Framing:	2x6

Foundation Options:

Crawlspace
(All plans can be built with your choice of foundation and framing. A generic conversion diagram is available. See order form.)

BLUEPRINT PRICE CODE:	E

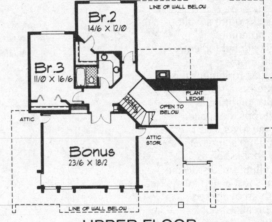

UPPER FLOOR

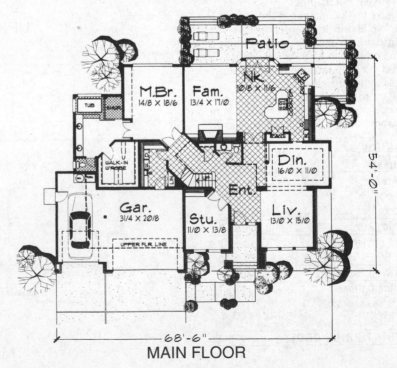

MAIN FLOOR

Plan R-2173-G

PRICES AND DETAILS
ON PAGES 12-15

Gentle Breezes

- With or without palm trees, this design invokes a breezy sense of tropical relaxation. A unique front porch and upper- and lower-level rear verandas embrace the open outdoors.
- From the foyer, an arched opening sweeps guests into the expansive Grand Room, which boasts a fireplace, a 14-ft. tray ceiling and an optional aquarium.
- The breakfast nook flows into the kitchen, which shares an eating bar with the Grand Room. A large pantry and easy access to the formal dining room add to its practicality.
- A versatile study, to the left of the foyer, provides the perfect haven for you and your favorite books. It can also be converted to an extra bedroom.
- The master suite encompasses the entire left wing of the home. Its fantastic features treat you as though you are at a spa resort!
- When you wake, throw open the French doors to the veranda for a breath of fresh air. Large walk-in closets connect the bedroom to its opulent private bath. Here, a garden tub, a separate shower, a dual-sink vanity and a compartmentalized toilet keep you feeling sane.
- Two additional bedrooms across the home share another full bath.
- Unless otherwise specified, all main-floor rooms feature 9-ft., 4-in. ceilings.

Plan SG-6622	
Bedrooms: 3+	**Baths:** 2
Living Area:	
Main floor	2,190 sq. ft.
Lower floor	1,383 sq. ft.
Total Living Area:	**3,573 sq. ft.**
Tuck-under garage	583 sq. ft.
Exterior Wall Framing:	2x6
Foundation Options:	
Slab	

(All plans can be built with your choice of foundation and framing. A generic conversion diagram is available. See order form.)

BLUEPRINT PRICE CODE:	F

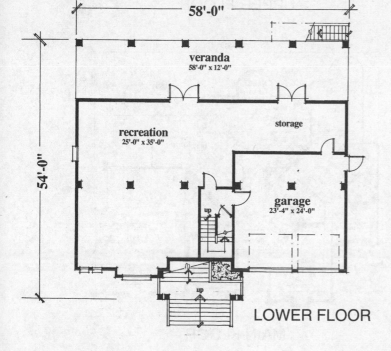

LOWER FLOOR

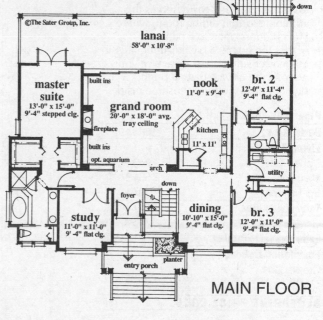

MAIN FLOOR

ORDER BLUEPRINTS ANYTIME!
CALL TOLL-FREE 1-888-626-2026

Plan SG-6622

PRICES AND DETAILS
ON PAGES 12-15

173

As You Like It

- This creative two-story will serve you well in its many roles—as a comforting refuge, a stylish spot for entertaining, and maybe even a dignified office.
- Inside, the vaulted entry bids guests an airy welcome. Built-in shelves in the den hold a growing library, and the window seat is a great place to read.
- When company calls, settle down in the beautiful sunken living room for a visit. A built-in bookcase displays wedding and graduation photos, while a warm fireplace flickers in the background.
- At the rear of the home, casual activities have a place of their own. In the family room, shelves on either side of the fireplace hold multimedia equipment.
- Fresh orange juice will taste even better in the sunny breakfast nook. The kitchen boasts an island cooktop and a snack bar that is fun for after-school treats. The kitchen easily serves the adjoining formal dining room, where French doors open to a patio.
- Across the home, a bayed sitting area in the master suite offers a place of your own. In the private bath, a bright skylight draws natural sunshine inside.

Plan CDG-2089

Bedrooms: 3+	Baths: 2½
Living Area:	
Upper floor	949 sq. ft.
Main floor	2,531 sq. ft.
Bonus room	497 sq. ft.
Total Living Area:	**3,977 sq. ft.**
Garage	735 sq. ft.
Exterior Wall Framing:	2x6

Foundation Options:

Crawlspace
(All plans can be built with your choice of foundation and framing. A generic conversion diagram is available. See order form.)

BLUEPRINT PRICE CODE:	F

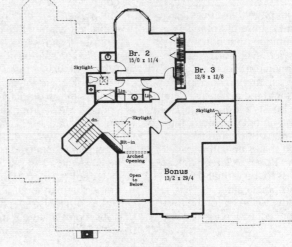

UPPER FLOOR

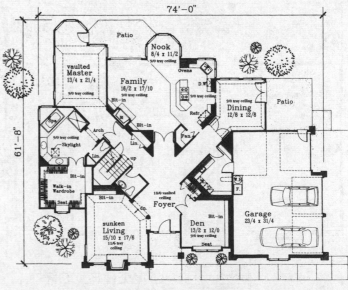

MAIN FLOOR

ORDER BLUEPRINTS ANYTIME!
CALL TOLL-FREE 1-888-626-2026

Plan CDG-2089

PRICES AND DETAILS
ON PAGES 12-15

Hallowed Halls

- Angled passages unfold within this breathtaking home, leading you to its wide-open rooms and peaceful refuges.
- On either side of the 17-ft., 4-in.-high raised entry, the formal living and dining rooms await pleasant conversation and elegant cuisine.
- Crowned by an 18-ft., 4-in. ceiling, the showpiece family room resides at the crux of the home. A legion of windows flanks the central fireplace.
- Two space-saving islands grace the thoroughly modern kitchen: one hosts a cooktop; the other, a small sink and a serving counter. The adjoining breakfast nook easily accesses a covered lanai.
- The master suite is unbelievably posh, featuring a two-way fireplace between the sleeping chamber and a bow-windowed sitting room. The private bath boasts an oval tub nestled into a glass-block wall, plus a separate shower and a segregated walk-in closet.
- Unless otherwise noted, all main-floor rooms are topped by 9-ft., 4-in. ceilings.
- Upstairs, the luxury continues. A fitting counterpart to the two secondary bedrooms, the guest suite flaunts a private bath, a roomy walk-in closet and private access to an exquisite deck.

Plan B-91020

Bedrooms: 4	Baths: 3½
Living Area:	
Upper floor	1,374 sq. ft.
Main floor	3,158 sq. ft.
Total Living Area:	**4,532 sq. ft.**
Garage	758 sq. ft.
Exterior Wall Framing:	2x6

Foundation Options:

Slab
(All plans can be built with your choice of foundation and framing. A generic conversion diagram is available. See order form.)

BLUEPRINT PRICE CODE: H

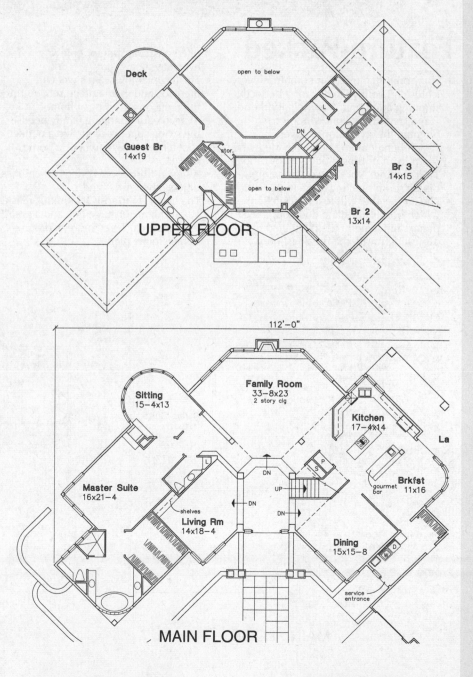

Feature-Packed

- This comfortable design combines every feature on your wish list, for a perfectly stunning addition to any neighborhood.
- Transom and sidelight windows brighten the stylish, open foyer.
- Tasteful entertaining begins in the living room, with its boxed-out window and 18-ft. ceiling. Not to be outdone, the dining room's ceiling soars to 22 feet.
- The family chef will love the kitchen, which boasts an island cooktop, a big pantry and a menu desk. Defined by a 36-in.-high wall, the breakfast nook

offers a casual spot for enjoying everyday meals.
- The large family room's wet bar, fireplace and media niche set you up for a relaxing evening at home.
- Available for changing family needs, the swing suite would make a perfect spot for an aging parent or a home office.
- All main-floor rooms offer 9-ft. ceilings, unless otherwise noted.
- The upper floor hosts a fabulous master suite with an 11-ft. ceiling and a great exercise area. Three more bedrooms complete the plan.

Plan B-93020

Bedrooms: 4+	**Baths:** 4

Living Area:	
Upper floor	1,590 sq. ft.
Main floor	1,890 sq. ft.
Total Living Area:	**3,480 sq. ft.**
Standard basement	1,890 sq. ft.
Garage and storage	629 sq. ft.
Exterior Wall Framing:	2x6

Foundation Options:

Standard basement
(All plans can be built with your choice of foundation and framing. A generic conversion diagram is available. See order form.)

BLUEPRINT PRICE CODE:	E

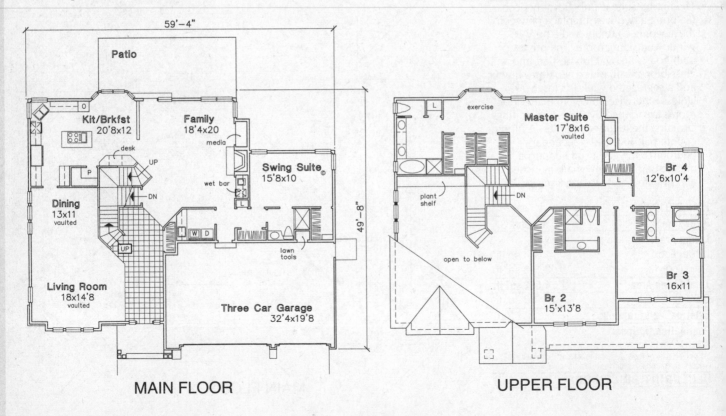

MAIN FLOOR

UPPER FLOOR

Plan B-93020

PRICES AND DETAILS
ON PAGES 12-15

REAR VIEW

Flexible Design

- Designed for flexibility, this home can be built on a narrow or sloping lot, with either two bedrooms or three.
- The living room boasts a 16-ft.-high sloped ceiling and is warmed by a handsome woodstove. Sliding glass doors open to an inviting corner deck.
- The skylighted, passive-solar dining room is wrapped by windows and has a slate floor to capture and retain solar heat. A French door opens to the deck.
- The kitchen is open to the dining room but is separated from the living room by a 7½-ft.-high wall.
- The main-floor bedroom is located across the hall from a full bath with laundry facilities.
- In the plan's two-bedroom version, the upper-floor loft hosts a spacious master suite with a 12-ft. sloped ceiling, a huge walk-in closet and a private bath.
- In the plan's three-bedroom version, two bedrooms share the upper floor.

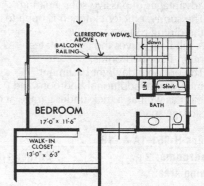

FRONT VIEW

Plans H-946-1A, -1B, -2A & -2B

Bedrooms: 2+	Baths: 1-2
Living Area:	
Upper floor (3-bedroom plan)	290 sq. ft.
Upper floor (2-bedroom plan)	381 sq. ft.
Main floor	814 sq. ft.
Total Living Area:	**1,104/1,195 sq. ft.**
Daylight basement	814 sq. ft.
Garage	315 sq. ft.
Exterior Wall Framing:	2x6
Foundation Options:	Plan #
Daylight basement (2 bedrooms)	H-946-1B
Daylight basement (3 bedrooms)	H-946-2B
Crawlspace (2 bedrooms)	H-946-1A
Crawlspace (3 bedrooms)	H-946-2A

(All plans can be built with your choice of foundation and framing. A generic conversion diagram is available. See order form.)

BLUEPRINT PRICE CODE:	**A**

MAIN FLOOR

UPPER FLOOR
(TWO-BEDROOM PLAN)

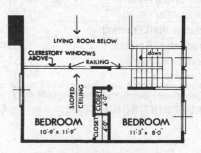

UPPER FLOOR
(THREE-BEDROOM PLAN)

Suspended Sun Room

- This narrow-lot design is a perfect combination of economical structure and luxurious features.
- The living and dining rooms flow together to create a great space for parties or family gatherings. A 16-ft. sloped ceiling and clerestory windows add drama and brightness. A fabulous deck expands the entertaining area.
- An exciting sun room provides the advantages of passive-solar heating.
- The sunny, efficient kitchen is open to the dining room.
- A full bath serves the two isolated main-floor bedrooms.
- The optional daylight basement includes an additional bedroom and bath as well as a tuck-under garage and storage space.

Plans H-951-1A & -1B

Bedrooms: 2+	Baths: 1-2
Living Area:	
Main floor	1,075 sq. ft.
Sun room	100 sq. ft.
Daylight basement	662 sq. ft.
Total Living Area:	**1,175/1,837 sq. ft.**
Tuck-under garage	311 sq. ft.
Exterior Wall Framing:	2x6
Foundation Options:	**Plan #**
Daylight basement	H-951-1B
Crawlspace	H-951-1A

(All plans can be built with your choice of foundation and framing. A generic conversion diagram is available. See order form.)

BLUEPRINT PRICE CODE:	**A/B**

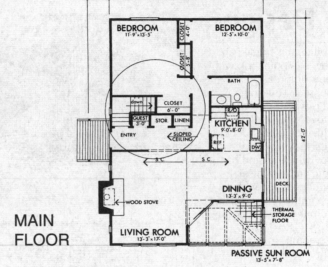

MAIN FLOOR

PASSIVE SUN ROOM
13'-5" x 7'-8"

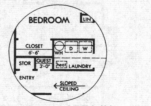

STAIRWAY AREA IN CRAWLSPACE VERSION

CLERESTORY WINDOWS OVER HALLWAY

TOP OF CLOSETS

CLERESTORY WINDOW AT CORNER OF LIVING ROOM

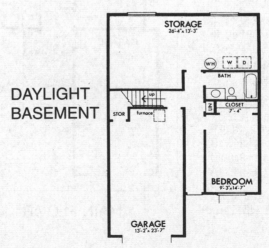

DAYLIGHT BASEMENT

Sun-Splashed One-Story

- This unique angled design offers spectacular backyard views, a delightful sun room and two enticing terraces.
- The high-ceilinged reception hall is open to the huge combination living and dining area. Here, more high ceilings, a stone fireplace and walls of glass add to the expansive look and the inviting atmosphere.

- The adjoining family room, kitchen and nook are just as appealing. The family room features a built-in entertainment center and sliding glass doors that access the energy-saving sun room. The comfortable kitchen has a handy snack counter facing the sunny dinette.
- The sleeping wing offers three bedrooms and two baths. The master suite boasts a sloped ceiling, a private terrace, a large walk-in closet and a personal bath with a whirlpool tub. The two remaining bedrooms are just steps away from another full bath.

See this plan on our "One-Story" VideoGraphic Tour!
Order form on page 9

Plan AHP-9330	
Bedrooms: 3	**Baths:** 2
Living Area:	
Main floor	1,626 sq. ft.
Sun room	146 sq. ft.
Total Living Area:	**1,772 sq. ft.**
Standard basement	1,542 sq. ft.
Garage	427 sq. ft.
Exterior Wall Framing:	2x4 or 2x6

Foundation Options:
Standard basement
Crawlspace
Slab
(All plans can be built with your choice of foundation and framing. A generic conversion diagram is available. See order form.)

BLUEPRINT PRICE CODE:	B

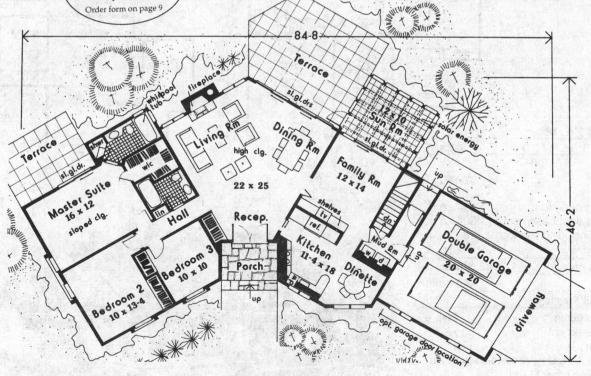

MAIN FLOOR

FRONT VIEW

Sun Lovers' Hideaway

- Attractive, cozy and sunny are only three adjectives that come immediately to mind as one looks at this plan. Energy efficiency is also a major element.
- An air-lock entry helps seal heated or cooled air inside, and the home is well-insulated in walls, ceilings and floors for tight control of energy bills.
- The major portion of the main floor is devoted to a spacious living/dining/kitchen area with easy access to the large sun room.
- Two downstairs bedrooms share a full bath and include large double-glazed windows.
- Upstairs, the master suite features a private bath and large closet, plus a balcony overlook into the living room.
- An optional daylight basement offers potential for an additional bedroom as well as a large recreation room and general use area. In this version, the sun room is on the lower level, and a dramatic spiral staircase ascends to the main floor.

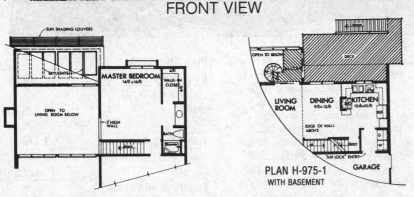

UPPER FLOOR

PLAN H-975-1
WITH BASEMENT

MAIN FLOOR
PLAN H-975-1A
WITHOUT BASEMENT

BASEMENT

Plans H-975-1 & -1A

Bedrooms: 3	**Baths:** 2

Space:

Upper floor	370 sq. ft.
Main floor (including sun room)	1,394 sq. ft.
Optional daylight basement	1,394 sq. ft.
Finished (including sun room)	782 sq. ft.
Unfinished	612 sq. ft.
Total Living Area	**1,764/2,546 sq. ft.**
Garage	448 sq. ft.
Exterior Wall Framing	2x6

Foundation options:	**Plan #**
Daylight Basement	H-975-1
Crawlspace	H-975-1A
(Foundation & framing conversion diagram available—see order form.)	
Blueprint Price Code	B/D

REAR VIEW

Plans H-975-1 & -1A

PRICES AND DETAILS
ON PAGES 12-15

Visual Surprises

- The exterior of this home is accented with a dramatic roof cavity, while the inside uses angles to enhance the efficiency and variety of the floor plan.
- The double-door entry opens to a reception area, which unfolds to the spacious living room. A 16½-ft. sloped ceiling and an angled fireplace add drama to the living room and the adjoining bayed dining room, where sliding doors access a backyard terrace.
- The efficient kitchen easily serves both the formal dining room and the cheerful dinette, which offers sweeping outdoor views. A fireplace in the adjoining family room warms the entire area. A second terrace is accessible via sliding glass doors.
- The oversized laundry room could be finished as a nice hobby room.
- A skylighted stairway leads up to the sleeping areas. The master suite is fully equipped with a private bath, a separate dressing area, a walk-in closet and an exciting sun deck alcoved above the garage. Three additional bedrooms share another full bath.

Plan K-540-L

Bedrooms: 4	**Baths:** 2½

Living Area:	
Upper floor	884 sq. ft.
Main floor	1,238 sq. ft.
Total Living Area:	**2,122 sq. ft.**
Standard basement	1,106 sq. ft.
Garage	400 sq. ft.
Storage	122 sq. ft.
Exterior Wall Framing:	2x4 or 2x6

Foundation Options:

Standard basement

Slab

(All plans can be built with your choice of foundation and framing. A generic conversion diagram is available. See order form.)

BLUEPRINT PRICE CODE: C

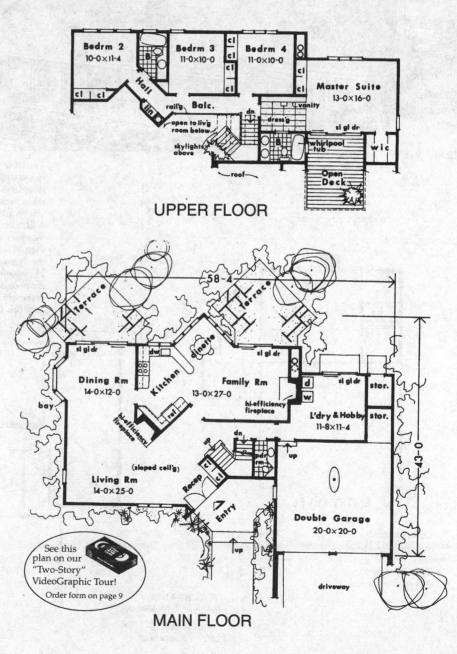

UPPER FLOOR

See this plan on our "Two-Story" VideoGraphic Tour! Order form on page 9

MAIN FLOOR

ORDER BLUEPRINTS ANYTIME!
CALL TOLL-FREE 1-888-626-2026

Plan K-540-L

PRICES AND DETAILS
ON PAGES 12-15
181

The Weather-Beater

INTERIOR

REAR VIEW

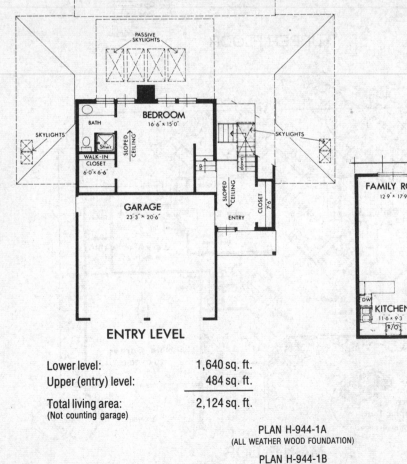

PASSIVE SKYLIGHTS

SKYLIGHTS

BATH

BEDROOM
16'6" x 15'0"

SLOPED CEILING

Shw'r.

WALK-IN CLOSET
6'0" x 6'6"

SKYLIGHTS

UP

down

SLOPED CEILING

CLOSET
7'6"

ENTRY

GARAGE
23'3" x 20'6"

ENTRY LEVEL

Lower level:	1,640 sq. ft.
Upper (entry) level:	484 sq. ft.
Total living area: (Not counting garage)	2,124 sq. ft.

PLAN H-944-1A
(ALL WEATHER WOOD FOUNDATION)

PLAN H-944-1B
(CONCRETE FOUNDATION)

Available with an all-weather wood foundation (H-944-1A) or with a concrete foundation (H-944-1B), this energy miser takes maximum advantage of the tempering affects offered through earth berming. Additional energy features such as the masonry trombe wall, passive sun roof and Plen-Wood heating system are but some of the features this plan offers. A careful inspection of this layout suggests that more and more homes of the future will resemble this innovative design, especially as more sloping building sites are utilized.

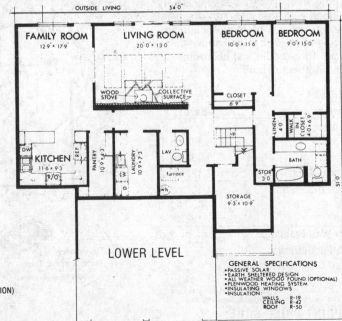

OUTSIDE LIVING   54'0"

FAMILY ROOM
12'9" x 17'9"

LIVING ROOM
20'0" x 13'0"

BEDROOM
10'0" x 11'6"

BEDROOM
9'0" x 15'0"

WOOD STOVE

COLLECTIVE SURFACE

CLOSET
6'9"

LINEN
4'0"

WALK-IN CLOSET
4'0" x 6'9"

KITCHEN
11'6" x 9'3"

REF

PANTRY
10'9" x 9'3"

DW

LAUNDRY
10'9" x 7'3"

LAV

furnace

BATH

STOR
3'0"

STORAGE
9'3" x 10'9"

LOWER LEVEL

GENERAL SPECIFICATIONS
• PASSIVE SOLAR
• EARTH SHELTERED DESIGN
• ALL WEATHER WOOD FOUND. (OPTIONAL)
• PLENWOOD HEATING SYSTEM
• INSULATING WINDOWS
• INSULATION
  WALLS   R-19
  CEILING   R-42
  ROOF   R-50

Blueprint Price Code C

Plans H-944-1A & -1B

Home with Sparkle

- This dynamite design simply sparkles, with the main living areas geared toward a gorgeous greenhouse at the back of the home.
- At the front of the home, a sunken foyer introduces the formal dining room, which is framed by a curved half-wall. The sunken living room boasts a 17-ft. vaulted ceiling and a nice fireplace.
- The spacious kitchen features a bright, two-story skywell above the island. The family room's ceiling rises to 17 feet. These rooms culminate at a solar greenhouse with an indulgent hot tub and a 12-ft. vaulted ceiling. The neighboring bath has a raised spa tub.
- Upstairs, the impressive master suite includes its own deck and a stairway to the greenhouse. A vaulted library with a woodstove augments the suite. Ceilings soar to 16 ft. in both areas.

Plan S-8217

Bedrooms: 3+	Baths: 2
Living Area:	
Upper floor	789 sq. ft.
Main floor	1,709 sq. ft.
Bonus room	336 sq. ft.
Total Living Area:	**2,834 sq. ft.**
Partial basement	1,242 sq. ft.
Garage	441 sq. ft.
Exterior Wall Framing:	2x6

Foundation Options:

Partial basement
Crawlspace
Slab

(All plans can be built with your choice of foundation and framing. A generic conversion diagram is available. See order form.)

BLUEPRINT PRICE CODE: D

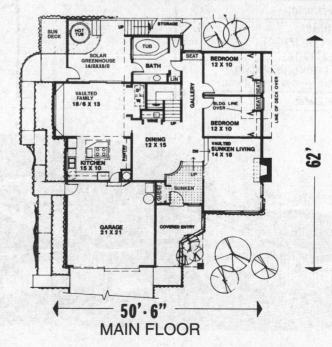

UPPER FLOOR

MAIN FLOOR

50'-6"

62'

Striking Octagonal Solarium

- The center of attraction in this dramatic design is the sunsoaking passive sun room. This 20' diameter solarium reaches above the roofline to capture the most possible solar energy from any direction.
- For passive cooling, several of the vertical windows in the dome can be opened. The room also includes a "splash pool" to provide humidity in the winter.
- Then rooms surrounding the solarium are equally striking, as well as spacious and convenient, providing plenty of space for casual family living as well as more formal entertaining.
- The master suite includes a bath fit for royalty and a huge walk-in closet. Two secondary bedrooms share a large second bath with separate tub and shower and double sinks.

Plans H-3719-1 & -1A

Bedrooms: 3	Baths: 2½

Space:

Total living area:	3,166 sq. ft.
(Includes 324 sq. ft. sun room)	
Basement (under bedrooms & family room):	approx. 1,400 sq. ft.
Garage:	850 sq. ft.
Storage:	132 sq. ft.

Exterior Wall Framing:	2x6

Foundation options:
Partial basement (H-3719-1).
Crawlspace (H-3719-1A)
(Foundation & framing conversion diagram available — see order form.)

Blueprint Price Code:	E

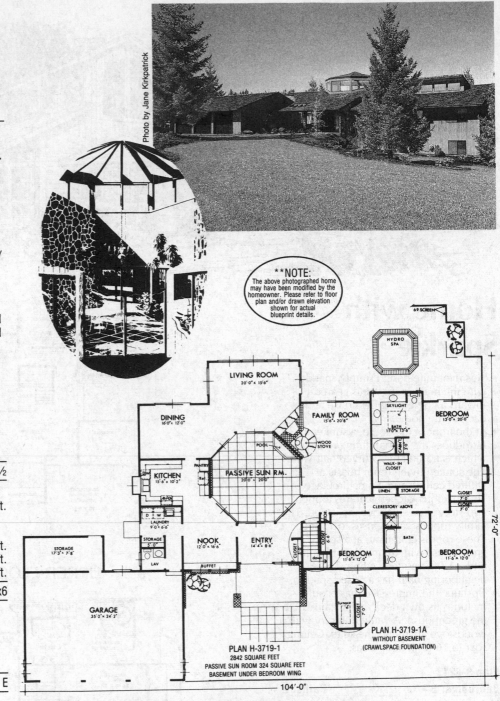

Photo by Jane Kirkpatrick

NOTE:
The above photographed home may have been modified by the homeowner. Please refer to floor plan and/or drawn elevation shown for actual blueprint details.

PLAN H-3719-1
2842 SQUARE FEET
PASSIVE SUN ROOM 324 SQUARE FEET
BASEMENT UNDER BEDROOM WING

PLAN H-3719-1A
WITHOUT BASEMENT
(CRAWLSPACE FOUNDATION)

Plans H-3719-1 & -1A

PRICES AND DETAILS ON PAGES 12-15

Dual-Function Atrium

Energy efficiency in a home is a concept which is currently widely sought and needs to be carefully considered in view of today's energy costs. The atrium or greenhouse featured in this home serves a dual function, both as a collecting room for passive solar heating and a venting area for summer cooling.

The living room features a massive masonry fireplace with a 5' opening. The family room also has a fireplace.

The plan provides several other convenience features: The nook adjacent to the kitchen can be used for informal dining or, if equipped with folding doors, can serve as a guest room with its own bath.

The laundry located directly off the kitchen is a welcome step-saver. The skylights in the second floor hall provide natural light to an area usually lighted only artificially.

A recessed entry is sheltered by the roof overhang that opens to the glazed atrium, the central feature of this passive solar home.

Exterior walls are 2x6 construction.

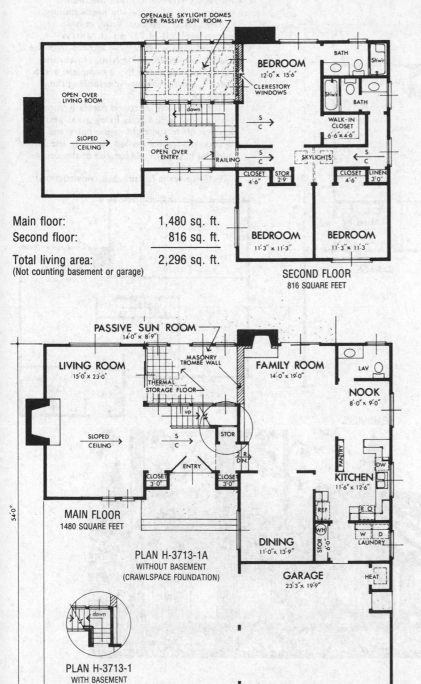

OPENABLE SKYLIGHT DOMES OVER PASSIVE SUN ROOM

OPEN OVER LIVING ROOM

SLOPED CEILING

OPEN OVER ENTRY

RAILING

down

BEDROOM
12'-0" x 15'-6"

CLERESTORY WINDOWS

BATH

Shwr

Shwr

BATH

WALK-IN CLOSET
6'-6" x 4'-6"

SKYLIGHTS

CLOSET 4'-6"

STOR 2'-9"

CLOSET 4'-6"

LINEN 3'-0"

BEDROOM
11'-3" x 11'-3"

BEDROOM
11'-3" x 11'-3"

SECOND FLOOR
816 SQUARE FEET

Main floor: 1,480 sq. ft.
Second floor: 816 sq. ft.

Total living area: 2,296 sq. ft.
(Not counting basement or garage)

PASSIVE SUN ROOM
14'-0" x 8'-9"

LIVING ROOM
15'-0" x 23'-0"

MASONRY TROMBE WALL

THERMAL STORAGE FLOOR

SLOPED CEILING

up

STOR

2 R DN.

CLOSET 3'-0"

ENTRY

CLOSET 3'-0"

MAIN FLOOR
1480 SQUARE FEET

FAMILY ROOM
14'-0" x 19'-0"

LAV

NOOK
8'-0" x 9'-0"

PANTRY

DW

KITCHEN
11'-6" x 12'-6"

REF

R.O.

W H

W D

LAUNDRY

DINING
11'-0" x 13'-9"

STOR 6'-0"

GARAGE
23'-3" x 19'-9"

HEAT

PLAN H-3713-1A
WITHOUT BASEMENT
(CRAWLSPACE FOUNDATION)

54'-0"

down

PLAN H-3713-1
WITH BASEMENT

54'-0"

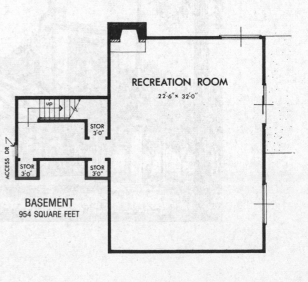

RECREATION ROOM
22'-6" x 32'-0"

up

STOR 3'-0"

ACCESS DR

STOR 3'-0"

STOR 3'-0"

BASEMENT
954 SQUARE FEET

ORDER BLUEPRINTS ANYTIME!
CALL TOLL-FREE 1-888-626-2026

Blueprint Price Code C
Plan H-3713-1 & -1A

PRICES AND DETAILS
ON PAGES 12-15

185

Solar Features Add to Striking Design

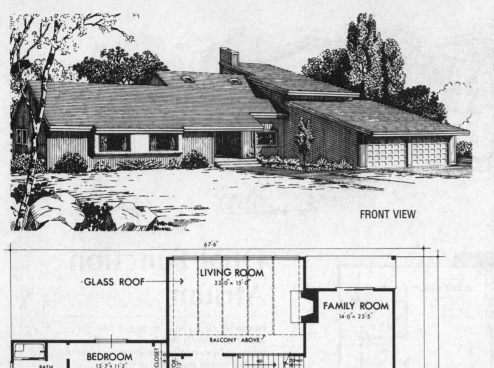

FRONT VIEW

The passive sun room in this plan has a full window wall and glass roof oriented to the south for gathering the sun's energy, and a plank hardwood floor and large stone fireplace which store the heat for later release.

Because this area also is the living room, the windows should be equipped with moveable screens to make the room comfortable when the sun needs muting.

The master bedroom suite, in an upper-level loft of 757 sq. ft., also is warmed by a window wall aligned with the glass roof. An adjoining bath, closets and skylighted den make this a complete adult retreat, with a balcony overlooking the living room.

The main floor is zoned carefully for easy traffic flow, with family living areas and the kitchen off to the right of the entry and the bedroom wing on the left. Stairs to the loft and the basement are located at the center of the home.

Exterior walls feature 2x6 construction.

MAIN FLOOR

GLASS ROOF

LIVING ROOM
22'-0" x 15'-0"

FAMILY ROOM
14'-0" x 22'-5"

BALCONY ABOVE

BEDROOM
13'-7" x 11'-2"

BATH

BATH

CLOSET

CLOSET 3'-3"

STOR. 3'-3"

CLOSET 3'-3"

LINEN 4'-3"

ENTRY

PANTRY

CHINA

DINING

BEDROOM
12'-2" x 11'-0"

CLOSET 5'-3"

CLOSET 5'-3"

BEDROOM
12'-2" x 11'-0"

KITCHEN
11'-0" x 12'-2"

LAV

LAUNDRY
10'-6" x 7'-6"

W D

STOR

DW

GARAGE
21'-3" x 21'-7"

67'-6"

57'-6"

MAIN FLOOR
PLAN H-3721-1
WITH BASEMENT

PLAN H-3721-1A
WITHOUT BASEMENT
(CRAWLSPACE FOUNDATION)

Upper floor:	757 sq. ft.
First floor:	1,888 sq. ft.
Total living area:	2,645 sq. ft.

(Not counting basement or garage)

UPPER FLOOR

OPEN TO LIVING RM

BALCONY RAILING

BEDROOM
11'-10" x 18'-9"

DEN
10'-7" x 15'-3"

WALK-IN CLOSET
8'-7" x 9'-2"

VANITY

SKYLIGHT

down

CLOSET 7'-6"

BATH

Sh'w'r

UPPER FLOOR
757 SQ. FT.

REAR VIEW

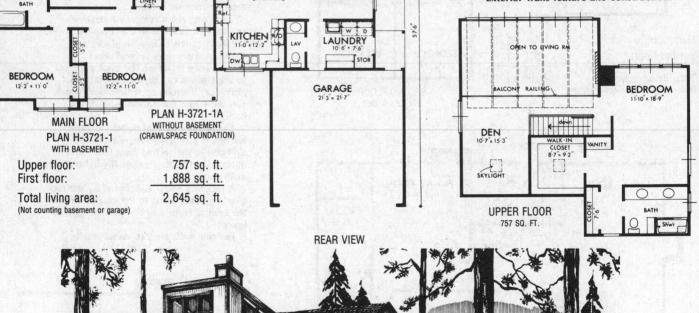

Blueprint Price Code D

Plans H-3721-1 & -1A

REAR VIEW

FRONT VIEW

Year-Round Comfort

- Designed for the energy-conscious, this passive-solar home provides year-round comfort with much lower fuel costs.
- The open, airy interior is a delight. In the winter, sunshine penetrates deep into the living spaces. In the summer, wide overhangs shade the interior.
- The central living and dining rooms flow together, creating a bright, open space. Sliding glass doors open to a terrace and an enclosed sun spot.
- In the airy casual space, the kitchen has an eating bar and a sunny breakfast nook. The adjoining family room boasts a woodstove that warms the entire area.
- The master bedroom suite includes a private terrace, a personal bath and a walk-in closet. Two other bedrooms share another full bath.

Plan K-392-T

Bedrooms: 3	Baths: 2½
Living Area:	
Main floor	1,592 sq. ft.
Sun spot	125 sq. ft.
Total Living Area:	**1,717 sq. ft.**
Partial basement	634 sq. ft.
Garage	407 sq. ft.
Exterior Wall Framing:	2x4 or 2x6

Foundation Options:

Partial basement

Slab

(All plans can be built with your choice of foundation and framing. A generic conversion diagram is available. See order form.)

BLUEPRINT PRICE CODE:	B

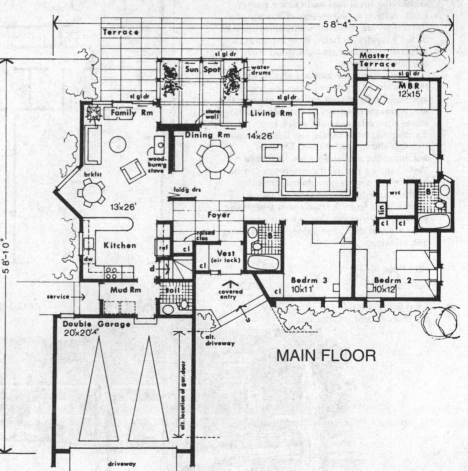

MAIN FLOOR

PRICES AND DETAILS ON PAGES 12-15

FRONT VIEW

Sun Room
Adds Warmth

At first glance this seems like just another very nice home, with crisp contemporary lines, a carefully conceived traffic flow and generous bedroom and living areas. What sets this home apart from most other houses is its passive sun room, a 13' x 11'6" solarium that collects, stores and distributes solar energy to warm the home, conserving fossil fuel and cutting energy costs. Adding to the energy efficiency of the design are 2x6 stud walls, allowing use of R-19 insulation batts, R-30 insulation in the ceiling, and an air-tight wood stove in the family room.

The passive sun room has glazing on three walls as it juts out from the home, and has a fully glazed ceiling to capture the maximum solar energy. A masonry tile floor stores the collected heat which is distributed to the family and living rooms through sliding glass doors. The wall adjoining the dining area also is glazed. With hanging plants, the sun room can be a visually stunning greenhouse extension of the vaulted-ceilinged living room. A French door from the sun room and sliding glass doors from the family room open onto a wood deck, for outdoor entertaining and relaxing.

First floor:	2,034 sq. ft.
Sun room:	159 sq. ft.
Total living area:	2,193 sq. ft.
(Not counting basement or garage)	

PLAN H-3720-1
WITH BASEMENT

PLAN H-3720-1A
WITHOUT BASEMENT
(CRAWLSPACE FOUNDATION)

62'0"

PASSIVE SUN ROOM (13'0" x 11'6")

FAMILY ROOM 14'0" x 16'6"

LIVING ROOM 14'0" x 22'0"

BEDROOM 12'0" x 18'0"

WALK-IN CLOSET 6'6" x 6'6"

THERMAL STORAGE MASS

WOOD STOVE

DINING 13'5" x 11'0"

VAULTED CEILING

BATH

Shwr

KITCHEN 10'6" x 9'0"

PANTRY 3'0"

down

CLERESTORY ABOVE

LINEN 6'9"

BATH

DW

R/O Ref

STOR

61'0"

D W

LAUNDRY 11'6" x 6'0"

LAV

CLOSET 6'0"

ENTRY

CLOSET 5'9"

GARAGE 23'3" x 23'8"

BEDROOM 10'0" x 12'0"

CLOSET 5'9"

BEDROOM 10'0" x 12'0"

PANTRY

heat w h

STOR 4'0"

REAR VIEW

Blueprint Price Code C

Plans H-3720-1 & -1A

FRONT VIEW

Sun Chaser

A passive sun room with two fully glazed walls and an all-glass roof offers leeway when siting this comfortable, contemporary leisure home. Orientation is towards the south to capture maximum solar warmth. The window wall in the living room and a bank of clerestory windows high on the master bedroom wall soak up the winter rays for direct heat gain, yet are shaded with overhangs to block out the higher sun in the summer.

The 165 sq. ft. sun room is a focal point from the living and family rooms, through windows and sliding glass doors between these rooms. A dining table in the family room would command a sweeping view, or meals could be enjoyed in the sun room.

Sloping ceilings in the living and sun rooms allow balcony railings to open the master bedroom partially for a view down to these rooms, and let warm air flow up from the masonry storage floor of the sun room.

Accent walls of solid board paneling add visual warmth and texture to the rooms. Western cedar bevel siding adds beauty and individuality to the exterior. Exterior walls are of 2x6 construction.

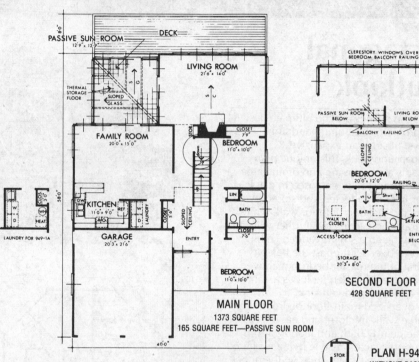

MAIN FLOOR
1373 SQUARE FEET
165 SQUARE FEET—PASSIVE SUN ROOM

SECOND FLOOR
428 SQUARE FEET

PLAN H-949-1A
WITHOUT BASEMENT
(CRAWLSPACE FOUNDATION)

PLAN H-949-1B
DAYLIGHT BASEMENT

PLAN H-949-1
STANDARD BASEMENT

First floor:	1,373 sq. ft.
Passive sun room:	165 sq. ft.
Second floor:	428 sq. ft.
Total living area:	1,966 sq. ft.

(Not counting basement or garage)

Blueprint Price Code B

ORDER BLUEPRINTS ANYTIME!
CALL TOLL-FREE 1-888-626-2026

Plans H-949-1, -1A & -1B

**PRICES AND DETAILS
ON PAGES 12-15**

189

Octagonal Outlook

- Octagon homes are the ultimate design for providing stunning panoramic views. Besides an expansive wraparound deck, this unique plan features a huge living and dining area that is almost fully enclosed in glass!
- Solar heat is collected and stored by a dramatic masonry interior wall, while a central woodstove adds further warmth. The living area's high vaulted ceiling soars to over 15 ft., past the balcony railing of the master bedroom above.
- The efficient kitchen includes a pantry and a nice windowed sink.
- The oversized main-floor bedroom has a large walk-in closet and easy access to the nearby bath and laundry room.
- Luxurious vacation-style living is offered in the private master suite on the upper floor. An enormous bedroom with a cozy woodstove, a private bath and a gigantic separate dressing area make this retreat hard to beat!
- Space for a recreation room, a hobby room or extra bedrooms is available in the daylight basement.

Plans H-948-1A & -1B

Bedrooms: 2+	Baths: 2
Living Area:	
Upper floor	700 sq. ft.
Main floor	1,236 sq. ft.
Daylight basement	1,236 sq. ft.
Total Living Area:	**1,936/3,172 sq. ft.**
Garage	552 sq. ft.
Exterior Wall Framing:	2x6
Foundation Options:	**Plan #**
Daylight basement	H-948-1B
Crawlspace	H-948-1A

(All plans can be built with your choice of foundation and framing. A generic conversion diagram is available. See order form.)

BLUEPRINT PRICE CODE:	**B/E**

REAR VIEW

MAIN FLOOR

STAIRWAY AREA IN CRAWLSPACE VERSION

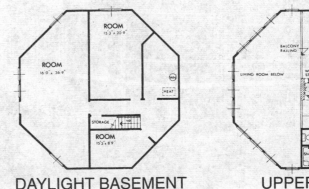

DAYLIGHT BASEMENT   UPPER FLOOR

Solar Design that Shines

- A passive-solar sun room, an energy-efficient woodstove and a panorama of windows make this design really shine.

- The open living/dining room features a 16-ft.-high vaulted ceiling, glass-filled walls and access to the dramatic decking. A balcony above gives the huge living/dining area definition while offering spectacular views.

- The streamlined kitchen has a convenient serving bar that connects it to the living/dining area.

- The main-floor bedroom features dual closets and easy access to a full bath. The laundry room, located just off the garage, doubles as a mudroom and includes a handy coat closet.

- The balcony hallway upstairs is bathed in natural light. The two nice-sized bedrooms are separated by a second full bath.

Plans H-855-3A & -3B

Bedrooms: 3		**Baths:** 2-3
Living Area:		
Upper floor		586 sq. ft.
Main floor		1,192 sq. ft.
Sun room		132 sq. ft.
Daylight basement		1,192 sq. ft.
Total Living Area:		**1,910/3,102 sq. ft.**
Garage		520 sq. ft.
Exterior Wall Framing:		2x6
Foundation Options:		**Plan #**
Daylight basement		H-855-3B
Crawlspace		H-855-3A

(All plans can be built with your choice of foundation and framing. A generic conversion diagram is available. See order form.)

BLUEPRINT PRICE CODE: B/E

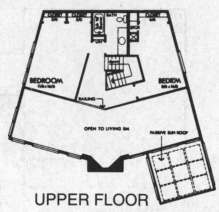

UPPER FLOOR

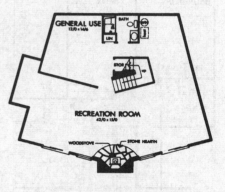

DAYLIGHT BASEMENT

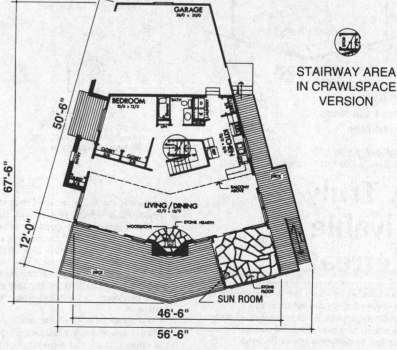

MAIN FLOOR

STAIRWAY AREA
IN CRAWLSPACE
VERSION

FRONT VIEW

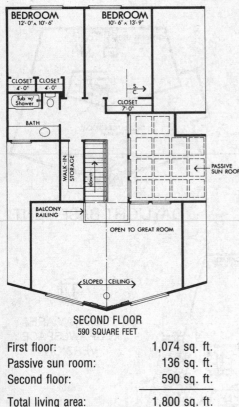

BEDROOM 12'-0" x 10'-6"
BEDROOM 10'-6" x 13'-9"

CLOSET 4'-0"   CLOSET 4'-0"
Tub w/ Shower
BATH
CLOSET 7'-0"
WALK-IN STORAGE
down
PASSIVE SUN ROOF
BALCONY RAILING
OPEN TO GREAT ROOM
SLOPED CEILING

SECOND FLOOR
590 SQUARE FEET

First floor:	1,074 sq. ft.
Passive sun room:	136 sq. ft.
Second floor:	590 sq. ft.
Total living area:	**1,800 sq. ft.**

(Not counting basement or garage)

A Truly Livable Retreat

For a number of years the A-Frame idea has enjoyed great acceptance and popularity, especially in recreational areas. Too often, however, hopeful expectations have led to disappointment because

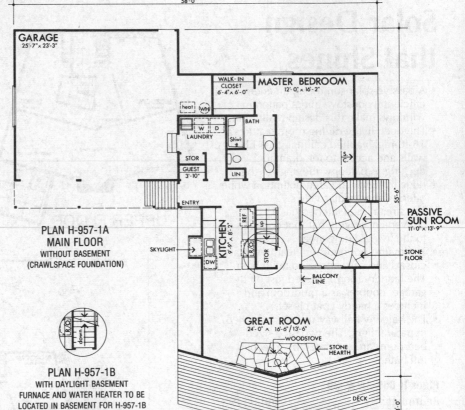

GARAGE 25'-7" x 23'-3"

WALK-IN CLOSET 6'-4" x 6'-0"
MASTER BEDROOM 12'-0" x 16'-2"
heat   WH
BATH
W D
LAUNDRY
Sh'w'r
STOR
GUEST 3'-10"
LIN
ENTRY
PASSIVE SUN ROOM 11'-0" x 13'-9"
STONE FLOOR
REF
KITCHEN 9'-0" x 8'-2"
SKYLIGHT
DW
STOR
UP
BALCONY LINE
GREAT ROOM 24'-0" x 16'-6"/13'-6"
WOODSTOVE
STONE HEARTH
DECK

58'-0"
55'-6"
8'-0"

PLAN H-957-1A
MAIN FLOOR
WITHOUT BASEMENT
(CRAWLSPACE FOUNDATION)

R/O   down

PLAN H-957-1B
WITH DAYLIGHT BASEMENT
FURNACE AND WATER HEATER TO BE
LOCATED IN BASEMENT FOR H-957-1B

economic necessity resulted in small and restricted buildings. Not so with this plan. Without ignoring the need for economy, the designers allowed themselves enough freedom to create a truly livable and practical home with a main floor of 1,210 sq. ft., exclusive of the garage area. The second floor has 590 sq. ft., and includes two bedrooms, a bath and ample storage space.

Take special note of the multi-use passive sun room. Its primary purpose is to collect, store and redistribute the sun's heat, not only saving a considerable

amount of money but contributing an important function of keeping out dampness and cold when the owners are elsewhere. Otherwise the room might serve as a delightful breakfast room, a lovely arboretum, an indoor exercise room or any of many other functions limited only by the occupants' ingenuity.

A truly livable retreat, whether for weekend relaxation or on a daily basis as a primary residence, this passive solar A-Frame is completely equipped for the requirements of today's active living.

Exterior walls are framed with 2x6 studs.

Blueprint Price Code B

Plans H-957-1A & -1B

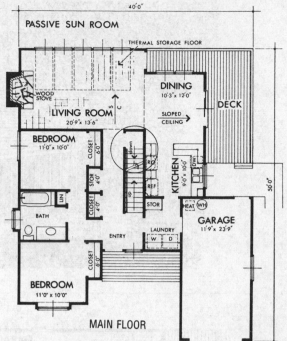

FRONT VIEW

MAIN FLOOR

Sunny Family Living

- Pleasant-looking and unassuming from the front, this plan breaks into striking, sun-catching angles at the rear.
- The living room sun roof gathers passive solar heat, which is stored in the tile floor and the two-story high masonry backdrop to the wood stove.
- A 516-square-foot master suite with private bath and balcony makes up the second floor.
- The main floor offers two more bedrooms and a full bath.

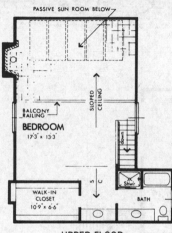

UPPER FLOOR

WITHOUT BASEMENT
(CRAWLSPACE FOUNDATION)

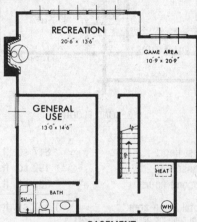

BASEMENT

Plans H-947-1A & -1B

Bedrooms: 3	Baths: 2-3

Space:

Upper floor:	516 sq. ft.
Main floor:	1,162 sq. ft.
Total without basement:	**1,678 sq. ft.**
Daylight basement:	966 sq. ft.
Total with basement:	**2,644 sq. ft.**
Garage:	279 sq. ft.
Exterior Wall Framing:	**2x6**

Foundation options:
Daylight basement (H-947-1B).
Crawlspace (H-947-1A).
(Foundation & framing conversion diagram available — see order form.)

Blueprint Price Code:

Without basement:	B
With basement:	D

REAR VIEW

Plans H-947-1A & -1B

PRICES AND DETAILS ON PAGES 12-15

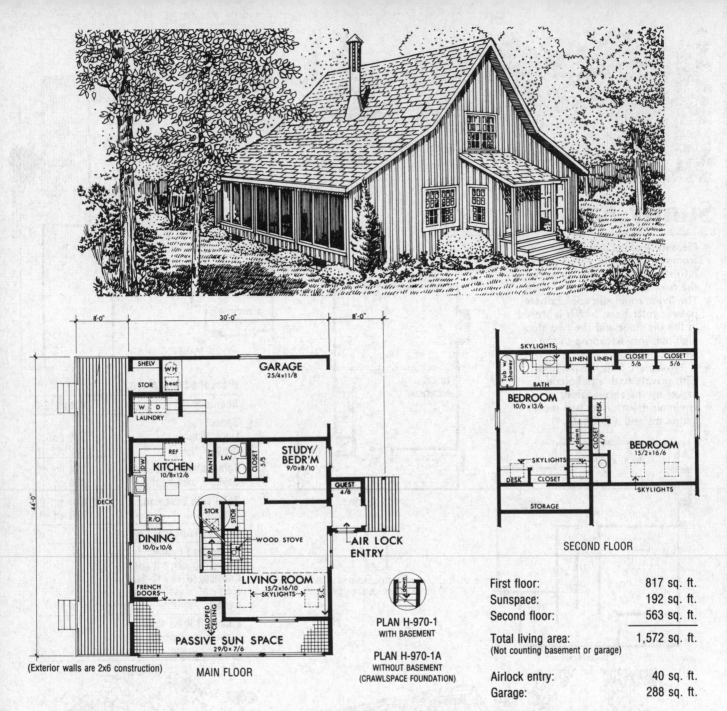

GARAGE 25/4x11/8

SHELV · WH
STOR · heat
W D
LAUNDRY

REF
KITCHEN 10/8x12/6

DW

PANTRY · LAV · CLOSET 5/5

STUDY/ BEDR'M 9/0x8/10

GUEST 4/6

R/O

STOR · STOR

DECK

DINING 10/0x10/6

WOOD STOVE

UP

AIR LOCK ENTRY

FRENCH DOORS

LIVING ROOM 15/2x16/10 SKYLIGHTS

SLOPED CEILING

PASSIVE SUN SPACE 29/0 x 7/6

(Exterior walls are 2x6 construction)

MAIN FLOOR

8'-0" · 30'-0" · 8'-0"

44'-0"

PLAN H-970-1 WITH BASEMENT

PLAN H-970-1A WITHOUT BASEMENT (CRAWLSPACE FOUNDATION)

down

SKYLIGHTS

Tub w/ Shower · LINEN · LINEN · CLOSET 5/6 · CLOSET 5/6

BATH

BEDROOM 10/0 x 13/6

DESK

down · CLOSET 4/9

DESK · CLOSET

BEDROOM 15/2x16/6

STORAGE

SKYLIGHTS · SKYLIGHTS

SECOND FLOOR

First floor:	817 sq. ft.
Sunspace:	192 sq. ft.
Second floor:	563 sq. ft.
Total living area: (Not counting basement or garage)	1,572 sq. ft.
Airlock entry:	40 sq. ft.
Garage:	288 sq. ft.

The Simple Life at Its Best in a Passive Solar Design

This home's rustic exterior is suggestive of Carpenter Gothic Style homes or early barn designs. The wood shake roof and "board-and-batten" style siding help to carry out this theme. An air-lock entry provides a protected place to remove outer garments as well as serving as an energy-conserving heat loss barrier. As you pass from the entry into the cozy living room, there is an immediate perception of warmth and light. This room features a centrally located woodstove and two skylights.

Between the living room and the sun space are two double-hung windows to provide heat circulation as well as admit natural light. Further inspection of the ground floor reveals a delightful flow of space. From the dining room it is possible to view the kitchen, the wider portion of the sun space and part of the living room. An open staircase connects this room with the second floor.

The kitchen boasts modern appliances, large pantry and storage closets and a convenient peninsula open to the dining room. The remainder of the first floor includes a handy laundry room, an easily accessible half-bath and a bonus room with an unlimited number of possibilities. One such use may be as a home computer/study area. Upstairs, two bedrooms with an abundance of closet space share the fully appointed, skylighted bathroom.

A word about the passive sun room: It seems that solar design has come full circle, returning us to the concept that less is more. This sun room uses masonry floor pavers as heat storage and natural convection as the primary means of heat circulation. This serves to reduce both the potential for system failures and the heavy operating workload often found in more elaborate solar designs, not to mention the high cost of such systems.

Blueprint Price Code B

Plans H-970-1 & H-970-1A

Stunning Stucco

- A stunning columned porch and bright stucco adorn the exterior of this attractive one-story home.
- The bold foyer leads to the formal living room, which is set off with decorative half-walls and a high plant shelf. The room is further enhanced by a 14-ft. vaulted ceiling and an energy-efficient fireplace. A 36-in.-high counter to the right of the fireplace is open to the adjoining dining room.
- The spacious kitchen, which includes a space-saving island cooktop, merges with the cheery bayed breakfast nook.
- The nearby family room boasts a 13-ft. vaulted ceiling, a nice fireplace and a French door to an expansive rear patio.
- The lovely den located off the foyer could double as a guest room.
- Dramatic 10-ft. ceilings brighten the den, the kitchen and the breakfast nook.
- A 13-ft., 9-in. vaulted ceiling adorns the sun-drenched master suite, which features a huge walk-in closet. His-and-hers vanities and a platform garden tub highlight the private master bath.
- The second bedroom features a walk-in closet and a nearby full bath.

Plan B-93032

Bedrooms: 2+	Baths: 2½
Living Area:	
Main floor	2,029 sq. ft.
Total Living Area:	**2,029 sq. ft.**
Standard basement	2,029 sq. ft.
Garage	682 sq. ft.
Exterior Wall Framing:	2x6

Foundation Options:

Standard basement

(All plans can be built with your choice of foundation and framing. A generic conversion diagram is available. See order form.)

BLUEPRINT PRICE CODE:	C

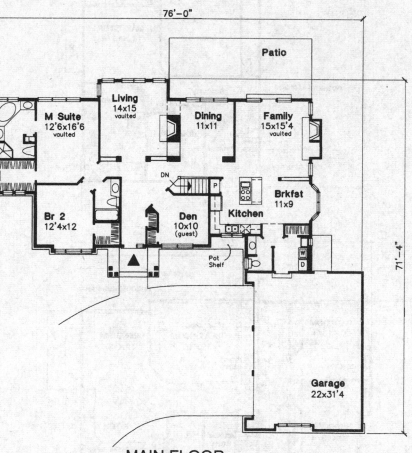

MAIN FLOOR

ORDER BLUEPRINTS ANYTIME!
CALL TOLL-FREE 1-888-626-2026

Plan B-93032

PRICES AND DETAILS
ON PAGES 12-15

195

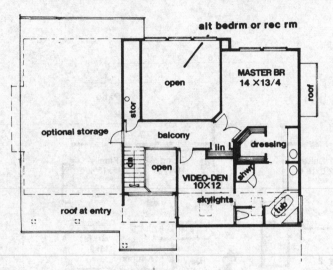

alt bedrm or rec rm

MASTER BR
14 X 13/4

open

stor

roof

optional storage

balcony

dressing

lin

open

db

VIDEO-DEN
10 X 12

shwr

skylights

roof at entry

t ub

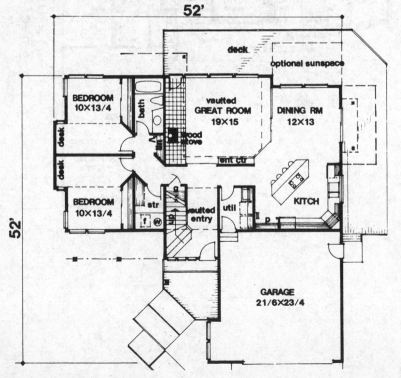

52'

deck

optional sunspace

BEDROOM
10 X 13/4

bath

vaulted
GREAT ROOM
19 X 15

DINING RM
12 X 13

desk

wood
stove

desk

ent ctr

desk

52'

BEDROOM
10 X 13/4

str

KITCH

vaulted
entry

util

f

w

p

GARAGE
21/6 X 23/4

Convenient Contemporary Design

- A thoroughly contemporary front elevation includes a sheltered porch as a traditional, homey touch.
- A vaulted Great Room makes this home look extra spacious.
- A large, open kitchen gives plenty of working space and avoids the confined feeling often found in kitchens.
- The second floor is really an "adult retreat," with its master bedroom, video/den area and balcony hallway.
- The master suite features a walk-through closet and dressing area leading to a generous master bath, which is also accessible from the video room.
- As an alternate, the vaulted area over the Great Room can be enclosed to make a fourth bedroom or upstairs rec room.

Plan S-72485

Bedrooms: 3-4	Baths: 2
Space:	
Upper floor:	650 sq. ft.
Main floor:	1,450 sq. ft.
Total living area:	**2,100 sq. ft.**
Basement:	1,450 sq. ft.
Garage:	502 sq. ft.
Exterior Wall Framing:	2x6

Foundation options:
Standard basement.
Crawlspace.
(Foundation & framing conversion diagram available — see order form.)

Blueprint Price Code:	C

REAR VIEW

Eye-Catching Executive Home

- This eye-catching executive home boasts a two-story bay window and unique transoms above both the front door and the garage doors.
- An equally dramatic interior is prefaced by a two-story-high foyer, which leads into the bayed living room and the adjoining dining room.
- The gourmet kitchen features an island cooktop, a sunny double sink and plenty of counter space.
- The bright breakfast area and the sunken family room each have sliding glass doors to the optional deck. A half-wall separates the two rooms and a fireplace warms the entire area.
- Upstairs, a balcony hall overlooks the foyer. The dazzling master suite has a 10-ft.-high tray ceiling in the sleeping area, a sloped ceiling in the skylighted master bath and a cathedral ceiling in the intimate sitting room.
- Three more spacious bedrooms, one with a bay window and a 10-ft. vaulted ceiling, share a second full bath.

Plan AX-2319

Bedrooms: 4	Baths: 2½
Living Area:	
Upper floor	1,501 sq. ft.
Main floor	1,366 sq. ft.
Total Living Area:	**2,867 sq. ft.**
Standard basement	1,366 sq. ft.
Garage	460 sq. ft.
Exterior Wall Framing:	2x6

Foundation Options:
Standard basement
Slab
(All plans can be built with your choice of foundation and framing. A generic conversion diagram is available. See order form.)

BLUEPRINT PRICE CODE: D

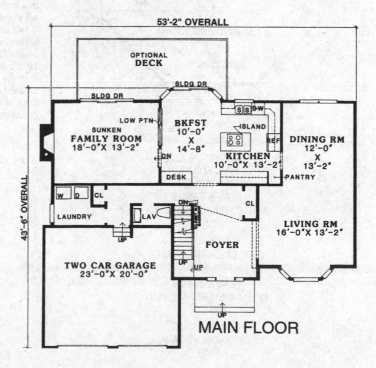

UPPER FLOOR

MAIN FLOOR

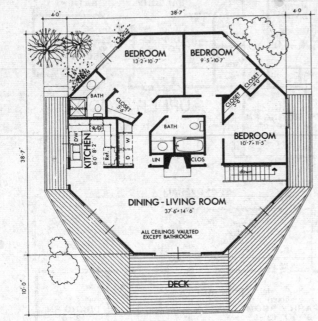

Octagon with Options

Four floor plans are available for this striking octagonal design. You might choose plan H-861-3C with a basement garage, or you might decide on Plan H-861-3B with a daylight basement. Whatever your choice, the main floor plan remains essentially the same. One of the attractions of an octagonal design such as this is the panavistic viewing possibilities. All except one of the eight sides has a view.

In Plans H-861-3B & 3C, the private bathroom in the master bedroom is omitted, allowing a sleeping area of 14' x 10'7". Another nice feature of this home is that the laundry facilities are conveniently located on the main floor. The total living area of this home is 1,236 sq. ft., not counting the basement.

Main floor plan labels
BEDROOM 13'2" x 10'7"
BEDROOM 9'5" x 10'7"
BEDROOM 10'7" x 11'5"
BATH
CLOSET 5'0"
CLOSET 5'6"
CLOSET 2'0"
BATH
LIN
CLOS
KITCHEN 8'0" x 8'2"
Ref.
DW
D/W
Shower
down
DINING - LIVING ROOM 37'6" x 14'6"
ALL CEILINGS VAULTED EXCEPT BATHROOM
DECK

PLAN H-861-2B & 2C
MAIN FLOOR
1236 SQUARE FEET

PLAN H-861-3B
WITH DAYLIGHT BASEMENT
2,472 SQ. FT.

PLAN H-861-3C
WITH BASEMENT GARAGE
2,141 SQ. FT.

PLAN H-861-2B
WITH DAYLIGHT BASEMENT
2,472 SQ. FT.

PLAN H-861-2C
WITH BASEMENT GARAGE
2,141 SQ. FT.

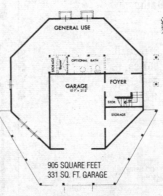

GENERAL USE
STORAGE
OPTIONAL BATH
GARAGE 15'7" x 21'3"
FOYER
STORAGE
STOR.

905 SQUARE FEET
331 SQ. FT. GARAGE

PLAN H-861-2C & 3C
BASEMENT WITH GARAGE

GENERAL USE
BATH
Shower
FOYER
STORAGE
RECREATION 37'0" x 14'6"

PLAN H-861-2B & 3B
DAYLIGHT BASEMENT

Blueprint Price Code C

Plans H-861-2B, -2C, -3B & -3C

PRICES AND DETAILS
ON PAGES 12-15

REAR VIEW

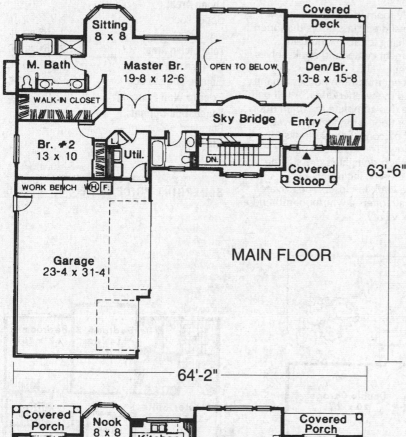

Covered Deck

Sitting 8 x 8

M. Bath

Master Br. 19-8 x 12-6

OPEN TO BELOW

Den/Br. 13-8 x 15-8

WALK-IN CLOSET

Sky Bridge

Entry

Br. #2 13 x 10

Util.

DN.

Covered Stoop

WORK BENCH

63'-6"

Garage 23-4 x 31-4

MAIN FLOOR

64'-2"

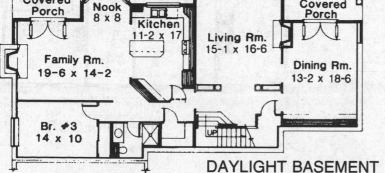

Covered Porch

Nook 8 x 8

Kitchen 11-2 x 17

Living Rm. 15-1 x 16-6

Covered Porch

Family Rm. 19-6 x 14-2

Dining Rm. 13-2 x 18-6

Br. #3 14 x 10

UP

DAYLIGHT BASEMENT

Wonderful Walkout

- Not your ordinary two-story, this wonderful walkout plan creates excitement from the top down.
- The main motorcourt level houses a stunning master suite, a second bedroom and a den/bedroom with French doors to a covered deck. The entry of the main level opens to a dramatic view from a sky bridge to the lower-level living room with two-story window wall.
- The lower level contains the living areas of the house including the formal living and dining rooms and the family room, which is open to the island kitchen and the breakfast bay. There is also a third bedroom and full bath nearby.

Plan NW-915

Bedrooms: 3-4	Baths: 3
Space:	
Main floor	1,522 sq. ft.
Daylight basement	1,267 sq. ft.
Total Living Area	**2,789 sq. ft.**
Garage	731 sq. ft.
Exterior Wall Framing	2x6

Foundation options:

Daylight Basement
(Foundation & framing conversion diagram available—see order form.)

Blueprint Price Code	D

ORDER BLUEPRINTS ANYTIME!
CALL TOLL-FREE 1-888-626-2026

Plan NW-915

PRICES AND DETAILS
ON PAGES 12-15

199

Colonial for Today

- Designed for a growing family, this handsome traditional home offers four bedrooms plus a den and three complete baths. The Colonial exterior is updated by a covered front entry porch with a fanlight window above.
- The dramatic tiled foyer is two stories high and provides direct access to all of the home's living areas. The spacious living room has an inviting brick fireplace and sliding pocket doors to the adjoining dining room.
- Overlooking the backyard, the huge combination kitchen/family room is the

home's hidden charm. The kitchen features a peninsula breakfast bar with seating for six.
- The family room includes a window wall with sliding glass doors that open to an enticing terrace. A built-in entertainment center and bookshelves line another wall.
- The adjacent mudroom houses a pantry closet and the washer/dryer. A full bath and a big den complete the main floor.
- The upper floor is highlighted by a beautiful balcony that overlooks the foyer below. The luxurious master suite boasts a skylighted dressing area and two closets, including an oversized walk-in closet. The private master bath offers a whirlpool tub and a dual-sink vanity.

Plan AHP-7050

Bedrooms: 4+	Baths: 3
Living Area:	
Upper floor	998 sq. ft.
Main floor	1,153 sq. ft.
Total Living Area:	**2,151 sq. ft.**
Standard basement	1,067 sq. ft.
Garage and storage	439 sq. ft.
Exterior Wall Framing:	2x6

Foundation Options:

Standard basement
Crawlspace
Slab
(All plans can be built with your choice of foundation and framing. A generic conversion diagram is available. See order form.)

BLUEPRINT PRICE CODE:	C

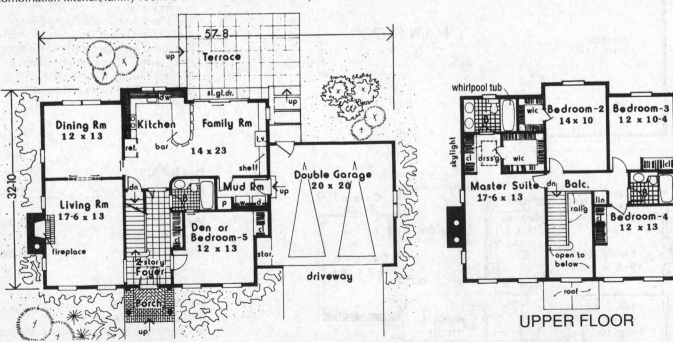

MAIN FLOOR

UPPER FLOOR

ORDER BLUEPRINTS ANYTIME!
CALL TOLL-FREE 1-888-626-2026

Plan AHP-7050

PRICES AND DETAILS
ON PAGES 12-15

Elegant Entry Gazebo

- An elegant gazebo-shaped entry portico awaits guests arriving at the turn-around.
- The elegance continues inside with a curved staircase in the two-story entry foyer.
- To the left of the entry is a sunken living room with vaulted ceiling, round-top transom window and fireplace. To the left of the entry is a double-doored study with built-in bookshelves.
- The rear of the main floor accommodates everyday activities in the island kitchen, breakfast nook and family room with fireplace and second stairway to the upper floor.
- There are three bedrooms and two full baths on the upper floor, plus a bonus room above the garage which can be used as a play room, additional bedroom or storage.
- The master suite is a dazzler, with private sitting bay, corner fireplace, rear-facing deck, and stunning bath retreat.

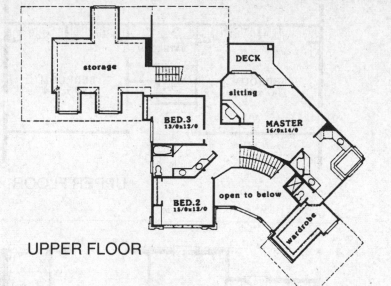

UPPER FLOOR

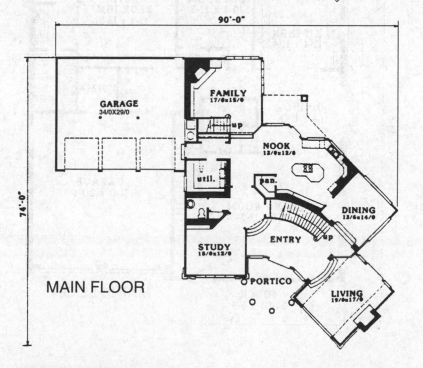

MAIN FLOOR

Plan R-2120

Bedrooms: 3-5	Baths: 2 ½
Space:	
Upper floor	2,028 sq. ft.
Main floor	2,390 sq. ft.
Total Living Area	**4,418 sq. ft.**
Garage	986 sq. ft.
Exterior Wall Framing	2x6
Foundation options:	
Crawlspace	
(Foundation & framing conversion diagram available—see order form.)	
Blueprint Price Code	G

Easy-Going Design

- A relaxing front porch and airy, easy-going spaces inside make a wonderful combination in this charming country-style design.

- Family and visitors alike will gather in front of the fireplace in the large living room. The adjoining dining room features a bay window and opens to the efficiently designed kitchen. A back door leads to another covered porch.

- The main-floor master suite is brightened by a bay window overlooking the backyard. The private, compartmentalized bath includes a dual-sink vanity, a garden tub and a large walk-in closet.

- Another full bath is just across the hall from the second main-floor bedroom.

- Upstairs, two large bedrooms with double closets have private access to a nice-sized bathroom.

Plan J-91006

Bedrooms: 4	**Baths: 3**
Living Area:	
Upper floor	698 sq. ft.
Main floor	1,467 sq. ft.
Total Living Area:	**2,165 sq. ft.**
Standard basement	1,467 sq. ft.
Garage	459 sq. ft.
Exterior Wall Framing:	2x6

Foundation Options:

Standard basement

Crawlspace

Slab

(Typical foundation & framing conversion diagram available—see order form.)

BLUEPRINT PRICE CODE:	**C**

UPPER FLOOR

46-6

53-6

BATHROOM

BEDROOM
17-0 x 12-4

BEDROOM
16-8 x 12-4

KITCHEN
12-4 x 11-4

BEDROOM
10-4 x 12-2

MASTER BEDROOM
13-8 x 15-0

STORAGE

DINING
11-8 x 11-0

GARAGE
21-0 x 20-0

LIVING ROOM
19-5 x 17-2

PORCH
24-10 x 6-6

MAIN FLOOR

202

ORDER BLUEPRINTS ANYTIME!
CALL TOLL-FREE 1-888-626-2026

Plan J-91006

PRICES AND DETAILS
ON PAGES 12-15

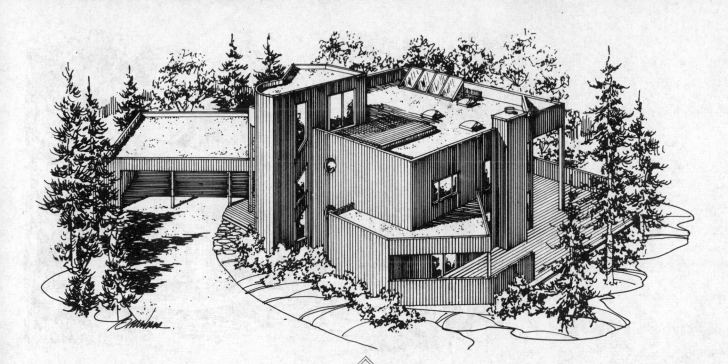

Striking Vertical Design

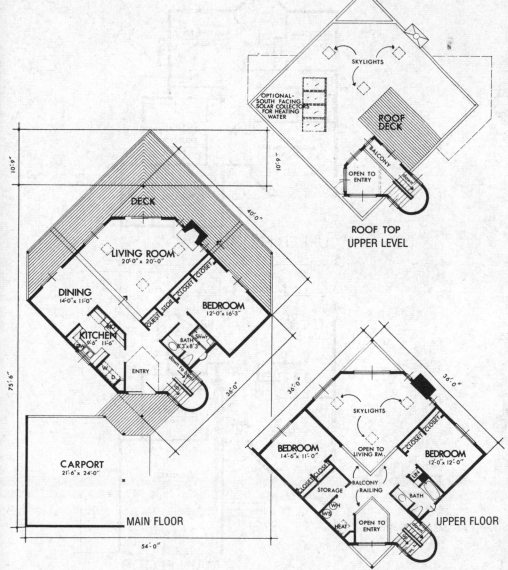

SKYLIGHTS

OPTIONAL-
SOUTH FACING
SOLAR COLLECTORS
FOR HEATING
WATER

ROOF
DECK

BALCONY

OPEN
TO ENTRY

down

**ROOF TOP
UPPER LEVEL**

DECK

LIVING ROOM
20'-0" x 20'-0"

DINING
14'-0" x 11'-0"

GUEST   STOR   CLOSET   CLOSET

BEDROOM
12'-0" x 16'-3"

KITCHEN
9'-6" x 11'-6"

ENTRY

BATH SHWR
8'-3" x 8'-3"

down to basement

CARPORT
21'-6" x 24'-0"

MAIN FLOOR

54'-0"

SKYLIGHTS

BEDROOM
14'-6" x 11'-0"

OPEN TO
LIVING RM.

CLOSET CLOSET

BEDROOM
12'-0" x 12'-0"

CLOSET   CLOSET

STORAGE

BALCONY
RAILING

LIN.

WH
WS

BATH

HEAT

OPEN TO
ENTRY

down

UPPER FLOOR

- Unique roof deck and massive wrap-around main level deck harbor an equally exciting interior.
- Large sunken living room is brightened by a three-window skylight and also features a log-sized fireplace.
- U-shaped kitchen is just off the entry, adjacent to handy laundry area.
- Second-story balcony overlooks the large living room and entryway below.

Plans H-935-1 & -1A

Bedrooms: 3	Baths: 2

Space:

Upper floor:	844 sq. ft.
Main floor:	1,323 sq. ft.
Total living area:	2,167 sq. ft.
Basement:	approx. 1,323 sq. ft.
Carport:	516 sq. ft.

Exterior Wall Framing:	2x6

Foundation options:
Standard basement (Plan H-935-1).
Crawlspace (Plan H-935-1A).
(Foundation & framing conversion diagram available — see order form.)

Blueprint Price Code:	C

ORDER BLUEPRINTS ANYTIME!
CALL TOLL-FREE 1-888-626-2026

Plans H-935-1 & -1A

PRICES AND DETAILS
ON PAGES 12-15

203

Upscale Home for Narrow Lot

- A dramatic living room with floor-to-ceiling windows and a large fireplace is the showpiece of this narrow-lot home.
- A second fireplace warms the family room, dining room and kitchen, which feature outdoor views, an island cooktop, a built-in desk and a French door to the backyard.
- A den or guest room has private access to a half-bath.
- Upstairs, the master suite boasts a walk-in closet and a garden tub.
- A bonus room could be finished and used as a bedroom, a hobby room or an exercise area.

Plan S-21188

Bedrooms: 3-5	Baths: 2½
Living Area:	
Upper floor	845 sq. ft.
Main floor	1,140 sq. ft.
Bonus room	182 sq. ft.
Total Living Area:	**2,167 sq. ft.**
Standard basement	1,140 sq. ft.
Garage	428 sq. ft.
Exterior Wall Framing:	2x6

Foundation Options:
Standard basement
Crawlspace
Slab
(Typical foundation & framing conversion diagram available—see order form.)

BLUEPRINT PRICE CODE: C

UPPER FLOOR

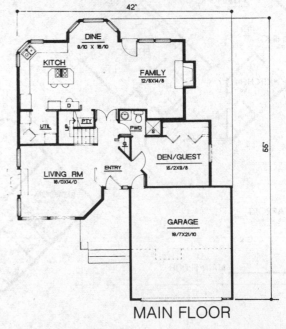

BASEMENT STAIRWAY LOCATION

MAIN FLOOR

REAR VIEW

A Striking Contemporary

A multiplicity of decks and outcroppings along with unusual window arrangements combine to establish this striking contemporary as a classic type of architecture. To adapt to the sloping terrain, the structure has three levels of living space on the downhill side. As one moves around the house from the entry to the various rooms and living areas, both the appearance and function of the different spaces change, as do the angular forms and cutouts that define the floor plan arrangement. Almost all the rooms are flooded with an abundance of daylight, yet are shielded by projections of wing walls and roof surfaces to assure privacy as well as to block undesirable direct rays of sunshine.

The design projects open planning of a spacious living room that connects with the dining and kitchen area. The home features four large bedrooms, two of which have walk-in closets and private baths. The remaining two bedrooms also have an abundance of wardrobe space, and the rooms are of generous proportions.

For energy efficiency, exterior walls are framed with 2x6 studs.

First floor:	1,216 sq. ft.
Second floor:	958 sq. ft.
Total living area: (Not counting basement or garage)	2,174 sq. ft.
Daylight basement:	1,019 sq. ft.

PLAN H-914-1A
WITHOUT BASEMENT
(CRAWLSPACE FOUNDATION)

PLAN H-914-1
WITH DAYLIGHT BASEMENT

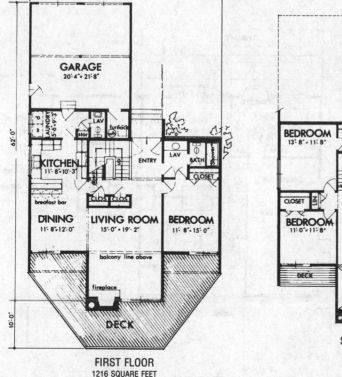

FIRST FLOOR
1216 SQUARE FEET

SECOND FLOOR
958 SQUARE FEET

ORDER BLUEPRINTS ANYTIME!
CALL TOLL-FREE 1-888-626-2026

Blueprint Price Code C
Plans H-914-1 & -1A

PRICES AND DETAILS
ON PAGES 12-15

205

A Move Up

- Narrow lap siding and repeated round-top windows with divided panes give this traditional home a different look.
- The roomy interior offers space for the upwardly mobile family, with four to five bedrooms and large activity areas.
- The two-story foyer welcomes guests into a spacious formal area that combines the living and dining rooms. The rooms share a dramatic 13-ft. cathedral ceiling, while a handsome fireplace adds a peaceful glow.
- Behind double doors is a cozy study or fifth bedroom.
- A second fireplace and a media center make the family room a fun retreat. French doors open to a lovely terrace.
- Adjoining the family room is a well-designed kitchen with a bayed dinette.
- Double doors introduce the secluded master suite, which boasts a 12-ft. sloped ceiling and a quiet terrace. The private bath offers an invigorating whirlpool tub under a skylight.
- Three more bedrooms and another bath occupy the upper floor.

Plan AHP-9396

Bedrooms: 4+	Baths: 2½
Living Area:	
Upper floor	643 sq. ft.
Main floor	1,553 sq. ft.
Total Living Area:	**2,196 sq. ft.**
Standard basement	1,553 sq. ft.
Garage and storage	502 sq. ft.
Exterior Wall Framing:	2x4 or 2x6

Foundation Options:

Standard basement

Crawlspace

Slab

(All plans can be built with your choice of foundation and framing. A generic conversion diagram is available. See order form.)

BLUEPRINT PRICE CODE: C

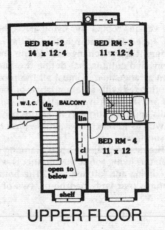

UPPER FLOOR

VIEW INTO LIVING AND DINING ROOMS

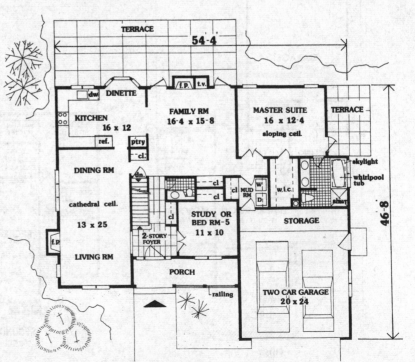

MAIN FLOOR

Classic Styling

- This handsome one-story traditional would look great in town or in the country. The shuttered and paned windows, narrow lap siding and brick accents make it a classic.
- The sprawling design begins with the spacious, central living room, featuring a beamed ceiling that slopes up to 14 feet. A window wall overlooks the covered backyard porch, and an inviting fireplace includes an extra-wide hearth and built-in bookshelves.
- The galley-style kitchen features a snack bar to the sunny eating area and a raised-panel door to the dining room.
- The isolated master suite is a quiet haven offering a large walk-in closet, a dressing room and a spacious bath.
- Three more bedrooms, two with walk-in closets, and a compartmentalized bath are located at the opposite side of the home.

Plan E-2206	
Bedrooms: 4	**Baths:** 2
Living Area:	
Main floor	2,200 sq. ft.
Total Living Area:	**2,200 sq. ft.**
Standard basement	2,200 sq. ft.
Garage and storage	624 sq. ft.
Exterior Wall Framing:	2x6

Foundation Options:
Standard basement
Crawlspace
Slab
(All plans can be built with your choice of foundation and framing. A generic conversion diagram is available. See order form.)

BLUEPRINT PRICE CODE: C

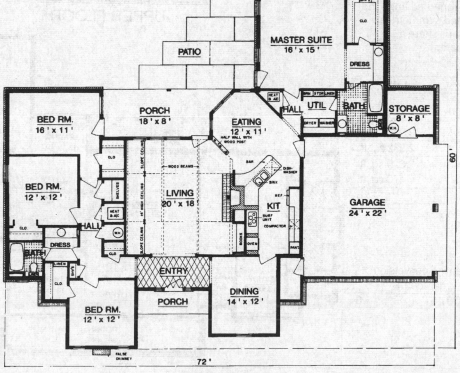

MAIN FLOOR

ORDER BLUEPRINTS ANYTIME!
CALL TOLL-FREE 1-888-626-2026

Plan E-2206

PRICES AND DETAILS
ON PAGES 12-15

207

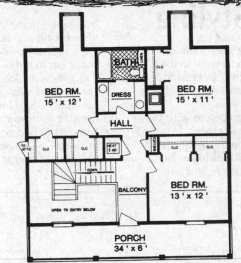

Verandas Add Extra Charm

- Porches, columns and dormers give this home a charming facade.
- The interior is equally appealing, with its beautiful two-story foyer and practical room arrangement.
- The central living room has a fireplace and access to a covered porch.
- A great island kitchen is conveniently situated between the two dining areas.
- A multipurpose room and an office are perfect for hobbies and projects.
- The secluded master suite offers a private study with a sloped ceiling. The master bath is large and symmetrical.
- Three bedrooms upstairs share a compartmentalized bath.

Plan E-2900	
Bedrooms: 4	**Baths: 2½**
Living Area:	
Upper floor	903 sq. ft.
Main floor	2,029 sq. ft.
Total Living Area:	**2,932 sq. ft.**
Standard basement	2,029 sq. ft.
Garage and storage	470 sq. ft.
Exterior Wall Framing:	2x6

Foundation Options:
Standard basement
Crawlspace
Slab
(Typical foundation & framing conversion diagram available—see order form.)

BLUEPRINT PRICE CODE: D

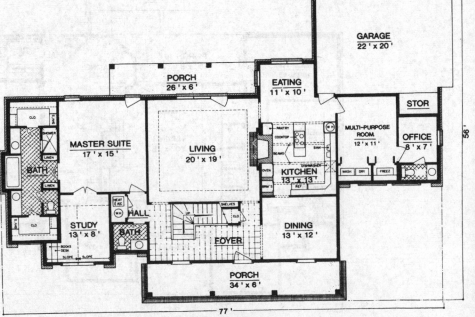

UPPER FLOOR

MAIN FLOOR

Plan E-2900

PRICES AND DETAILS
ON PAGES 12-15

Graceful Facade

- Elegant half-round transoms spruce up the wood-shuttered facade of this charming traditional two-story.
- The wide front porch opens to a two-story foyer that flows between the formal dining room and a two-story-high library or guest room. Sliding French doors close off the library from the Great Room.
- Perfect for entertaining, the spacious Great Room shows off a handsome fireplace and a TV center. Beautiful French doors on either side extend the room to a large backyard deck.
- The adjoining dinette has its own view of the backyard through a stunning semi-circular glass wall, which sheds light on the nice-sized attached kitchen.
- A pantry and a laundry room are neatly housed near the two-car garage. The adjacent full bath could be downsized to a half-bath with storage space.
- The master suite and its private whirlpool bath are isolated from the three upper-floor bedrooms and features a 14-ft.-high cathedral ceiling.
- Unless otherwise specified, all main-floor ceilings are 9 ft. high.

Plan AHP-9490

Bedrooms: 4+	Baths: 2½-3
Living Area:	
Upper floor	722 sq. ft.
Main floor	1,497 sq. ft.
Total Living Area:	**2,219 sq. ft.**
Standard basement	1,165 sq. ft.
Garage	420 sq. ft.
Exterior Wall Framing:	2x4 or 2x6

Foundation Options:

Standard basement

Crawlspace

Slab

(All plans can be built with your choice of foundation and framing. A generic conversion diagram is available. See order form.)

BLUEPRINT PRICE CODE: **C**

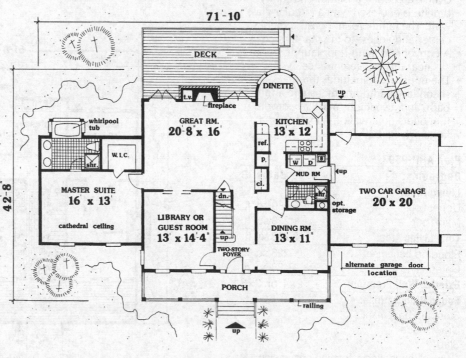

UPPER FLOOR

MAIN FLOOR

ORDER BLUEPRINTS ANYTIME!
CALL TOLL-FREE 1-888-626-2026

Plan AHP-9490

PRICES AND DETAILS
ON PAGES 12-15

209

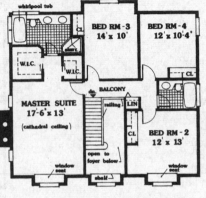

Tradition Recreated

- Classic traditional styling is recreated in this home with its covered porch, triple dormers and half-round windows.
- A central hall stems from the two-story-high foyer and accesses each of the main living areas.
- A large formal space is created with the merging of the living room and the dining room. The living room boasts a fireplace and a view of the front porch.
- The informal spaces merge at the rear of the home. The kitchen features an oversized cooktop island. The sunny dinette is enclosed with a circular glass wall. The family room boasts a media center and access to the rear terrace.
- A convenient main-floor laundry room sits near the garage entrance.
- The upper floor includes three secondary bedrooms that share a full bath, and a spacious master bedroom that offers dual walk-in closets and a large private bath.

Plan AHP-9393

Bedrooms: 4+	Baths: 3
Living Area:	
Upper floor	989 sq. ft.
Main floor	1,223 sq. ft.
Total Living Area:	**2,212 sq. ft.**
Standard basement	1,223 sq. ft.
Garage and storage	488 sq. ft.
Exterior Wall Framing:	2x4 or 2x6

Foundation Options:

Standard basement
Crawlspace
Slab
(Typical foundation & framing conversion diagram available—see order form.)

BLUEPRINT PRICE CODE:	C

UPPER FLOOR

MAIN FLOOR

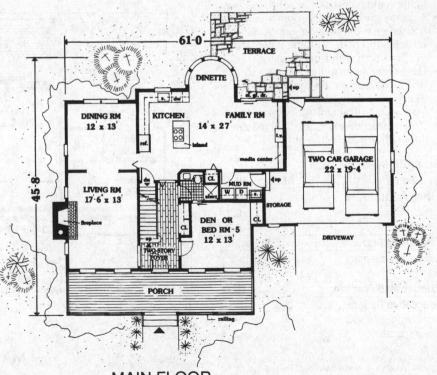

Plan AHP-9393

PRICES AND DETAILS
ON PAGES 12-15

UPPER FLOOR

Modern Traditional-Style Home

- Covered porch and decorative double doors offer an invitation into this three or four bedroom home.
- Main floor bedroom may be used as a den, home office, or guest room, with convenient bath facilities.

- Adjoining dining room makes living room seem even more spacious; breakfast nook enlarges the look of the attached kitchen.
- Brick-size concrete block veneer and masonry tile roof give the exterior a look of durability.

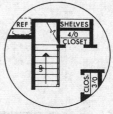

PLAN H-1351-M1A
WITHOUT BASEMENT
(CRAWLSPACE FOUNDATION)

Plans H-1351-M1 & -M1A

Bedrooms: 3-4	Baths: 3

Space:	
Upper floor:	862 sq. ft.
Main floor:	1,383 sq. ft.
Total living area:	**2,245 sq. ft.**
Basement:	1,383 sq. ft.
Garage:	413 sq. ft.

Exterior Wall Framing:	2x6

Foundation options:
Standard basement (Plan H-1351-M1).
Crawlspace (Plan H-1351-M1A).
(Foundation & framing conversion diagram available — see order form.)

Blueprint Price Code:	C

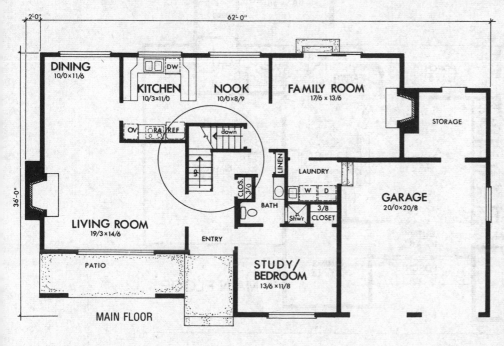

MAIN FLOOR

ORDER BLUEPRINTS ANYTIME!
CALL TOLL-FREE 1-888-626-2026

Plans H-1351-M1 & -M1A

PRICES AND DETAILS
ON PAGES 12-15

211

Luxurious Living on One Level

- The elegant exterior of this spacious one-story presents a classic air of quality and distinction.
- Three French doors brighten the inviting entry, which flows into the spacious living room. Boasting a 13-ft. ceiling, the living room enjoys a fireplace with a wide hearth and adjoining built-in bookshelves. A wall of glass, including

a French door, provides views of the sheltered backyard porch.
- A stylish angled counter joins the spacious kitchen to the sunny bay-windowed eating nook.
- Secluded for privacy, the master suite features a nice dressing area, a large walk-in closet and private backyard access. A convenient laundry/utility room is adjacent to the master bath.
- At the opposite end of the home, double doors lead to three more bedrooms, a compartmentalized bath and lots of closet space.

Plan E-2208

Bedrooms: 4	**Baths:** 2

Living Area:

Main floor	2,252 sq. ft.
Total Living Area:	**2,252 sq. ft.**
Standard basement	2,252 sq. ft.
Garage and storage	592 sq. ft.
Exterior Wall Framing:	2x6

Foundation Options:

Standard basement
Crawlspace
Slab

(All plans can be built with your choice of foundation and framing. A generic conversion diagram is available. See order form.)

BLUEPRINT PRICE CODE:	C

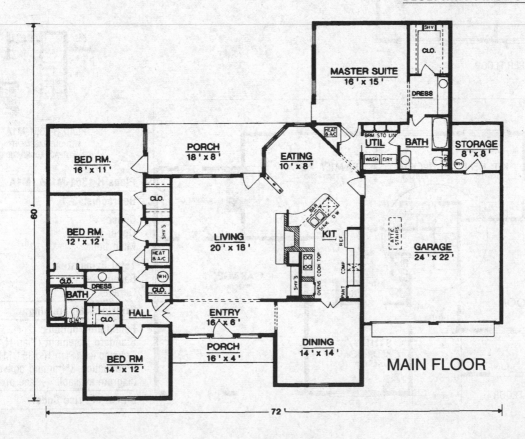

MAIN FLOOR

Sun Nook Brightens Split-Level Contemporary

A breakfast nook splashed with sunlight through a glass roof and windows on two walls serve as passive solar collectors in this spacious four-bedroom, split-level contemporary home.

Traffic is directed along a central hall, turning right at the top of the stairs to the sun nook and kitchen, or straight ahead to the vaulted-ceiling living room.

Clerestory windows at one end and a sliding glass door and window at the other end lighten the living room, warmed by a corner fireplace.

A wide wood deck extends along the back of the home, with sliding glass doors off the living room and master bedroom. The two other bedrooms have window seats and share the second bath.

Exterior walls are framed with 2x6 studs for energy efficiency.

Main floor:	1,408 sq. ft.
Lower level:	855 sq. ft.
Total living area: (Not counting garage)	**2,263 sq. ft.**

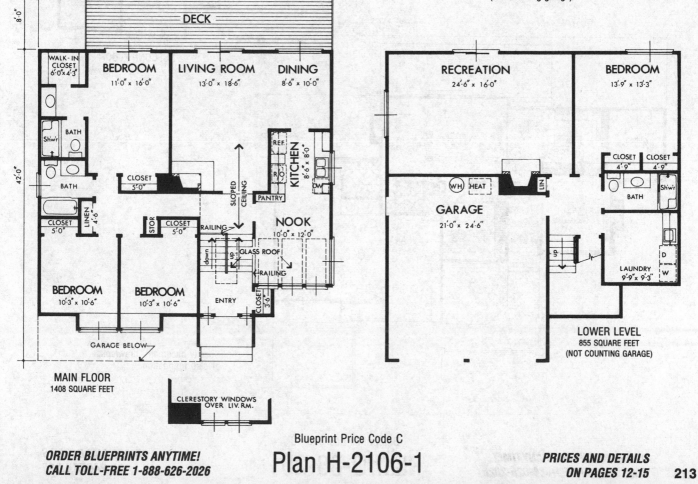

MAIN FLOOR
1408 SQUARE FEET

CLERESTORY WINDOWS OVER LIV. RM.

LOWER LEVEL
855 SQUARE FEET
(NOT COUNTING GARAGE)

Blueprint Price Code C
Plan H-2106-1

PRICES AND DETAILS
ON PAGES 12-15

Two-Story Features
Deluxe Master Bedroom

First floor:	1,442 sq. ft.
Second floor:	823 sq. ft.
Total living area:	2,265 sq. ft.
Basement (Optional):	688 sq. ft.

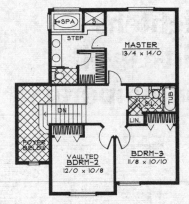

SECOND FLOOR

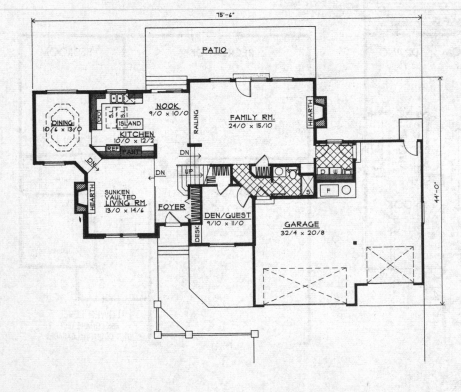

Specify basement, crawlspace
or slab foundation.

Blueprint Price Code C

Plan U-88-201

FRONT VIEW

Something Old, Something New

"Something old, something new" aptly describes the flavor and sentiment of this replica of earlier times.

Beveled oval plate glass with heavy oak surrounds and appropriate hand-carved wreaths and borders make entering the home the delightful experience it was meant to be. Inside one finds the huge central entry hall with the magnificent open staircase with turned balusters and shapely handrails.

With all bedrooms being on the second floor, the main level is entirely devoted to daily living in a generous atmosphere. The 14' x 23' living room and 14' x 13' dining room give one an idea of the spaciousness of this home.

Notice the 80 cubic foot pantry closet and the adjacent storage closet with an equal amount of space. A two-thirds bath and well equipped laundry room complete the mechanical area of the home.

Certainly the most provocative room on the main floor is the beautiful glass-enclosed morning or breakfast room. Huge skylight panels augment the bank of windows and sliding doors to create a delightful passive solar room suitable for many uses while contributing greatly to the heating efficiency of the entire building.

Upstairs two good-sized bedrooms with adjoining bathroom serve the junior members of the family while the parents enjoy the spacious master suite with walk-in wardrobes and private bath.

REAR VIEW

UPPER FLOOR

PLAN H-3729-1A
WITHOUT BASEMENT
(CRAWLSPACE FOUNDATION)

FURNACE AND WATER HEATER TO BE
LOCATED IN LAUNDRY ROOM

PLAN H-3729-1
WITH BASEMENT

MAIN FLOOR

First floor:	1,116 sq. ft.
Sun nook:	132 sq. ft.
Second floor:	1,026 sq. ft.
Total living area:	2,274 sq. ft.

(Not counting basement or garage)
(Exterior walls are 2x6 construction.)

Blueprint Price Code C

ORDER BLUEPRINTS ANYTIME!
CALL TOLL-FREE 1-888-626-2026

Plans H-3729-1 & -1A

**PRICES AND DETAILS
ON PAGES 12-15**

215

Comfortable Cape Cod

- This comfortable, family-sized home is reminiscent of a classic Cape Cod. The covered front porch, repeating gables and brick trim give it plenty of character.
- A gracious two-story foyer separates the formal rooms. The living room offers a cathedral ceiling, while the dining room has an optional built-in hutch.
- Family gatherings will center around the warm fireplace in the family room and around the oversized island in the efficiently designed kitchen.
- The master suite features a tray ceiling, a large walk-in closet, a private bath and an optional window seat. An alternate master bath design is included in the blueprints.
- Upstairs, three secondary bedrooms share a nice hall bath. Storage space is provided underneath the window seats in two of the bedrooms.
- The blueprints include an alternate three-bedroom plan and an alternate plan for the mudroom/entry area near the garage.

Plan GL-2275

Bedrooms: 4	Baths: 2½
Living Area:	
Upper floor	714 sq. ft.
Main floor	1,561 sq. ft.
Total Living Area:	**2,275 sq. ft.**
Standard basement	1,561 sq. ft.
Garage	462 sq. ft.
Exterior Wall Framing:	2x6

Foundation Options:

Standard basement
(Typical foundation & framing conversion diagram available—see order form.)

BLUEPRINT PRICE CODE:	C

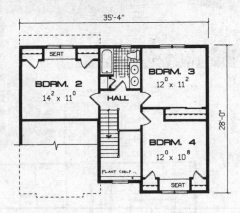

UPPER FLOOR

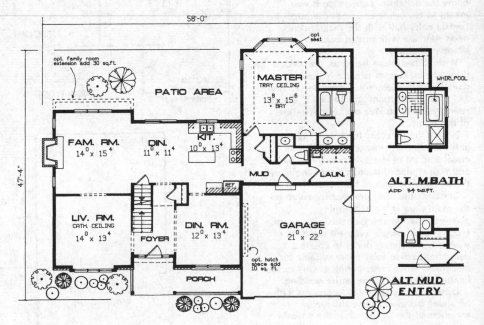

MAIN FLOOR

PLAN H-2107-1B

Solarium for Sloping Lots

This plan is available in two versions. Plan H-2107-1B, shown above, is most suitable for a lot sloping upward from front to rear, providing a daylight front for the lower floor. The other version, Plan H-2107-1 (at right), is more suitable for a lot that slopes from side to side.

Either way, this moderately sized home has a number of interesting and imaginative features. Of these, the passive sun room will provoke the most comment. Spanning two floors between recreation and living rooms, this glass-enclosed space serves the practical purpose of collecting, storing and redistributing the sun's natural heat, while acting as a conservatory for exotic plants, an exercise room, or any number of other uses. A link between the formal atmosphere of the living room and the carefree activities of the recreation area is created by this two-story solarium by way of an open balcony railing. Living, dining, and entry blend together in one huge space made to seem even larger by the vaulted ceiling spanning the entire complex of rooms.

PLAN H-2107-1

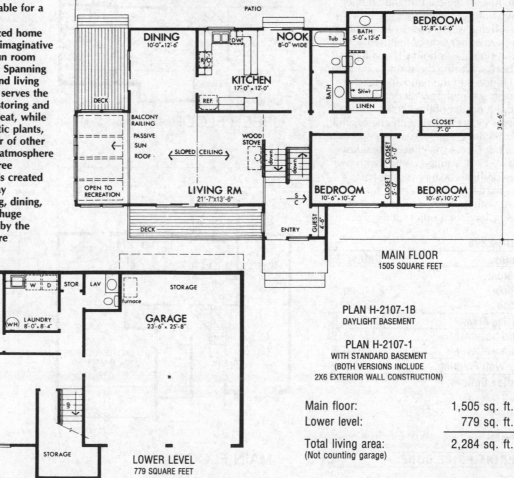

MAIN FLOOR
1505 SQUARE FEET

LOWER LEVEL
779 SQUARE FEET

PLAN H-2107-1B
DAYLIGHT BASEMENT

PLAN H-2107-1
WITH STANDARD BASEMENT
(BOTH VERSIONS INCLUDE
2X6 EXTERIOR WALL CONSTRUCTION)

Main floor:	1,505 sq. ft.
Lower level:	779 sq. ft.
Total living area: (Not counting garage)	2,284 sq. ft.

Blueprint Price Code C

ORDER BLUEPRINTS ANYTIME!
CALL TOLL-FREE 1-888-626-2026

Plans H-2107-1 & -1B

PRICES AND DETAILS
ON PAGES 12-15

217

Brighten Up!

- Multiple skylights and many oversized arched windows draw natural sunshine into this wonderful two-story design.
- The 17-ft.-high foyer welcomes guests inside, where a 16-ft., 8-in. vaulted ceiling with skylights crowns the living room. For special affairs, this is the spot.
- An 8-ft. coffered ceiling lends unmistakable style to the formal dining room. Just imagine a romantic dinner for two in this elegant setting.
- Casual living reigns in the nearby family room. On either side of the fireplace, built-in bookcases hold CDs, videos and books. During the spring, open the French doors to the patio and take in the fresh scent of new blooms.
- The open design of the kitchen allows the family chef to visit with guests while preparing that night's feast. An optional snack bar serves the cheery breakfast nook. A 17-ft. vaulted ceiling with two sunny skylights soars over the area.
- In the master suite upstairs, a sunny alcove with an arched window is the perfect place for a quiet sitting area.

Plan SUN-2290

Bedrooms: 4	Baths: 2½
Living Area:	
Upper floor	1,148 sq. ft.
Main floor	1,137 sq. ft.
Total Living Area:	**2,285 sq. ft.**
Standard basement	1,154 sq. ft.
Garage and storage	580 sq. ft.
Exterior Wall Framing:	**2x6**

Foundation Options:

Standard basement
Crawlspace
Slab
(All plans can be built with your choice of foundation and framing. A generic conversion diagram is available. See order form.)

BLUEPRINT PRICE CODE:	C

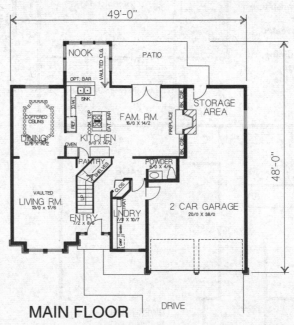

REAR VIEW

UPPER FLOOR

MAIN FLOOR

Plan SUN-2290

PRICES AND DETAILS ON PAGES 12-15

Contemporary Elegance

- This striking contemporary design combines vertical siding with elegant traditional overtones.
- Inside, an expansive activity area is created with the joining of the vaulted living room, the family/dining room and the kitchen. The openness of the rooms creates a spacious, dramatic feeling, which extends to an exciting two-story sun space and a patio beyond.

- A convenient utility/service area near the garage includes a clothes-sorting counter, a deep sink and ironing space.
- Two bedrooms share a bright bath to round out the main floor.
- Upstairs, the master suite includes a sumptuous skylighted bath with two entrances. The tub is positioned on an angled wall, while the shower and toilet are secluded behind a pocket door. An optional overlook provides views down into the sun space, which is accessed by a spiral staircase.
- A versatile loft area and a large bonus room complete this design.

Plan LRD-1971

Bedrooms: 3+	Baths: 2
Living Area:	
Upper floor	723 sq. ft.
Main floor	1,248 sq. ft.
Sun space	116 sq. ft.
Bonus room	225 sq. ft.
Total Living Area:	**2,312 sq. ft.**
Standard basement	1,248 sq. ft.
Garage	483 sq. ft.
Exterior Wall Framing:	2x6

Foundation Options:

Standard basement
Crawlspace
(All plans can be built with your choice of foundation and framing. A generic conversion diagram is available. See order form.)

BLUEPRINT PRICE CODE: C

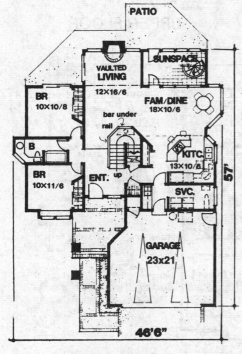

MAIN FLOOR

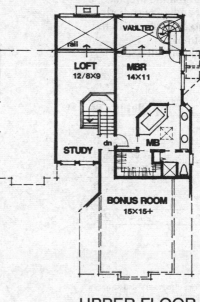

UPPER FLOOR

ORDER BLUEPRINTS ANYTIME!
CALL TOLL-FREE 1-888-626-2026

Plan LRD-1971

PRICES AND DETAILS
ON PAGES 12-15

219

Grand Colonial Home

- This grand Colonial home boasts a porch entry framed by bay windows and gable towers.
- The two-story foyer flows to the dining room on the left and adjoins the bayed living room on the right, with its warm fireplace and flanking windows.
- At the rear, the family room features a 17-ft. ceiling, a media wall, a bar and terrace access through French doors.
- Connected to the family room is a high-tech kitchen with an island work area, a pantry, a work desk and a circular dinette.
- A private terrace, a romantic fireplace, a huge walk-in closet and a lavish bath with a whirlpool tub are featured in the main-floor master suite.
- Three bedrooms and two full baths share the upper floor.

Plan AHP-9120

Bedrooms: 4	Baths: 3½
Living Area:	
Upper floor	776 sq. ft.
Main floor	1,551 sq. ft.
Total Living Area:	**2,327 sq. ft.**
Standard basement	1,580 sq. ft.
Garage	440 sq. ft.
Exterior Wall Framing:	2x4 or 2x6

Foundation Options:

Standard basement

Crawlspace

Slab

(All plans can be built with your choice of foundation and framing. A generic conversion diagram is available. See order form.)

BLUEPRINT PRICE CODE: C

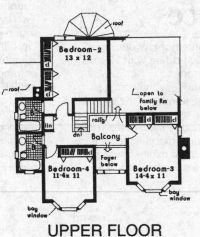

UPPER FLOOR

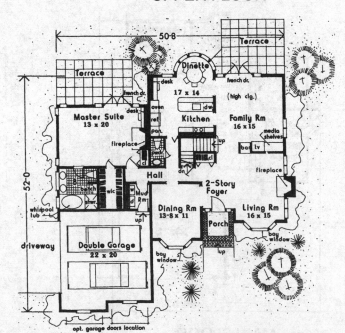

MAIN FLOOR

Charming Design for Hillside Site

- Split-level design puts living room on entry level, other rooms up or down a half-flight of steps.
- Kitchen includes work/eating island and combines with dining/family room for informal living.
- Vaulted master suite includes private bath and large closet.
- Daylight basement includes two bedrooms, bath, utility area and a rec room.

48'-0"

Deck

Kitchen 14-6x9-0

Den 11-4x10-4 vaulted

Master Br 11-2x16-8 vaulted

Desk

Dining/Family 16-4x14-4 vaulted

UP DN

Entry

Living Rm 14-10x12-8 vaulted

39'-6

MAIN FLOOR

Bedroom 3 14x10-2

Rec Room 23-2x12-10

Shelves

Br 2 10-10x12-4

D W

UP

F W

Crawlspace

Garage

DAYLIGHT BASEMENT

Plan B-89037

Bedrooms: 3+	Baths: 3

Living Area:

Main floor	1,422 sq. ft.
Partial daylight basement	913 sq. ft.
Total Living Area:	**2,335 sq. ft.**
Garage	480 sq. ft.
Exterior Wall Framing:	2x6

Foundation Options:

Partial daylight basement
(Typical foundation & framing conversion diagram available—see order form.)

BLUEPRINT PRICE CODE:	**C**

ORDER BLUEPRINTS ANYTIME!
CALL TOLL-FREE 1-888-626-2026

Plan B-89037

PRICES AND DETAILS
ON PAGES 12-15

221

One More Time!

- The character and excitement of our most popular plan in recent years, E-3000, have been recaptured in this smaller version of the design.
- The appealing facade is distinguished by a covered front porch and accented with decorative columns, triple dormers and rail-topped corner windows.
- Off the foyer, a central gallery leads to the spacious family room, where a corner fireplace and a 17-ft. vaulted ceiling are highlights. Columns in the gallery introduce the kitchen and the dining areas.
- The kitchen showcases a walk-in pantry, a built-in desk and a long snack bar that serves the eating nook and the dining room.
- The stunning main-floor master suite offers a quiet sitting area and a private angled bath with dual vanities, a corner garden tub and a separate shower.
- A lovely curved stairway leads to a balcony that overlooks the family room and the foyer. Two large bedrooms, a split bath and easily accessible attics are also found upstairs.

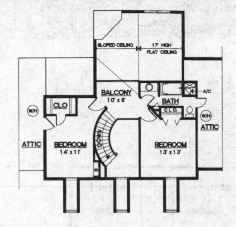

UPPER FLOOR

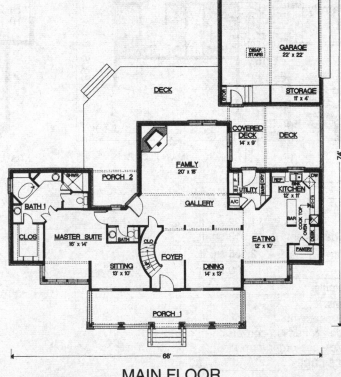

MAIN FLOOR

Plan E-2307-A

Bedrooms: 3	Baths: 2½
Living Area:	
Upper floor	595 sq. ft.
Main floor	1,765 sq. ft.
Total Living Area:	**2,360 sq. ft.**
Standard basement	1,765 sq. ft.
Garage and storage	528 sq. ft.
Exterior Wall Framing:	2x6

Foundation Options:

Standard basement

Crawlspace

Slab

(All plans can be built with your choice of foundation and framing. A generic conversion diagram is available. See order form.)

BLUEPRINT PRICE CODE: C

222

ORDER BLUEPRINTS ANYTIME!
CALL TOLL-FREE 1-888-626-2026

Plan E-2307-A

PRICES AND DETAILS
ON PAGES 12-15

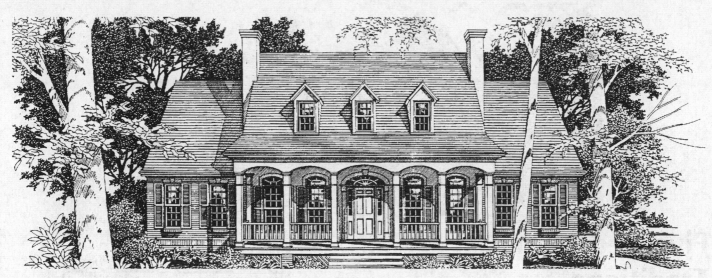

Wonderful Detailing

- The wonderfully detailed front porch, with its graceful arches, columns and railings, gives this home a character all its own. Dormer windows and arched transoms further accentuate the porch.
- The floor plan features a central living room with a 10-ft.-high ceiling and a fireplace framed by French doors. These doors open to a covered porch or a sun room, and a sheltered deck beyond.
- Just off the living room, the island kitchen and breakfast area provide a spacious place for family or guests. The nearby formal dining room has arched transom windows and a 10-ft. ceiling, as does the bedroom off the foyer. All of the remaining rooms have 9-ft. ceilings.
- The unusual master suite includes a window alcove, access to the porch and a fantastic bath with a garden tub.
- A huge utility room, a storage area off the garage and a 1,000-sq.-ft. attic space are other bonuses of this design.

Plan J-90019

Bedrooms: 3	**Baths:** 2½
Living Area:	
Main floor	2,410 sq. ft.
Total Living Area:	**2,410 sq. ft.**
Standard basement	2,410 sq. ft.
Garage	512 sq. ft.
Storage	86 sq. ft.
Exterior Wall Framing:	2x6

Foundation Options:
Standard basement
Crawlspace
Slab
(All plans can be built with your choice of foundation and framing. A generic conversion diagram is available. See order form.)

BLUEPRINT PRICE CODE: C

64' 4"

GARAGE
20' 4" X 23' 4"

DECK
20' 0" X 14' 0"

STORAGE
12' 8" X 5' 8"

PORCH OR SUNROOM
21' 6" X 12' 2"

UTILITY

MASTER BEDROOM
17' 8" X 16' 8"

LIVING
21' 9" X 17' 2"

KITCHEN

71' 6"

BREAKFAST
12' 9" X 11' 6"

BEDROOM
11' 0" X 12' 0"

BEDROOM
11' 0" X 13' 6"

FOYER

DINING
11' 0" X 16' 4"

PORCH
29' 8" X 6' 2"

MAIN FLOOR

ORDER BLUEPRINTS ANYTIME!
CALL TOLL-FREE 1-888-626-2026

Plan J-90019

PRICES AND DETAILS
ON PAGES 12-15

223

Five-Bedroom Traditional

- This sophisticated traditional home makes a striking statement both inside and out.
- The dramatic two-story foyer is flanked by the formal living spaces. The private dining room overlooks the front porch, while the spacious living room has outdoor views on two sides.
- A U-shaped kitchen with a snack bar, a sunny dinette area and a large family room flow together at the back of the home. The family room's fireplace warms the open, informal expanse, while sliding glass doors in the dinette access the backyard terrace.
- The second floor has five roomy bedrooms and two skylighted bathrooms. The luxurious master suite has a high ceiling with a beautiful arched window, a dressing area and a huge walk-in closet. The private bath offers dual sinks, a whirlpool tub and a separate shower.
- Attic space is located above the garage.

Plan AHP-9392

Bedrooms: 5	**Baths:** 2½

Living Area:	
Upper floor	1,223 sq. ft.
Main floor	1,193 sq. ft.
Total Living Area:	**2,416 sq. ft.**
Standard basement	1,130 sq. ft.
Garage	509 sq. ft.
Storage	65 sq. ft.
Exterior Wall Framing:	2x4 or 2x6

Foundation Options:
Standard basement
Crawlspace
Slab
(Typical foundation & framing conversion diagram available—see order form.)

BLUEPRINT PRICE CODE:	**C**

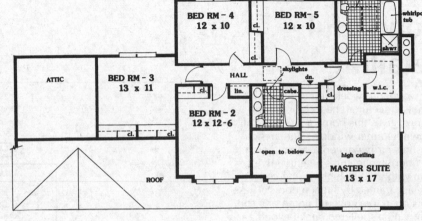

UPPER FLOOR

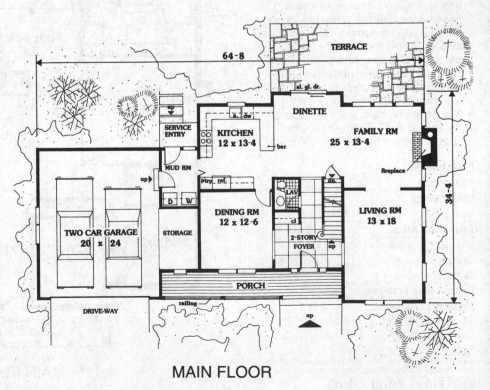

MAIN FLOOR

Plan AHP-9392

PRICES AND DETAILS
ON PAGES 12-15

Timeless Style

- The dramatic two-story entry porch and stately pillars add a timeless style and presence to this exciting two-story.
- The interior is pleasantly updated with features designed for the '90s. Open living areas extend from the unique raised entry, which offers direct access to each. The formal living room and dining room sit on either side, while a spacious two-story family room with a fireplace and a built-in entertainment center is showcased ahead.
- A handy snack counter extends from the adjoining kitchen, which also features a bayed breakfast nook, a pantry and sliding glass doors to the deck.
- A quiet den or extra bedroom is located at the other end of the home, near a half-bath.
- The upper-floor balcony overlooks the family room and foyer, and connects two secondary bedrooms to a large master suite. The master bedroom boasts a tray ceiling and corner windows. The master bath has an oval tub and a separate shower.
- The big, skylighted bonus room above the garage could serve as a playroom, hobby room or extra bedroom.

Plan B-92016

Bedrooms: 3+	Baths: 2½
Living Area:	
Upper floor	1,000 sq. ft.
Main floor	1,416 sq. ft.
Total Living Area:	**2,416 sq. ft.**
Standard basement	1,416 sq. ft.
Garage	692 sq. ft.
Exterior Wall Framing:	2x6

Foundation Options:

Standard basement
(Typical foundation & framing conversion diagram available—see order form.)

BLUEPRINT PRICE CODE: C

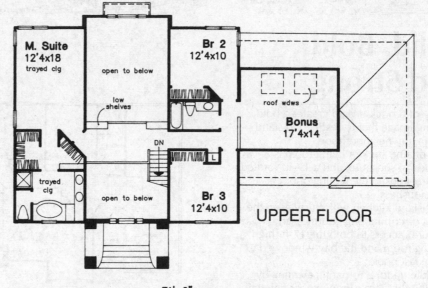

UPPER FLOOR

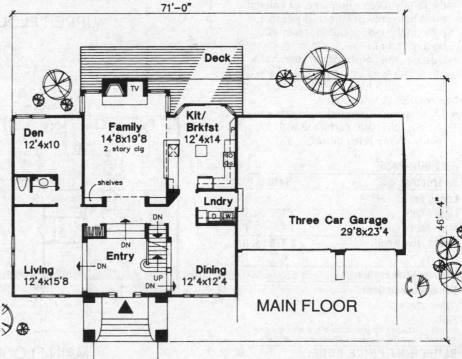

MAIN FLOOR

ORDER BLUEPRINTS ANYTIME!
CALL TOLL-FREE 1-888-626-2026

Plan B-92016

PRICES AND DETAILS
ON PAGES 12-15

225

Solid, Bold and Strong

- This solid brick design creates a bold, strong image that is destined to stand out in any neighborhood.
- The quaint, sunken living room is bathed in sunshine, and a 17-ft. vaulted ceiling adds to the feeling of bright spaciousness.
- The island kitchen will satisfy even the most discriminating gourmet, and features access to both the 17-ft.-high dining room and the bay-windowed breakfast nook.
- Cuddle up for a romantic evening by the family room's fireplace, or entertain the whole crowd; French doors to a patio make indoor/outdoor parties breezy and fun.
- Upstairs, the lavish master suite has a bay-windowed sitting area, dual walk-in closets, and a lush, skylighted bath with an opulent garden tub.
- Three spacious secondary bedrooms share a split bath, complete with a handy corner linen closet.

Plan SUN-2485

Bedrooms: 4+	Baths: 2½
Living Area:	
Upper floor	1,190 sq. ft.
Main floor	1,230 sq. ft.
Total Living Area:	**2,420 sq. ft.**
Garage	699 sq. ft.
Exterior Wall Framing:	2x6

Foundation Options:

Crawlspace
Slab
(All plans can be built with your choice of foundation and framing. A generic conversion diagram is available. See order form.)

BLUEPRINT PRICE CODE:	C

UPPER FLOOR

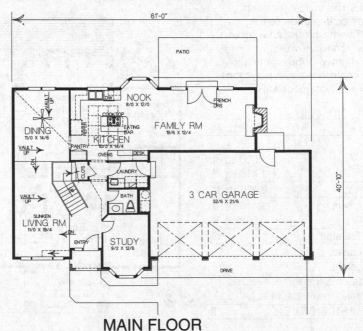

MAIN FLOOR

Plan SUN-2485

PLAN U-8503-T

Specify basement, crawlspace or slab foundation.
Both 2x4 and 2x6 options included in blueprints.

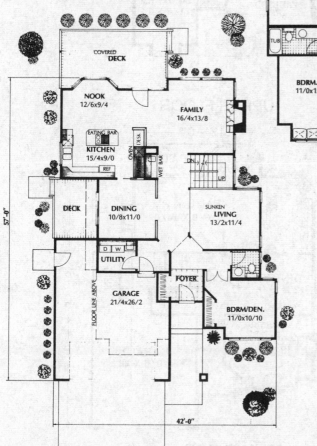

Tantalizing Design

Interesting roof lines and delicately arched windows tantalize the neighbors of this exquisite two-story. Careful planning combines rich accents with function to create a fantastic layout. You can enjoy a dream world in the master suite with a private deck. All-in-all, this is a home that makes the most out of living.

First floor:	1,349 sq. ft.
Second floor:	1,090 sq. ft.
Total living area:	2,439 sq. ft.
(Not counting basement or garage)	
Basement (optional):	1,241 sq. ft.

Blueprint Price Code C

Plan U-8503-T

Tasteful Style

- Traditional lines and a contemporary floor plan combine to make this home a perfect choice for the '90s.
- The two-story-high entry introduces the formal living room, which is warmed by a fireplace and brightened by a round-top window arrangement. The living room's ceiling rises to 13 ft., 9 inches.
- A handy pocket door separates the formal dining room from the kitchen for special occasions. The U-shaped kitchen features an eating bar, a work desk and a bayed nook with access to an outdoor patio.
- The spacious family room includes a second fireplace and outdoor views.
- Ceilings in all main-floor rooms are at least 9 ft. high for added spaciousness.
- Upstairs, the master suite features a 12-ft. vaulted ceiling, two walk-in closets and a compartmentalized bath with a luxurious tub in a window bay.
- Two additional bedrooms share a split bath. A versatile bonus room could serve as an extra bedroom or as a sunny area for hobbies or paperwork.

Plan S-8389

Bedrooms: 3+	Baths: 2½
Living Area:	
Upper floor	932 sq. ft.
Main floor	1,290 sq. ft.
Bonus room	228 sq. ft.
Total Living Area:	**2,450 sq. ft.**
Standard basement	1,290 sq. ft.
Garage	429 sq. ft.
Exterior Wall Framing:	2x6

Foundation Options:

Standard basement

Crawlspace

Slab

(All plans can be built with your choice of foundation and framing. A generic conversion diagram is available. See order form.)

BLUEPRINT PRICE CODE: C

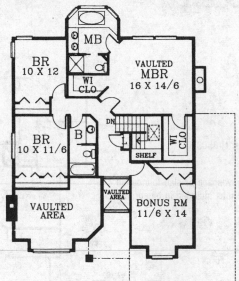

UPPER FLOOR

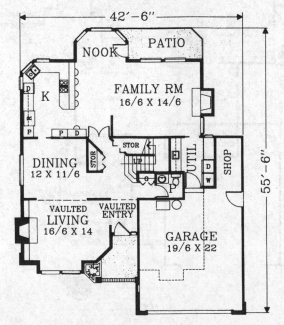

MAIN FLOOR

ORDER BLUEPRINTS ANYTIME!
CALL TOLL-FREE 1-888-626-2026

Plan S-8389

PRICES AND DETAILS
ON PAGES 12-15

Contemporary Return to Yesterday

- Bold rooflines complemented by crisply angled windows blend the traditional with the new, a theme that is increasingly popular with today's home builders. Rough-sawn corner trim and the use of brick coupled with vertical cedar siding give this home an unusual look.
- The floor plan is based on an owner-proven concept, and is filled with many amenities.

- Note the balcony library situated above the vaulted entry and the bonus space above the garage that could be a fourth bedroom or a rec room. A separate utility room with clothes-sorting counter is close to the kitchen and activity area.
- The master bath features double vanities, a raised platform tub set in a bay-windowed area and a separate shower.

Plan LRD-2180	
Bedrooms: 3-5	**Baths: 2½**
Living Area:	
Upper floor	1,051 sq. ft.
Main floor	1,184 sq. ft.
Bonus room	232 sq. ft.
Total Living Area:	**2,467 sq. ft.**
Standard basement	1,184 sq. ft.
Garage	374 sq. ft.
Exterior Wall Framing:	2x6

Foundation Options:
Standard basement
Crawlspace
(Typical foundation & framing conversion diagram available—see order form.)

BLUEPRINT PRICE CODE: C

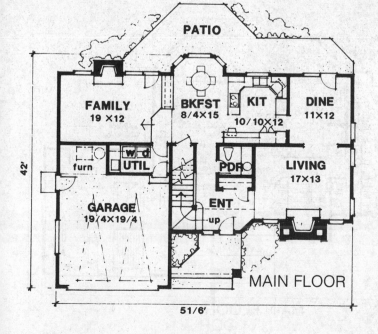

MAIN FLOOR

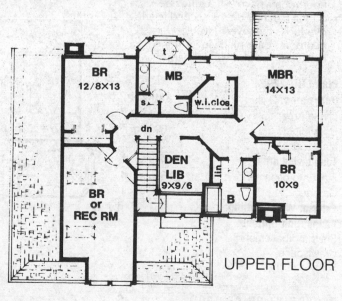

UPPER FLOOR

ORDER BLUEPRINTS ANYTIME!
CALL TOLL-FREE 1-888-626-2026

Plan LRD-2180

PRICES AND DETAILS
ON PAGES 12-15

229

Comfortable Contemporary

- This home's contemporary facade and roofline give way to an impressive Great Room for ultimate comfort.
- The sidelighted two-story foyer unfolds directly to the spectacular sunken Great Room, which is highlighted by a 10-ft., open-beam ceiling. A wood-burning stove, a pair of ceiling fans and two French doors that open to a rear wraparound deck are also showcased.
- Sharing the Great Room's 10-ft. ceiling, the open kitchen boasts an eating bar and a pass-through to the dining area.
- The secluded master bedroom features a TV wall with his-and-hers dressers. A French door provides access to a covered deck. The master bath flaunts a relaxing whirlpool tub and two vanities.
- Where not otherwise noted, the main-floor rooms have 9-ft. ceilings.
- A long balcony on the second level overlooks the foyer. Two good-sized bedrooms offer nice views of the backyard and share a full bath.

Plan LRD-22994

Bedrooms: 3	Baths: 2½
Living Area:	
Upper floor	692 sq. ft.
Main floor	1,777 sq. ft.
Total Living Area:	**2,469 sq. ft.**
Standard basement	1,655 sq. ft.
Garage	550 sq. ft.
Exterior Wall Framing:	2x6

Foundation Options:

Standard basement

Crawlspace

Slab

(All plans can be built with your choice of foundation and framing. A generic conversion diagram is available. See order form.)

BLUEPRINT PRICE CODE: C

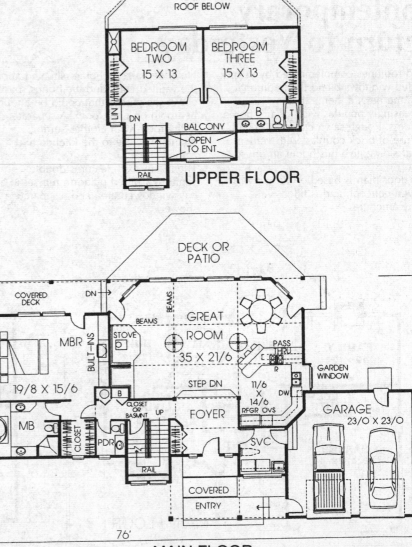

UPPER FLOOR

MAIN FLOOR

Plan LRD-22994

**PRICES AND DETAILS
ON PAGES 12-15**

Fantastic Facade, Stunning Spaces

- Matching dormers and a generous covered front porch give this home its fantastic facade. Inside, the open living spaces are just as stunning.
- A two-story foyer bisects the formal living areas. The living room offers three bright windows, an inviting fireplace and sliding French doors to the Great Room. The formal dining room overlooks the front porch and has easy access to the kitchen.
- The Great Room is truly grand, featuring a fireplace and a TV center flanked by French doors that lead to a large deck.
- A circular dinette connects the Great Room to the kitchen, which is handy to a mudroom and a powder room.
- The main-floor master suite boasts a 14-ft. cathedral ceiling, a walk-in closet and a private bath with a whirlpool tub.
- Upstairs, four large bedrooms share another whirlpool bath. One bedroom offers a 12-ft. sloped ceiling.

Plan AHP-9397

Bedrooms: 5	Baths: 2½
Living Area:	
Upper floor	928 sq. ft.
Main floor	1,545 sq. ft.
Total Living Area:	**2,473 sq. ft.**
Standard basement	1,545 sq. ft.
Garage and storage	432 sq. ft.
Exterior Wall Framing:	2x4 or 2x6

Foundation Options:
Standard basement
Crawlspace
Slab
(All plans can be built with your choice of foundation and framing. A generic conversion diagram is available. See order form.)

BLUEPRINT PRICE CODE:	C

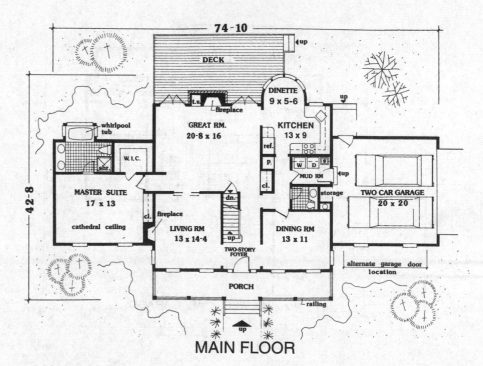

UPPER FLOOR

MAIN FLOOR

ORDER BLUEPRINTS ANYTIME!
CALL TOLL-FREE 1-888-626-2026

Plan AHP-9397

PRICES AND DETAILS
ON PAGES 12-15

231

Bright and Spacious

- Vaulted ceilings, plenty of windows and two rear decks make this home bright, spacious and perfect for entertaining.
- The vaulted foyer leads guests to the vaulted, sunken living room with fireplace. The adjacent dining room features French doors to the huge wraparound deck, which is partially covered.
- The informal family room, nook and kitchen are open and sunny, and boast a second fireplace, an island cooktop and easy access to both the deck and the garage.
- The highlight of the upper floor is the central balcony, which overlooks the foyer on one side and the living room on the other.
- The vaulted master suite opens onto a private deck. A walk-in closet leads to a 19' x 7' storage room. The deluxe bath is compartmentalized for dual use.
- The remaining bedrooms share another full bath. The vaulted den on the main floor could serve as a fourth bedroom.

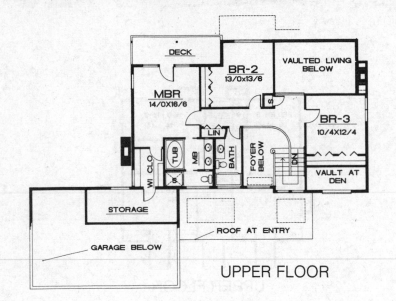

UPPER FLOOR

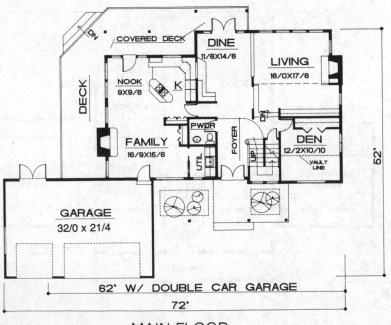

MAIN FLOOR

Plan LRD-9186

Bedrooms: 3-4	Baths: 2½
Living Area:	
Upper floor	1,025 sq. ft.
Main floor	1,460 sq. ft.
Total Living Area:	**2,485 sq. ft.**
Standard basement	1,460 sq. ft.
Two-car garage	425 sq. ft.
Three-car garage	680 sq. ft.
Storage room	133 sq. ft.
Exterior Wall Framing:	2x6

Foundation Options:
Standard basement
Crawlspace
(Typical foundation & framing conversion diagram available—see order form.)

BLUEPRINT PRICE CODE: C

Picture-Perfect

- Those tall, cold glasses of summertime lemonade will taste even better when enjoyed on the shady front porch of this picture-perfect home.
- Inside, the two-story, sidelighted foyer unfolds to the formal living areas and the Great Room beyond.
- Fireplaces grace the living room and the Great Room, which are separated by French pocket doors. A TV nook borders the fireplace in the Great Room, letting the kids catch their favorite show while Mom and Dad fix dinner in the kitchen. Two sets of French doors swing wide to reveal a backyard deck.
- A glassy dinette with an 8-ft. ceiling makes breakfasts cozy and comfortable.
- Restful nights will be the norm in the master suite, which boasts a 14-ft. cathedral ceiling. Next to the walk-in closet, the private bath has a whirlpool tub in a fabulous boxed-out window.
- Unless otherwise noted, all main-floor rooms are topped by 9-ft. ceilings.
- At day's end, guests and children may retire to the upper floor, where four big bedrooms and a full bath await them.

Plan AHP-9512

Bedrooms: 5	Baths: 2½
Living Area:	
Upper floor	928 sq. ft.
Main floor	1,571 sq. ft.
Total Living Area:	**2,499 sq. ft.**
Standard basement	1,571 sq. ft.
Garage and storage	420 sq. ft.
Exterior Wall Framing:	2x4 or 2x6

Foundation Options:

Standard basement

Crawlspace

Slab

(All plans can be built with your choice of foundation and framing. A generic conversion diagram is available. See order form.)

BLUEPRINT PRICE CODE: **C**

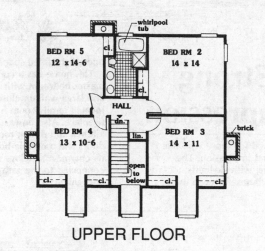

UPPER FLOOR

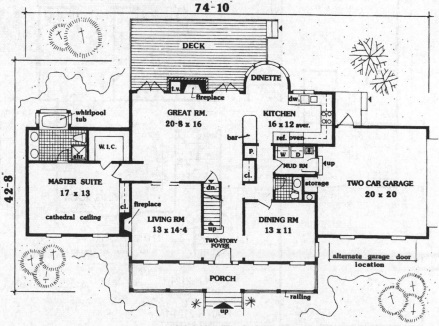

MAIN FLOOR

Plan AHP-9512

PRICES AND DETAILS
ON PAGES 12-15

For A Strong First Impression

This home is designed for those who like to make a strong first impression. The front entryway soars, with skylights providing the first glimpse of even more

open, light-filled space to come.

This home has a convenient lower level master bedroom with its own private bath and large walk-in closet. A centrally located family room has a bar counter and fireplace. Also downstairs is a sizable kitchen and dining room with French doors and a double-bow window enhancing its charm. A spacious utility room connected to the garage is a necessary convenience.

A second floor with dramatic views of the downstairs on almost every step of the upstairs passage bridge will delight you. Also upstairs is something every modern family should have — its own computer room complete with built-in desk. One bedroom has a deck off the side and both have more than enough storage space.

This two-story contemporary has 2,508 sq. ft. of living area, and an optional side- or front-entry double-car garage. Exterior walls feature 2x6 construction for energy efficiency.

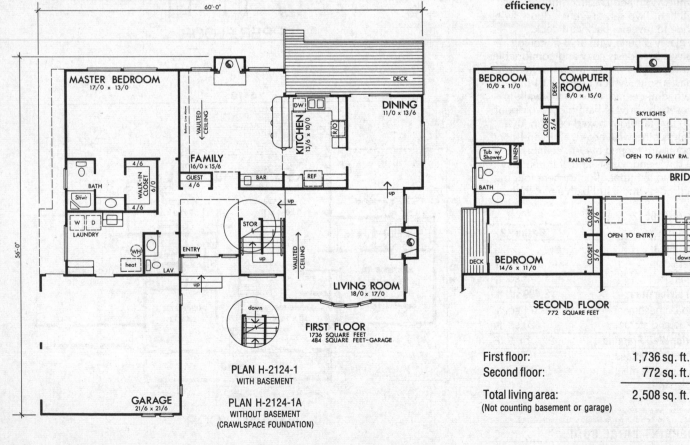

PLAN H-2124-1
WITH BASEMENT

PLAN H-2124-1A
WITHOUT BASEMENT
(CRAWLSPACE FOUNDATION)

First floor:	1,736 sq. ft.
Second floor:	772 sq. ft.
Total living area:	2,508 sq. ft.
(Not counting basement or garage)	

Blueprint Price Code D

Plans H-2124-1 & -1A

PRICES AND DETAILS
ON PAGES 12-15

Wonderful Ranch-Style

- This wonderful ranch-style home offers an L-shaped porch with ornate post detail, an interesting roofline and a classic cupola atop the garage.
- The open floor plan is ultra-modern, beginning with the huge living and dining area. The living room is highlighted by a raised ceiling with rustic beams. The dining room, one step up, is outlined by a railing.

- The super U-shaped kitchen has tons of counter and storage space, including an island cabinet, a desk, a pantry closet and two lazy Susans. The adjoining eating area offers views to the patio and access to the side porch.
- An oversized utility room, a sewing room and a game room are extra features, as are the two storage areas at the rear of the garage.
- The big master suite hosts plenty of closet space, plus a deluxe bath behind double doors. The two smaller bedrooms, each with double closets, share a compartmentalized bath.

Plan E-2502	
Bedrooms: 3+	**Baths:** 2½
Living Area:	
Main floor	2,522 sq. ft.
Total Living Area:	**2,522 sq. ft.**
Garage	484 sq. ft.
Storage	90 sq. ft.
Exterior Wall Framing:	2x6
Foundation Options:	
Crawlspace	
Slab	

(All plans can be built with your choice of foundation and framing. A generic conversion diagram is available. See order form.)

BLUEPRINT PRICE CODE: D

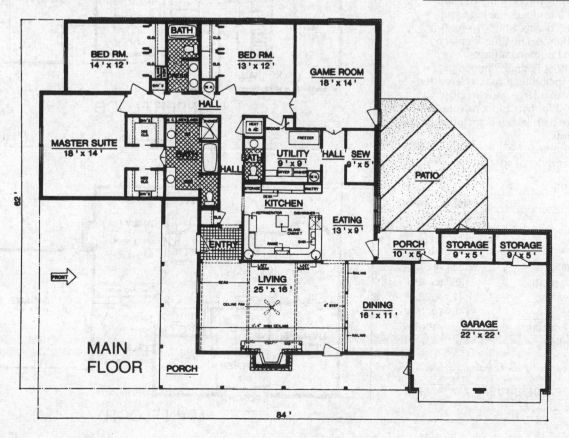

Plan E-2502

Stately Colonial

- This stately Colonial features a covered front entry and a secondary entry near the garage and the utility room.
- The main foyer opens to a comfortable den with elegant double doors.
- The formal living areas adjoin to the left of the foyer and culminate in a lovely bay window overlooking the backyard.
- The open island kitchen has a great central location, easily accessed from each of the living areas. Informal dining can be extended to the outdoors through sliding doors in the dinette.
- A half-wall introduces the big family room, which boasts a high 16-ft., 9-in. vaulted ceiling, an inviting fireplace and optional built-in cabinets.
- The upper floor is shared by four bedrooms, including a spacious master bedroom with a large walk-in closet, a dressing area for two and a private bath. An alternate bath layout is included in the blueprints.
- A bonus room may be added above the garage for additional space.

Plan A-2283-DS

Bedrooms: 4+	Baths: 2½
Living Area:	
Upper floor	1,137 sq. ft.
Main floor	1,413 sq. ft.
Total Living Area:	**2,550 sq. ft.**
Optional bonus room	280 sq. ft.
Standard basement	1,413 sq. ft.
Garage	484 sq. ft.
Exterior Wall Framing:	2x6

Foundation Options:

Standard basement
(All plans can be built with your choice of foundation and framing. A generic conversion diagram is available. See order form.)

BLUEPRINT PRICE CODE:	D

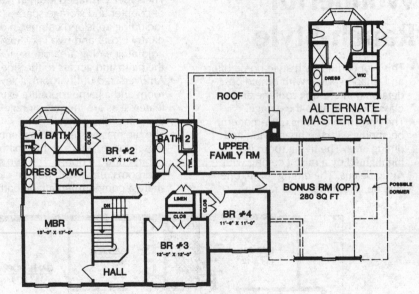

UPPER FLOOR

ALTERNATE MASTER BATH

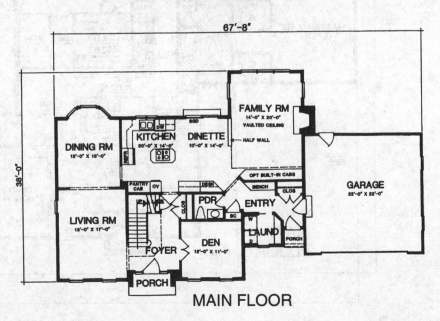

MAIN FLOOR

Plan A-2283-DS

PRICES AND DETAILS
ON PAGES 12-15

Hot Tub, Deck Highlighted

- Designed for indoor/outdoor living, this home features a skylighted spa room with a hot tub and a backyard deck that spans the width of the home.
- A central hall leads to the sunny kitchen and nook, which offer corner windows, a snack bar and a pantry.
- Straight ahead, the open dining and living rooms form one huge space, further pronounced by expansive windows. The 16-ft. vaulted living room also features a fireplace and sliding glass doors to the deck.
- The master suite includes a cozy window seat, a large walk-in closet, a private bath and access to the tiled spa room. The spa may also be entered from the deck and an inner hall.
- Upstairs, two more bedrooms share a full bath and a balcony that overlooks the living room below.
- The optional daylight basement offers a deluxe sauna, a fourth bedroom, a laundry room and a wide recreation room with a fireplace. A large game room and storage are also included.

See this plan on our "Two-Story" VideoGraphic Tour!

Order form on page 9

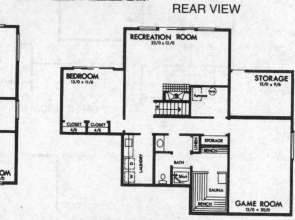

REAR VIEW

UPPER FLOOR

DAYLIGHT BASEMENT

MAIN FLOOR

STAIRWAY AREA IN CRAWLSPACE VERSION

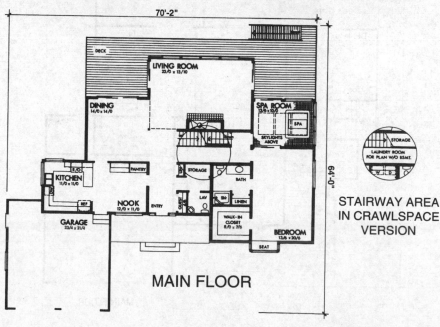

Plans H-2114-1A & -1B

Bedrooms: 3+	Baths: 2½-3½
Living Area:	
Upper floor	732 sq. ft.
Main floor	1,682 sq. ft.
Spa room	147 sq. ft.
Daylight basement	1,386 sq. ft.
Total Living Area:	**2,561/3,947 sq. ft.**
Garage	547 sq. ft.
Exterior Wall Framing:	2x6
Foundation Options:	**Plan #**
Daylight basement	H-2114-1B
Crawlspace	H-2114-1A

(All plans can be built with your choice of foundation and framing. A generic conversion diagram is available. See order form.)

BLUEPRINT PRICE CODE: D/F

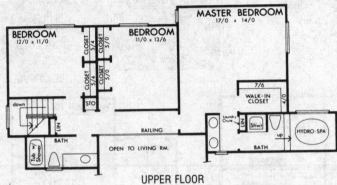

UPPER FLOOR

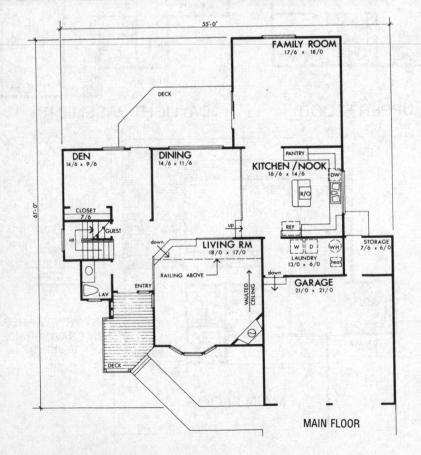

MAIN FLOOR

Grace and Prestige

- Dormer and bay windows and a hipped roof give this home a modern, yet traditional look.
- Tri-level room arrangement features a sunken living room, step-up U-shaped kitchen with island work center, and a second floor sleeping section with hallway balcony overlooking the living room.
- Living room boasts an entrance bordered by 3-ft. railings, corner fireplace, and vaulted ceilings.
- Master suite includes a convenient laundry chute, double-sink vanity, and a relaxing hydro-spa.

Plan H-2123-1A

Bedrooms: 3	Baths: 2½
Space:	
Upper floor:	989 sq. ft.
Main floor:	1,597 sq. ft.
Total living area:	2,586 sq. ft.
Garage:	441 sq. ft.
Storage:	45 sq. ft.
Exterior Wall Framing:	2x6

Foundation options:
Crawlspace only.
(Foundation & framing conversion diagram available — see order form.)

Blueprint Price Code:	D

Large Deck Wraps Home

- A full deck and an abundance of windows surround this exciting two-level contemporary.
- The brilliant living room boasts a huge fireplace and a 14-ft.-high cathedral ceiling, plus a stunning prow-shaped window wall.

- Skywalls brighten the island kitchen and the dining room. A pantry closet and laundry facilities are nearby.
- The master bedroom offers private access to the deck. The master bath includes a dual-sink vanity, a large tub and a separate shower. A roomy hall bath serves a second bedroom.
- A generous-sized family room, another full bath and two additional bedrooms share the lower level with a two-car garage and a shop area.

Plan NW-579

Bedrooms: 4	**Baths:** 3
Living Area:	
Main floor	1,707 sq. ft.
Daylight basement	901 sq. ft.
Total Living Area:	**2,608 sq. ft.**
Tuck-under garage	588 sq. ft.
Shop	162 sq. ft.
Exterior Wall Framing:	2x6

Foundation Options:

Daylight basement

(All plans can be built with your choice of foundation and framing. A generic conversion diagram is available. See order form.)

BLUEPRINT PRICE CODE: D

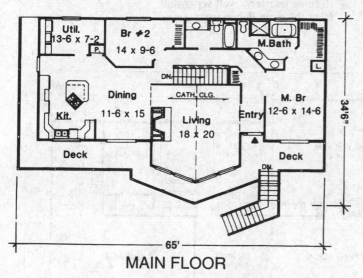

MAIN FLOOR

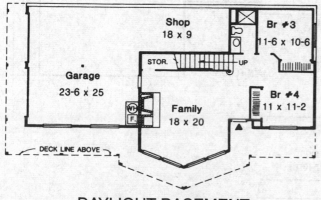

DAYLIGHT BASEMENT

VIEW INTO LIVING ROOM

ORDER BLUEPRINTS ANYTIME!
CALL TOLL-FREE 1-888-626-2026

Plan NW-579

PRICES AND DETAILS
ON PAGES 12-15

239

Southern Colonial with Authentic Style

- Porch columns, brick siding, and shuttered windows all contribute to this classic facade.
- This spacious home features large but detailed rooms, including a formal dining room and grand-sized

family room and living room, each with fireplaces.
- King-sized closets, large baths, and generous bedrooms make up the sleeping quarters, well separated from the main living areas.

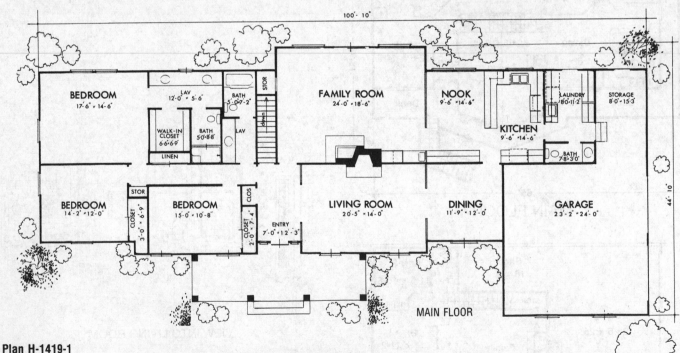

MAIN FLOOR

Plan H-1419-1

Bedrooms: 3	Baths: 2½

Total living area: 2,558 sq. ft.
Basement: approx. 2,558 sq. ft.
Garage: 556 sq. ft.

Exterior Wall Framing: 2x6

Foundation options:
Standard basement only.
(Foundation & framing conversion diagram available — see order form.)

Blueprint Price Code: D

Easy-Living Atmosphere

- Clean lines and a functional, well-designed floor plan create a relaxed, easy-living atmosphere for this sprawling ranch-style home.
- An inviting front porch with attractive columns and planter boxes opens to an airy entry, which flows into the living room and the family room.
- The huge central family room features a 14-ft. vaulted, exposed-beam ceiling and a handsome fireplace with a built-in wood box. A nice desk and plenty of

bookshelves give the room a distinguished feel. A French door opens to a versatile covered rear porch.
- The large gourmet kitchen is highlighted by an arched brick pass-through to the family room. Double doors open to the intimate formal dining room, which hosts a built-in china hutch. The sunny informal eating area features lovely porch views on either side.
- The isolated sleeping wing includes four bedrooms. The enormous master bedroom has a giant walk-in closet and a private bath. A compartmentalized bath with two vanities serves the remaining bedrooms.

Plan E-2700

Bedrooms: 4	Baths: 2½
Living Area:	
Main floor	2,719 sq. ft.
Total Living Area:	**2,719 sq. ft.**
Garage	533 sq. ft.
Storage	50 sq. ft.
Exterior Wall Framing:	2x6

Foundation Options:

Crawlspace
Slab
(All plans can be built with your choice of foundation and framing. A generic conversion diagram is available. See order form.)

BLUEPRINT PRICE CODE:	D

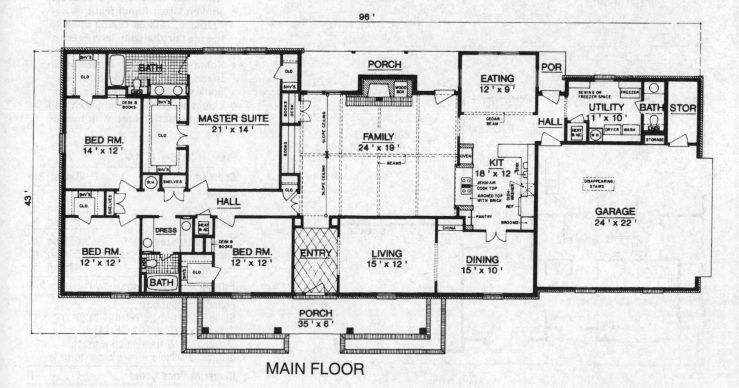

MAIN FLOOR

ORDER BLUEPRINTS ANYTIME!
CALL TOLL-FREE 1-888-626-2026

Plan E-2700

PRICES AND DETAILS
ON PAGES 12-15

241

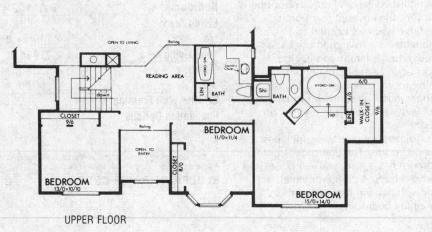

UPPER FLOOR

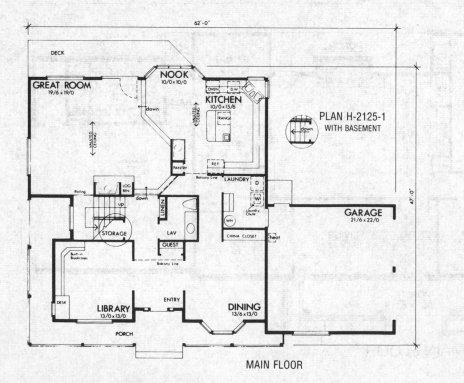

PLAN H-2125-1
WITH BASEMENT

MAIN FLOOR

Delightful Blend of Old and New

- A contemporary floor plan is hidden in a traditional farmhouse exterior.
- Vaulted entrance is open to the upper level; adjacent open stairwell is lit by a semi-circular window.
- French doors open into a library with built-in bookcase and deck.
- Sunken Great Room features a fireplace, vaulted ceiling open to the upstairs balcony, and French doors leading to a backyard deck.
- Roomy kitchen has center cooking island, eating bar, and attached nook with corner fireplace.
- Upper level has reading area and exciting master suite with hydro-spa.

Plans H-2125-1 & -1A

Bedrooms: 3	Baths: 2½

Space:	
Upper floor:	1,105 sq. ft.
Main floor:	1,554 sq. ft.
Total living area:	**2,659 sq. ft.**
Basement:	approx. 1,554 sq. ft.
Garage:	475 sq. ft.

Exterior Wall Framing:	2x6

Foundation options:
Standard basement (Plan H-2125-1).
Crawlspace (Plan H-2125-1A).
(Foundation & framing conversion diagram available — see order form.)

Blueprint Price Code:	D

Plans H-2125-1 & -1A

PRICES AND DETAILS
ON PAGES 12-15

Elegant, with a Country Heart

- A columned porch and a dramatic arched window help to create a country-style home with a twist of urbane elegance.
- The dramatic two-story foyer greets visitors with its sunlit brilliance.
- Entertaining big crowds can easily be done in the large family room or the even larger living room/dining room area. Take the party outdoors via sliding glass doors to a handy terrace.
- The master suite features its own secluded terrace, and is also highlighted by a 12-ft. cathedral ceiling, a walk-in closet and a skylighted private bath with a sensuous whirlpool tub under a dazzling glass-block wall.
- A majestic curved stairway leads gracefully to the upper floor, where four more bedrooms and a second full bath are featured.

Plan K-804-R

Bedrooms: 5	Baths: 2½
Living Area:	
Upper floor	937 sq. ft.
Main floor	1,808 sq. ft.
Total Living Area:	**2,745 sq. ft.**
Standard basement	1,795 sq. ft.
Garage	483 sq. ft.
Exterior Wall Framing:	2x4 or 2x6

Foundation Options:
Standard basement
Slab
(All plans can be built with your choice of foundation and framing. A generic conversion diagram is available. See order form.)

BLUEPRINT PRICE CODE: D

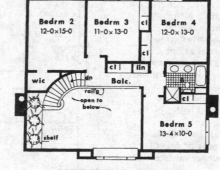

UPPER FLOOR

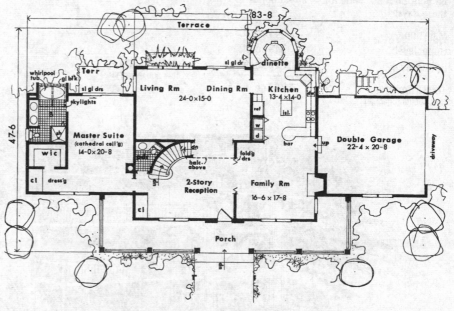

MAIN FLOOR

ORDER BLUEPRINTS ANYTIME!
CALL TOLL-FREE 1-888-626-2026

Plan K-804-R

**PRICES AND DETAILS
ON PAGES 12-15**

243

FRONT VIEW

Luxury on a Compact Foundation

Sky-lighted sloped ceilings, an intriguing stairway and overhead bridge and a carefully planned first floor arrangement combine to delight the senses as one explores this spacious 2737 sq. ft. home. A major element of the design is the luxurious master suite that is reached via the stairway and bridge. An abundance of closet space and an oversized bath are welcome features here.

Two bedrooms, generous bath facilities and a large family room provide lots of growing room for the younger members of the household.

All these features are available within a mere 36' width which allows the house to be built on a 50' wide lot — a real bonus these days.

Main floor:	1,044 sq. ft.
Upper level:	649 sq. ft.
Lower level:	1,044 sq. ft.
Total living area:	**2,737 sq. ft.**
(Not counting garage)	

(Exterior walls are 2x6 construction)

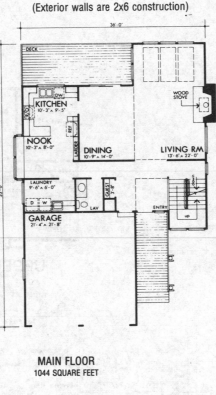

MAIN FLOOR
1044 SQUARE FEET

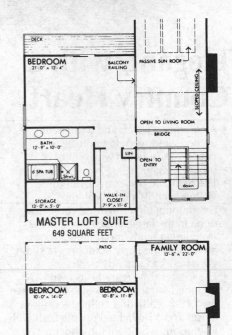

MASTER LOFT SUITE
649 SQUARE FEET

LOWER LEVEL
1044 SQUARE FEET

REAR VIEW

Blueprint Price Code D

Plan H-2110-1B

Gracious Days

- As it brings a touch of Victorian flair to this country-style home, a charming gazebo provides a gracious spot for afternoon visits and lemonade.
- Inside, the living and dining rooms flank the foyer, creating an elegant setting for parties. With a closet and private access to a bath, the living room could also be used as a bedroom or a home office.
- Straight ahead, handsome columns frame the Great Room, where puddles of sunshine will form under the two skylights. Sliding glass doors let in the fresh scent of spring blooms. A corner fireplace warms chilled fingers after an afternoon of raking leaves.
- In the kitchen, a sizable island doubles as a workstation and a snack bar. The sunny bay in the breakfast nook will rouse the sleepiest child.
- Across the home, the owners receive some extra special treatment in the master suite. Features here include a pair of walk-in closets, a linen closet and a bath with a dual-sink vanity.

Plan AX-95349

Bedrooms: 3+	Baths: 3
Living Area:	
Upper floor	728 sq. ft.
Main floor	2,146 sq. ft.
Total Living Area:	**2,874 sq. ft.**
Unfinished loft	300 sq. ft.
Standard basement	2,146 sq. ft.
Garage	624 sq. ft.
Exterior Wall Framing:	2x6

Foundation Options:

Standard basement
Crawlspace
Slab

(All plans can be built with your choice of foundation and framing. A generic conversion diagram is available. See order form.)

BLUEPRINT PRICE CODE:	D

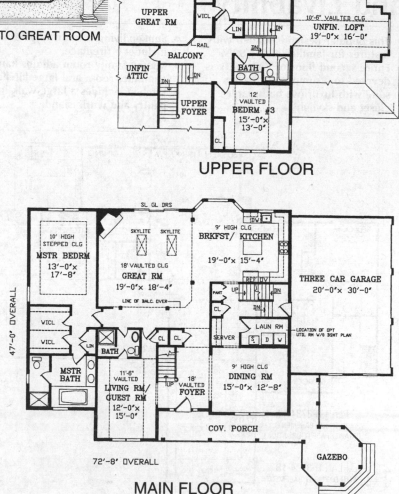

VIEW INTO GREAT ROOM

UPPER FLOOR

MAIN FLOOR

ORDER BLUEPRINTS ANYTIME!
CALL TOLL-FREE 1-888-626-2026

Plan AX-95349

PRICES AND DETAILS
ON PAGES 12-15

245

Ultimate in Luxury and Livability

- This popular design is loaded with features for families of the 90's.
- Entire second floor of 735 sq. ft. is devoted to a sumptuous master suite with luxurious bath, large closet and skylights.

- Sunken living room is large and includes a fireplace.
- Roomy family room adjoins handy computer room and large kitchen.
- Kitchen includes a large walk-in pantry and work island.

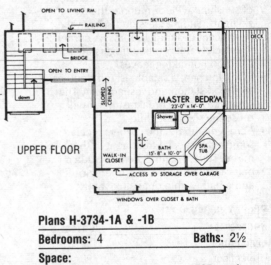

UPPER FLOOR

Plans H-3734-1A & -1B

Bedrooms: 4	Baths: 2½
Space:	
Upper floor:	735 sq. ft.
Main floor:	2,024 sq. ft.
Total living area:	2,759 sq. ft.
Basement:	2,024 sq. ft.
Garage:	687 sq. ft.
Exterior Wall Framing:	2x6

Foundation options:
Daylight basement, Plan H-3734-1B.
Crawlspace, Plan H-3734-1A.
(Foundation & framing conversion diagram available — see order form.)

Blueprint Price Code:	D

PLAN H-3734-1A
WITHOUT BASEMENT
(CRAWLSPACE FOUNDATION)

PLAN H-3734-1B
WITH DAYLIGHT BASEMENT

MAIN FLOOR

Spacious Great Room

- The efficient floor plan of this home centers around a stunning Great Room. The entire main floor is designed for those who enjoy casual living and entertaining, without the fuss of maintaining formal, rarely used living spaces.
- The Great Room is partially vaulted to the balcony overhead. The open-plan concept allows light, and traffic, to flow easily throughout the home.
- The two generous bedrooms on the lower level are separated from the

master suite, which is located on the second level. The future bonus space can be finished as needed.
- The covered patio can be eliminated in favor of a two-story sunspace, accessible from the master bedroom and the lower-level dining room.
- This is a home for all seasons and has a modest size of 2,542 sq. ft., excluding the bonus space over the garage.

Plan LRD-41389

Bedrooms: 2-4	Baths: 2-3

Space:	
Upper floor	910 sq. ft.
Main floor	1,632 sq. ft.
Bonus area	456 sq. ft.

Total Living Area:	**2,998 sq. ft.**

Standard basement	1,632 sq. ft.
Garage	567 sq. ft.

Exterior Wall Framing:	2x6

Foundation Options:
Standard basement
Crawlspace
(Typical foundation & framing conversion diagram available—see order form.)

BLUEPRINT PRICE CODE:	D

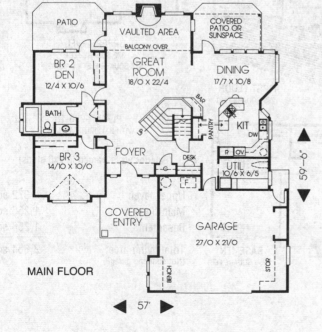

MAIN FLOOR

◄ 57' ►

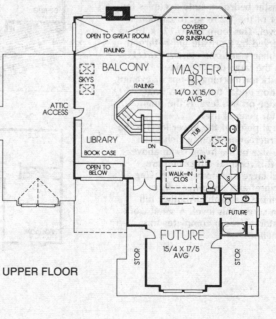

UPPER FLOOR

ORDER BLUEPRINTS ANYTIME!
CALL TOLL-FREE 1-888-626-2026

Plan LRD-41389

PRICES AND DETAILS
ON PAGES 12-15

247

Attractive Hillside Home

This three-level recreation home is designed to fit comfortably on a slope of approximately 20 degrees, with a fall of 15 to 17 feet for the depth of the building. Naturally the stability of the ground must be taken into consideration, and local professional advice should be sought. Otherwise, this home is designed to meet the requirements of the Uniform Building Code.

The pleasing contemporary nature of the exterior is calculated to blend into the surroundings as unobtrusively as possible, following the natural contours.

The modest roadside facade consisting of garage doors and a wooden entrance deck conceals the spacious luxury that lies beyond. Proceeding from the rustic deck into the skylighted entry hall, one is struck by the immensity of the living-dining room and the huge deck extending beyond. A massive masonry backdrop provides a setting for the pre-fab fireplace of your choice (this same structure incorporates the flue for a similar unit on the lower level).

Before descending from the entry hall, one must take notice of the balcony-type den, library, hobby or office room on this level — a private retreat from the activities below.

The efficient U-shaped kitchen has an adjoining attached breakfast bar for casual dining whenever the roomy dining room facilities are not required. A convenient laundry room is an important part of this housekeeping section.

The master bedroom suite occupies the remainder of the 1,256 sq. ft. contained on this level. The room itself, 12' x 16' in size, is served by a private full bathroom and two huge wardrobe closets. Direct access to the large deck provides opportunity for morning sit-ups or evening conversation under the stars. A final convenience on this level is the small lavatory for general use.

The focal point of the lower level is the spacious recreation room which is a duplicate size of the living room above. Flanking this room at either end are additional large bedrooms, one having a walk-in closet and the other a huge wall-spanning wardrobe. Another full bathroom serves this level. A small work shop or storage room completes this arrangement.

REAR VIEW

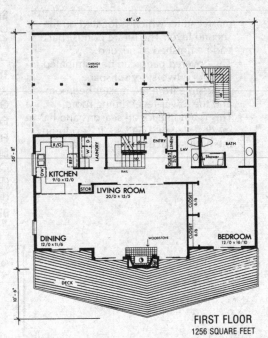

FIRST FLOOR
1256 SQUARE FEET

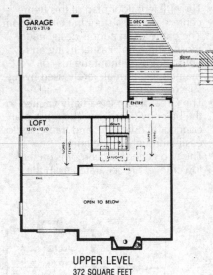

UPPER LEVEL
372 SQUARE FEET
528 SQUARE FEET - GARAGE

PLAN H-966-1B
WITH DAYLIGHT BASEMENT

(Exterior walls framed in 2x6 studs)

Upper level:	372 sq. ft.
Main floor:	1,256 sq. ft.
Basement:	1,256 sq. ft.
Total living area: (Not counting garage)	2,884 sq. ft.

BASEMENT
1256 SQUARE FEET

Blueprint Price Code D

Plan H-966-1B

FRONT VIEW

Geometric Sunshine

- Clean geometric lines join forces with wonderful windows and high ceilings to make this contemporary home bright and airy.
- The vaulted living room is warmed by a fireplace, while the dining room offers double doors to a sheltered patio.
- The spacious family room boasts an exposed-beam ceiling, an inviting woodstove and a bright window wall facing a delightful sun space.
- A hot tub or spa can be added to the sun space, which offers a spiral staircase to the upper-floor master suite.
- The kitchen is a gourmet cook's dream, with an angled cooktop/snack bar, a built-in pantry and a boxed-out window over the sink.
- The secluded den can perform double duty as a guest room or fourth bedroom when needed.
- The upper floor hosts three roomy bedrooms, including a luxurious master suite with a deluxe bath that includes a corner spa tub and a soothing sauna. A storage room is another nice extra.

REAR VIEW

Plan S-6777

Bedrooms: 3+	Baths: 2½
Living Area:	
Upper floor	1,342 sq. ft.
Main floor	1,514 sq. ft.
Sun space	160 sq. ft.
Total Living Area:	**3,016 sq. ft.**
Standard basement	1,500 sq. ft.
Garage	437 sq. ft.
Storage above den	146 sq. ft.
Exterior Wall Framing:	2x6

Foundation Options:

Standard basement

Crawlspace

Slab

(All plans can be built with your choice of foundation and framing. A generic conversion diagram is available. See order form.)

BLUEPRINT PRICE CODE:	E

UPPER FLOOR

MAIN FLOOR

ORDER BLUEPRINTS ANYTIME!
CALL TOLL-FREE 1-888-626-2026

Plan S-6777

PRICES AND DETAILS
ON PAGES 12-15

249

Pure Luxury in a Choice of Styles

- **Southwestern colonial or Western contemporary exteriors are available when deciding if this spacious design is for you.**
- **Elaborate master suite features attached screened spa room, regular and walk-in closets, and luxurious bath with skylight.**

- **Study, large family and living room with sloped ceilings and rear patio are other points of interest.**
- **Three additional bedrooms make up the second level.**
- **The Spanish version (M2A) offers a stucco exterior and slab foundation.**

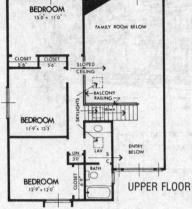

BEDROOM 15'0" x 11'0"

FAMILY ROOM BELOW

CLOSET 5'6" CLOSET 5'6"

SLOPED CEILING

BALCONY RAILING

SKYLIGHTS

down

BEDROOM 11'9" x 13'3"

LIN 3'0"

ENTRY BELOW

LAV

CLOSET 6'3"

BATH

BEDROOM 12'9" x 12'0"

UPPER FLOOR

Plans H-3714-1/1A/1B/M2A

Bedrooms: 4	Baths: 3

Space:	
Upper floor:	740 sq. ft.
Main floor:	2,190 sq. ft.

Total living area:	2,930 sq. ft.
Basement:	1,153 sq. ft.
Garage:	576 sq. ft.

Exterior Wall Framing:	2x6

Foundation options:
Daylight basement (Plan H-3714-1B).
Standard basement (Plan H-3714-1).
Crawlspace (Plan H-3714-1A).
Slab (Plan H-3714-M2A).
(Foundation & framing conversion diagram available — see order form.)

Blueprint Price Code:	D

MAIN FLOOR

78'0"

6" HIGH SCREEN WALL

52'0"

HYDRO SPA

BEDROOM 13'0" x 19'0"

FAMILY ROOM 15'6" x 20'6"

PATIO

HYDRO-SPA EQUIPMENT

SHWR

BATH

CLOSET 5'0"

SLOPED CEILING

DW

KITCHEN 11'9" x 11'0"

DINING 12'0" x 11'6"

UTILITY 7'0" x 13'6"

TUB

SKYLIGHT

WALK-IN CLOSET 5'6" x 7'0"

down up

REF R/O

SLOPED CEILING

HEAT

CLOSET 8'6"

STOR CLOSET 4'9"

GARAGE 23'6" x 24'6"

PULL DOWN LADDER FOR STORAGE ABOVE

W D

LAUNDRY

7'2 LINEN

BATH

ENTRY

SHWR

LIVING ROOM 23'6" x 15'0"

PLANTER

STUDY 15'6" x 10'0"

STOR up

STORAGE 5'3" CLOSET 4'3"

Plans H-3714-1/1A/1B/M2A
PRICES AND DETAILS
ON PAGES 12-15

PLAN H-3714-M2A FRONT VIEW

Shades of New England Seaside Homes

This home shows a traditional New England look to the world while the interior is very modern and open. Formal in exterior appearance, it is definitely a home that is designed for informal living throughout the interior.

A large two-story vaulted foyer greets guests upon arrival. Upon entering the Great Room, passing by either side of the fieldstone fireplace, they are then treated to a room flooded with light from the multiple window treatments. The large kitchen with central range island contains a secondary bar sink with room for four bar stools.

An open picketed staircase leads one to the "supersuite" complete with a gas-log fireplace, private deck, and luxurious master bath.

The study may be used as a bedroom or left as a study/library as shown. The utility area is part of the second floor design for easier access from the bedrooms.

First floor:	1,693 sq. ft.
Second floor:	1,361 sq. ft.
Total living area: (Not counting basement or garage)	3,054 sq. ft.

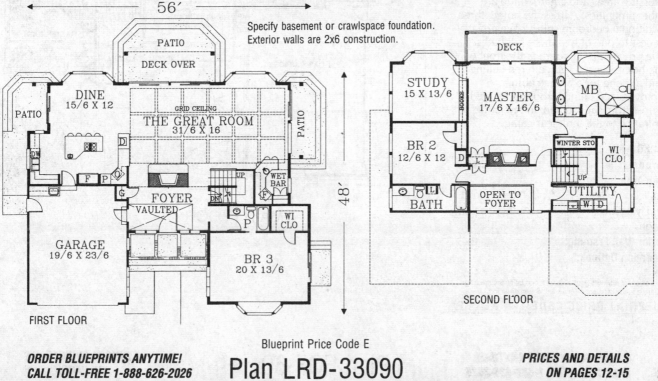

Specify basement or crawlspace foundation.
Exterior walls are 2x6 construction.

FIRST FLOOR

SECOND FLOOR

Blueprint Price Code E
Plan LRD-33090

PRICES AND DETAILS
ON PAGES 12-15

Master Suite Fit for a King

- This sprawling one-story features an extraordinary master suite that stretches from the front of the home to the back.
- Eye-catching windows and columns introduce the foyer, which flows back to the Grand Room. French doors open to the covered veranda, which offers a fabulous summer kitchen.
- The kitchen and bayed morning room are nestled between the Grand Room and a warm Gathering Room. A striking fireplace, an entertainment center and an ale bar are found here. This exciting core of living spaces also offers dramatic views of the outdoors.
- The isolated master suite features a stunning two-sided fireplace and an octagonal lounge area with veranda access. His-and-hers closets, separate dressing areas and a garden tub are other amenities. Across the home, three additional bedroom suites have private access to one of two more full baths.
- The private dining room at the front of the home has a 13-ft. coffered ceiling and a niche for a china cabinet.
- An oversized laundry room is located across from the kitchen and near the entrance to the three-car garage.

Plan EOF-60

Bedrooms: 4	Baths: 3
Living Area:	
Main floor	3,002 sq. ft.
Total Living Area:	**3,002 sq. ft.**
Garage	660 sq. ft.
Exterior Wall Framing:	2x6

Foundation Options:

Slab
(All plans can be built with your choice of foundation and framing. A generic conversion diagram is available. See order form.)

BLUEPRINT PRICE CODE:	E

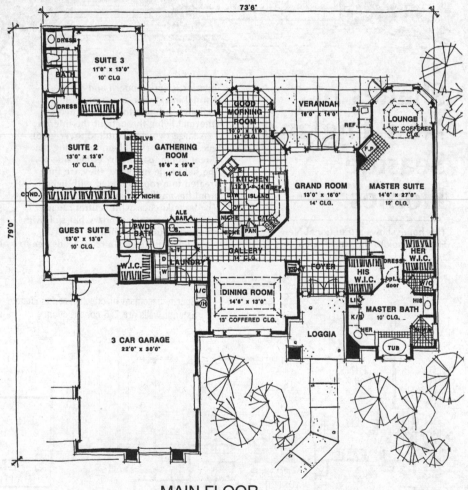

MAIN FLOOR

Plan EOF-60

PRICES AND DETAILS
ON PAGES 12-15

FRONT VIEW

Dramatic Western Contemporary

- Dramatic and functional building features contribute to the comfort and desire of this family home.
- Master suite offers a spacious private bath and luxurious hydro spa.
- Open, efficient kitchen accommodates modern appliances, a large pantry, and a snack bar.
- Skylights shed light on the entryway, open staircase, and balcony.
- Upper level balcony area has private covered deck, and may be used as a guest room or den.

REAR VIEW

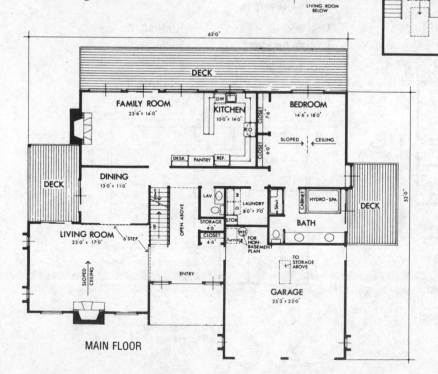

UPPER FLOOR

MAIN FLOOR

Plans H-3708-1 & -1A

Bedrooms: 4	Baths: 2½

Space:

Upper floor:	893 sq. ft.
Main floor:	2,006 sq. ft.

Total living area:	2,899 sq. ft.
Basement:	approx. 2,006 sq. ft.
Garage:	512 sq. ft.

Exterior Wall Framing:	2x6

Foundation options:
Daylight basement (Plan H-3708-1).
Crawlspace (Plan H-3708-1A).
(Foundation & framing conversion diagram available — see order form.)

Blueprint Price Code:	D

ORDER BLUEPRINTS ANYTIME!
CALL TOLL-FREE 1-888-626-2026

Plans H-3708-1 & -1A

PRICES AND DETAILS
ON PAGES 12-15

253

An Ever-Popular Floor Plan

The basic concept of this plan is to provide a simple straight-forward design for an uphill site. The plan is available with either a family room or dining room adjacent to the kitchen. Other features include a convenient laundry room, three bedrooms and two full baths. The living room features a fireplace and the wrap-around deck has access through the kitchen and laundry room. Total main floor area is 1,664 sq. ft.

Main floor:	1,664 sq. ft.
Daylight basement:	1,090 sq. ft.
Total living area:	2,754 sq. ft.
Garage:	573 sq. ft.

(Exterior walls are 2x6 construction)

PLAN H-2029-4
MAIN FLOOR
(DINING ROOM VERSION)
1664 SQUARE FEET

PLAN H-2029-5
MAIN FLOOR
(FAMILY ROOM VERSION)
1664 SQUARE FEET

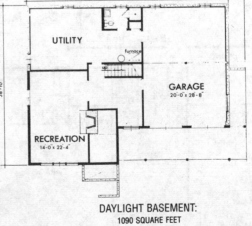

DAYLIGHT BASEMENT:
1090 SQUARE FEET

Blueprint Price Code D

Plans H-2029-4 & -5

Distinguished Living

- Beautiful arches, sweeping rooflines and a dramatic entry court distinguish this one-story from all the rest.
- Elegant columns outline the main foyer. To the right, the dining room has a 13-ft. coffered ceiling and an ale bar with a wine rack.
- The centrally located Grand Room can be viewed from the foyer and gallery. French doors and flanking windows allow a view of the veranda as well.
- A large island kitchen and sunny morning room merge with the casual Gathering Room. The combination offers a big fireplace, a TV niche, bookshelves and a handy snack bar.
- The extraordinary master suite flaunts a 12-ft. ceiling, an exciting three-sided fireplace and a TV niche shared with the private bayed lounge. A luxurious bath, a private library and access to the veranda are also featured.
- The two smaller bedroom suites have private baths and generous closets.

Plan EOF-62

Bedrooms: 3	Baths: 3½
Living Area:	
Main floor	3,090 sq. ft.
Total Living Area:	**3,090 sq. ft.**
Garage	660 sq. ft.
Exterior Wall Framing:	2x6

Foundation Options:

Slab
(All plans can be built with your choice of foundation and framing. A generic conversion diagram is available. See order form.)

BLUEPRINT PRICE CODE:	E

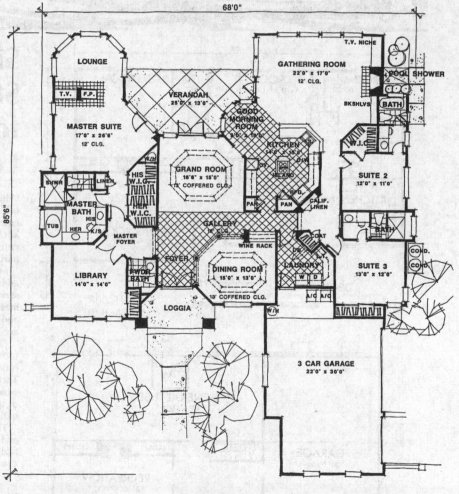

MAIN FLOOR

See this plan on our "One-Story" VideoGraphic Tour! Order form on page 9

ORDER BLUEPRINTS ANYTIME!
CALL TOLL-FREE 1-888-626-2026

Plan EOF-62

PRICES AND DETAILS
ON PAGES 12-15

255

Simple and Straightforward for an Uphill Lot

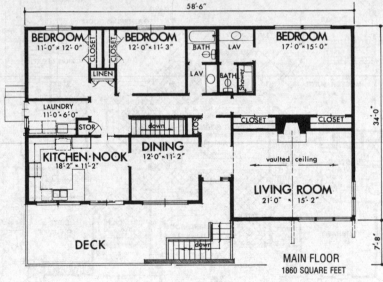

BEDROOM 11'-0" × 12'-0"
CLOSET
CLOSET
BEDROOM 12'-0" × 11'-3"
BATH
LAV
BEDROOM 17'-0" × 15'-0"

LINEN
LAV
BATH
Shower

LAUNDRY 11'-0" × 6'-0"
STOR
down
CLOSET
CLOSET

KITCHEN · NOOK 18'-2" × 11'-2"
DINING 12'-0" × 11'-2"
vaulted ceiling

LIVING ROOM 21'-0" × 15'-2"

DECK
down

MAIN FLOOR
1860 SQUARE FEET

58'-6"
34'-0"
7'-8"

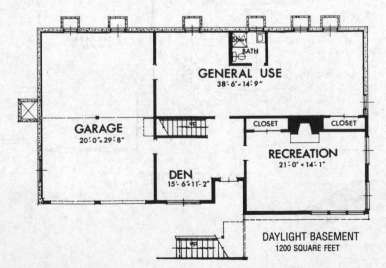

SK
BATH
GENERAL USE 38'-6" × 14'-9"

GARAGE 20'-0" × 29'-8"
UP
CLOSET
CLOSET

DEN 15'-6" × 11'-2"
RECREATION 21'-0" × 14'-1"

UP

DAYLIGHT BASEMENT
1200 SQUARE FEET

While relatively simple in design , this plan offers many attractive features. The huge entrance deck is accessible from both the kitchen and the dining nook, and a central entry area directs traffic to each separate part of the home.

In the living room, a vaulted ceiling adds a touch of drama, and the fireplace serves as a focal point. The spacious master bedroom features a private bath and ample closet space. Laundry facilities are on the main floor.

On the lower level, a large recreation room also has a fireplace, and another room can be used as a den or home office. There is also a large area for general use which could be finished as a family room, or used for a shop or hobby space. A third bath is also included.

The upper level includes 1,860 sq. ft. and the lower level adds about 1,200 additional sq. ft. of living space, not counting the garage.

Main floor:	1,860 sq. ft.
Daylight basement:	1,200 sq. ft.
Total living area:	3,060 sq. ft.

(Not counting garage)
(Exterior walls are 2X6 construction)

Blueprint Price Code E
Plan H-2028-4

PRICES AND DETAILS
ON PAGES 12-15

Spectacular View From Loft

- A soaring foyer and vaulted, step-down parlor with fireplace and decorative brick columns can be seen from an overhead loft in this distinguished two-story.
- Flanking the parlor are a vaulted library with built-in shelves along two walls and a formal dining room with brilliant 12' ceiling.
- Rich-looking brick borders the cooktop in the roomy island kitchen with a handy pantry; an adjoining bayed breakfast room offers a sunny patio.
- The exciting sunken family room off the kitchen features a unique gambrel ceiling, massive fireplace, corner windows and refreshing wet bar.
- Three steps up from the loft is the spacious master suite with private, bayed sitting area and lavish bath with separate vanities and walk-in closets, a garden tub and romantic deck.

UPPER FLOOR

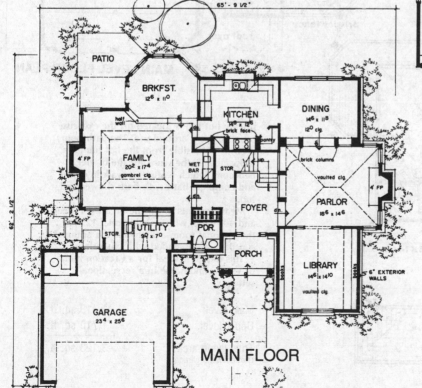

MAIN FLOOR

Plan DW-3108	
Bedrooms: 3	**Baths: 2 ½**
Space:	
Upper floor	1,324 sq. ft.
Main floor	1,784 sq. ft.
Total Living Area	**3,108 sq. ft.**
Basement	1,784 sq. ft.
Garage	595 sq. ft.
Exterior Wall Framing	2x6

Foundation options:
Standard Basement
Crawlspace
Slab
(Framing conversion diagram available—see order form.)

Blueprint Price Code	E

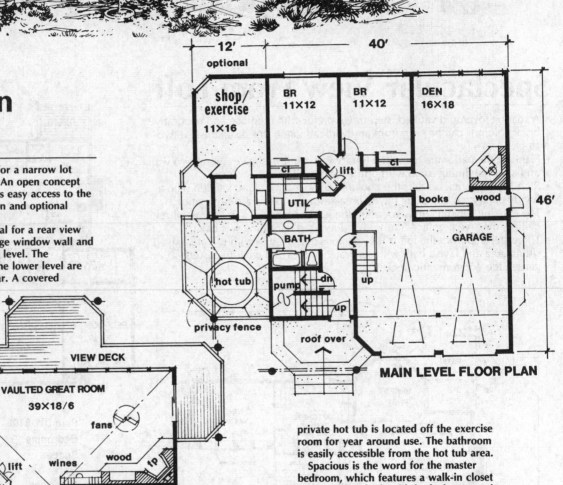

Deluxe Vacation Home

This residence is ideal for a narrow lot with solar possibilities. An open concept vaulted Great Room has easy access to the large, innovative kitchen and optional sunroom.

This home is also ideal for a rear view orientation, with its large window wall and upper-story main living level. The bedrooms and den in the lower level are also oriented to the rear. A covered

MAIN LEVEL FLOOR PLAN

- 12' optional
- 40'
- 46'
- shop/exercise 11×16
- BR 11×12
- BR 11×12
- DEN 16×18
- cl
- lift
- cl
- books
- wood
- UTIL
- GARAGE
- BATH
- hot tub
- pump
- dn
- up
- up
- privacy fence
- roof over

UPPER LEVEL FLOOR PLAN

- VIEW DECK
- optional SUNROOM 11/6×16
- VAULTED GREAT ROOM 39×18/6
- fans
- eating bar
- lift
- wines
- wood
- fp
- KIT
- PDR
- MB
- tub below
- g
- dn
- clos
- MBR 17/6×14/6
- roof below

private hot tub is located off the exercise room for year around use. The bathroom is easily accessible from the hot tub area.

Spacious is the word for the master bedroom, which features a walk-in closet and complete bath with both shower and tub.

Measurements of this home are 46' deep and 40' wide, with an additional 12' for the optional rooms. (Plans for the optional sunspace are included with blueprints.)

This design is ideal for a vacation home or year-round home in a recreational setting.

Main level:	1,413 sq. ft.
Upper level:	1,710 sq. ft.
Total living area: (Not counting garage)	3,123 sq. ft.

Blueprint Price Code E

Plan LRD-60983

PRICES AND DETAILS
ON PAGES 12-15

Victorian Farmhouse

- Fish-scale shingles and horizontal siding team up with the detailed front porch to create a look of yesterday. Brickwork enriches the sides and rear of the home.
- The main level features 10-ft.-high ceilings throughout the central living space. The front-oriented formal areas merge with the family room via three sets of French doors.

- The island kitchen and skylighted eating area have 16-ft. sloped ceilings.
- A breezeway off the deck connects the house to a roomy workshop. A two-car garage is located under the workshop and a large utility room is just inside the rear entrance.
- The main-floor master suite offers an opulent skylighted bath with a garden vanity, a spa tub, a separate shower and an 18-ft.-high sloped ceiling.
- The upper floor offers three more bedrooms, two full baths and a balcony that looks to the backyard.

Plan E-3103

Bedrooms: 4	Baths: 3½
Living Area:	
Upper floor	1,113 sq. ft.
Main floor	2,040 sq. ft.
Total Living Area:	**3,153 sq. ft.**
Daylight basement	2,040 sq. ft.
Tuck-under garage and storage	580 sq. ft.
Workshop and storage	580 sq. ft.
Exterior Wall Framing:	2x6

Foundation Options:

Daylight basement
Crawlspace
Slab

(All plans can be built with your choice of foundation and framing. A generic conversion diagram is available. See order form.)

BLUEPRINT PRICE CODE: E

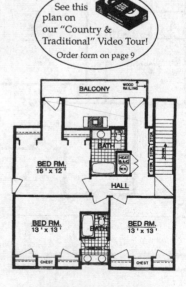

See this plan on our "Country & Traditional" Video Tour!
Order form on page 9

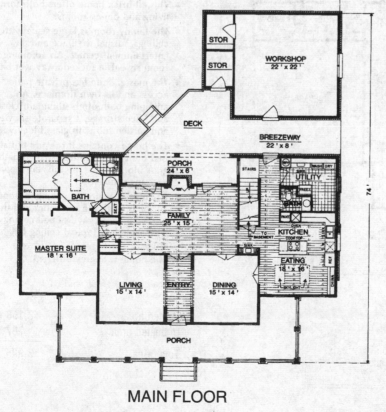

MAIN FLOOR

UPPER FLOOR

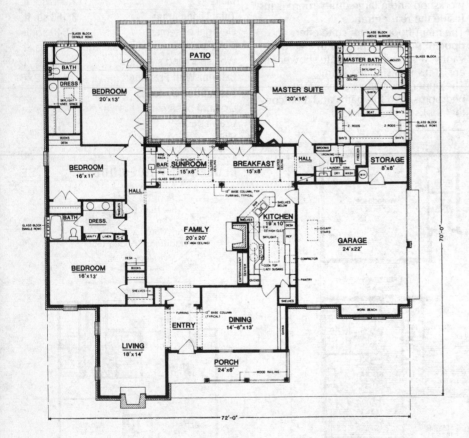

PLAN E-3102
WITHOUT BASEMENT

Exterior walls are 2x6 construction.
Specify crawlspace or slab foundation.

Ranch-Style Designed for Entertaining

- This all-brick home offers both formal living and dining rooms.
- The family room is large scale with 13' ceilings, formal fireplace and an entertainment center. An adjoining sun room reveals a tucked away wet bar.
- The master suite has private patio access and its own fireplace. An adjoining bath offers abundant closet and linen storage, a separate shower and garden tub with glass block walls.
- The home contains three additional bedrooms and two baths. Each bath has glass block above the tubs and separate dressing rooms.
- The master bedroom ceiling is sloped to 14' high. Both the sun room and the breakfast room have sloped ceilings with skylights. Typical ceiling heights are 9'.
- The home is energy efficient.

Heated area:	3,158 sq. ft.
Unheated area:	767 sq. ft.
Total area:	3,925 sq. ft.

Blueprint Price Code E

Plan E-3102

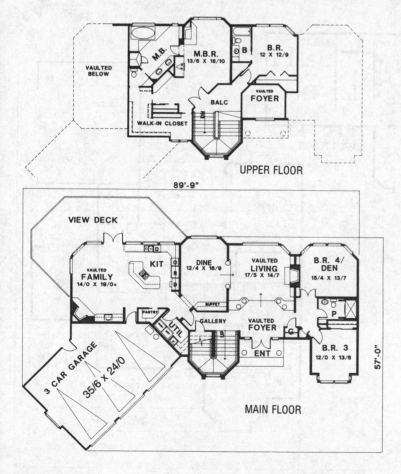

VAULTED BELOW

M.B.

M.B.R.
13/6 X 18/10

B

B.R.
12 X 12/9

BALC

VAULTED FOYER

WALK-IN CLOSET

DN

UPPER FLOOR

89'-9"

VIEW DECK

VAULTED FAMILY
14/0 X 19/0+

KIT

DINE
12/4 X 16/9

VAULTED LIVING
17/5 X 14/7

B.R. 4/ DEN
15/4 X 13/7

BUFFET

PANTRY

P

3 CAR GARAGE
35/6 X 24/0

UTIL

GALLERY

VAULTED FOYER

ENT

B.R. 3
12/0 X 13/6

57'-0"

MAIN FLOOR

Designed with Elegance in Mind

- This expansive home boasts 3,220 sq. ft. of living space designed with elegance in mind.
- The front of the home is finished in stucco, with the rest in lap siding for economy.
- The vaulted foyer leads directly into an impressive sunken and vaulted living room, guarded by columns that echo the exterior treatment.
- The formal dining room is visually joined to the living room to make an impressive space for entertaining.
- An unusually fine kitchen opens to a large family room, which boasts a vaulted ceiling, a corner fireplace and access to a sizable rear deck.
- In the front, the extra-wide staircase is a primary attraction, with its dramatic feature window.
- A terrific master suite includes a splendid master bath with double sinks and a huge walk-through closet.
- A second upstairs bedroom also includes a private bath.

Plan LRD-11388

Bedrooms: 3-4	Baths: 3

Living Area:

Upper floor:	1,095 sq. ft.
Main floor	2,125 sq. ft.
Total Living Area:	**3,220 sq. ft.**
Standard basement	2,125 sq. ft.
Garage	802 sq. ft.

Exterior Wall Framing:	2x6

Foundation Options:

Standard basement
Crawlspace
Slab
(Typical foundation & framing conversion diagram available—see order form.)

BLUEPRINT PRICE CODE: E

ORDER BLUEPRINTS ANYTIME!
CALL TOLL-FREE 1-888-626-2026

Plan LRD-11388

PRICES AND DETAILS
ON PAGES 12-15

261

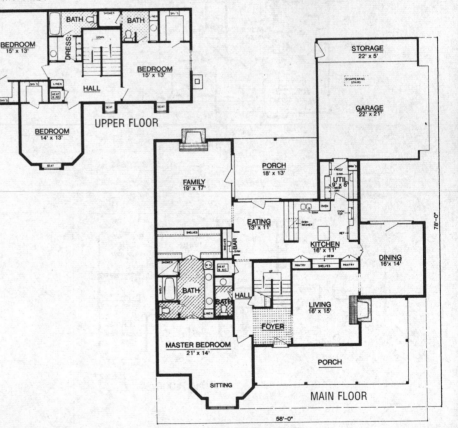

Striking Traditional Farmhouse

- This eye-catching design will attract compliments wherever it is built, with its wide front porch, decorative columns and gables.
- The interior is equally fascinating, with an abundance of space for formal entertaining and casual family living.
- A large kitchen and eating area are at the heart of the home, and a spacious family room with a fireplace opens onto a secluded back porch.
- For formal occasions, the living and dining rooms adjoin each other to create a fine space for entertaining.
- The master suite is fit for royalty, with its bright sitting area, majestic bath and enormous walk-in closet.
- The upstairs bedrooms are also roomy, and one boasts a private bath. All three feature walk-in closets.

Plan E-3101

Bedrooms: 4		**Baths:** 2½	
Space:			
Upper floor		1,074 sq. ft.	
Main floor		2,088 sq. ft.	
Total Living Area		**3,162 sq. ft.**	
Basement	(approx.)	2,088 sq. ft.	
Garage		462 sq. ft.	
Storage		110 sq. ft.	
Porches		598 sq. ft.	

Exterior Wall Framing   2x6

Foundation options:
Standard basement
Crawlspace
Slab
(Foundation & framing conversion diagram available—see order form.)

Blueprint Price Code   E

ORDER BLUEPRINTS ANYTIME!
CALL TOLL-FREE 1-888-626-2026

262

Plan E-3101

PRICES AND DETAILS
ON PAGES 12-15

Mediterranean Masterpiece

- A captivating roofline, a stucco facade and a columned porte cochere create a stunning exterior for this home.
- A tiled foyer leads into the expansive sunken living room, which is served by a wet bar that can be accessed from the outdoor pool area.
- Pocket doors close off the kitchen and breakfast area from the dining room and living room. The kitchen offers a preparation island, a nearby laundry room and a serving bar to the adjoining family room. The breakfast area overlooks the screened patio and pool.
- The spectacular master suite boasts a bright sitting room and a fireplace set along a curved glass wall that overlooks the pool, spa and summer kitchen. The private, compartmentalized bath shows off a step-up tub, a separate shower and a huge walk-in closet.
- Two secondary bedrooms and a unique observation room occupy the upper floor. Each bedroom offers sliding glass doors to the large balcony.
- A guest room with a private bath is near the master suite on the main floor.

Plan HDS-99-138

Bedrooms: 4	Baths: 3½
Living Area:	
Upper floor	621 sq. ft.
Main floor	2,669 sq. ft.
Total Living Area:	**3,290 sq. ft.**
Garage	479 sq. ft.
Exterior Wall Framing:	2x6

Foundation Options:
Slab
(Typical foundation & framing conversion diagram available—see order form.)

BLUEPRINT PRICE CODE: E

UPPER FLOOR

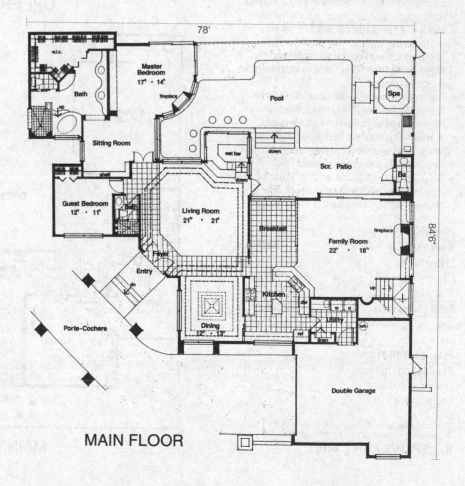

MAIN FLOOR

PRICES AND DETAILS
ON PAGES 12-15

Truly Nostalgic

- Designed after "Monteigne," an Italianate home near Natchez, Mississippi, this reproduction utilizes modern stucco finishes for the exterior.
- Columns and arched windows give way to a two-story-high foyer, which is accented by a striking, curved stairwell.
- The foyer connects the living room and the study, each boasting a 14-ft. ceiling and a cozy fireplace or woodstove.
- Adjacent to the formal dining room, the kitchen offers a snack bar and a bayed eating room. A unique entertainment center is centrally located to serve the main activity rooms of the home.
- A gorgeous sun room stretches across the rear of the main floor and overlooks a grand terrace.
- The plush master suite and bath boast his-and-hers vanities, large walk-in closets and a glassed-in garden tub.
- A main-floor guest bedroom features a walk-in closet and private access to another full main-floor bath.
- Two more bedrooms with private baths are located on the upper level. They share a sitting area and a veranda.

Plan E-3200

Bedrooms: 4	Baths: 4
Living Area:	
Upper floor	629 sq. ft.
Main floor	2,655 sq. ft.
Total Living Area:	**3,284 sq. ft.**
Standard basement	2,655 sq. ft.
Garage	667 sq. ft.
Exterior Wall Framing:	2x6

Foundation Options:

Standard basement

Crawlspace

Slab

(All plans can be built with your choice of foundation and framing. A generic conversion diagram is available. See order form.)

BLUEPRINT PRICE CODE: E

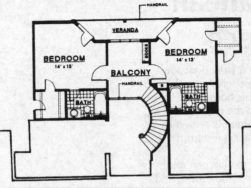

UPPER FLOOR

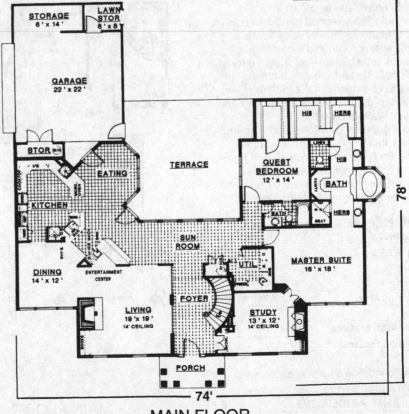

MAIN FLOOR

264

ORDER BLUEPRINTS ANYTIME!
CALL TOLL-FREE 1-888-626-2026

Plan E-3200

PRICES AND DETAILS
ON PAGES 12-15

Elegant Arches

- This gorgeous brick home is adorned by a plethora of elegant arches.
- The tiled foyer is expanded by a 13-ft. ceiling and unfolds beautifully to the parlour, which offers a 14-ft. ceiling and access to a skylighted lanai.
- Set off by an arched doorway, the elegant dining room boasts a functional built-in niche and an ale bar that is open to the main hallway.
- The gourmet kitchen features an island cooktop, an angled serving counter and a morning room with lanai access.
- The 13-ft. ceiling in the kitchen areas extends to the spacious Gathering Room, which includes impressive transom windows, an arched TV niche, an open-end fireplace and access to the lanai.
- Secluded on the opposite side of the home, the sun-drenched master suite flaunts a 13-ft. ceiling, a convenient morning kitchen and access to the lanai's summer kitchen. A three-sided fireplace separates the bedroom from the skylighted bath, which showcases a garden tub, a doorless shower, a dual-sink vanity with knee space and two walk-in closets.
- Each of the additional bedroom suites boasts private bath access.

Plan EOF-74

Bedrooms: 3+	Baths: 4
Living Area:	
Main floor	3,349 sq. ft.
Total Living Area:	**3,349 sq. ft.**
Garage	527 sq. ft.
Exterior Wall Framing:	2x6

Foundation Options:

Slab

(All plans can be built with your choice of foundation and framing. A generic conversion diagram is available. See order form.)

BLUEPRINT PRICE CODE: E

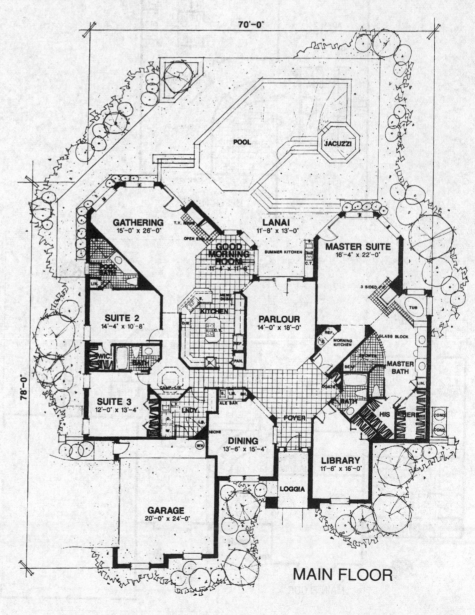

MAIN FLOOR

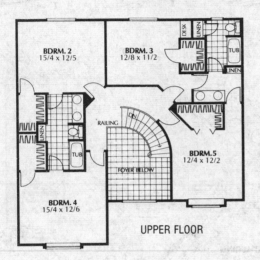

BDRM. 2
15/4 x 12/5

BDRM. 3
12/8 x 11/2

DESK LINEN

TUB

LINEN

RAILING

DN

BDRM. 4
15/4 x 12/6

LINEN

TUB

FOYER BELOW

BDRM.5
12/4 x 12/2

UPPER FLOOR

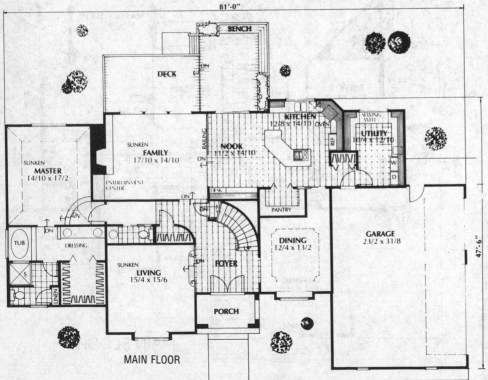

81'-0"

BENCH

DECK

DN

47'-6"

KITCHEN
12/8 x 14/10 OVEN

SEWING UTILITY
11/4 x 12/10

SUNKEN
FAMILY
17/10 x 14/10

RAILING

NOOK
11/2 x 14/10

REF

W
D

SUNKEN
MASTER
14/10 x 17/2

ENTERTAINMENT
CENTER

DN

DN

PANTRY

TUB

DRESSING

S

LINEN

DN

DN

DESK

DN

SUNKEN
LIVING
15/4 x 15/6

FOYER

DINING
12/4 x 13/2

GARAGE
23/2 x 31/8

PORCH

MAIN FLOOR

Spacious, Elegant Five-Bedroom

- Classic Tudor exterior design is reminiscent of bygone days of gracious traditions.
- Thoroughly modern interior provides all the amenities and features needed by today's families.
- Beginning at the impressive two-story-high foyer, everything is big on this spacious main floor — even including the utility/sewing room off the kitchen.
- Family room, nook and kitchen provide huge space, just right for a busy family.
- Downstairs master suite includes deluxe bath and large walk-in closet.
- Upstairs includes four more bedrooms and two more baths.

Plan U-87-206

Bedrooms: 5	Baths: 3½
Space:	
Upper floor:	1,243 sq. ft.
Main floor:	2,152 sq. ft.
Total living area:	3,395 sq. ft.
Basement:	2,152 sq. ft.
Garage:	733 sq. ft.
Exterior Wall Framing:	2x4/2x6

Foundation options:
Standard basement.
Crawlspace.
Slab.
(Foundation & framing conversion diagram available — see order form.)

Blueprint Price Code:	E

Plan U-87-206

PRICES AND DETAILS
ON PAGES 12-15

Elegant Arches

- Gracious arched windows and an entry portico create rhythm and style for this home's brick-clad exterior.
- An elegant curved staircase lends interest to the raised, two-story foyer.
- Two steps down to the left of the foyer lies the living room, with its dramatic 14-ft. cathedral ceiling. Lovely columns define the adjoining dining room. A cozy fireplace warms the entire area.
- The island kitchen overlooks the bayed breakfast room and offers a handy pass-through to the adjoining family room.
- The two-story-high family room boasts a second fireplace and a wall of windows topped by large transoms.
- The quiet master bedroom features a bay window and an 11-ft. sloped ceiling. The master bath shows off a garden tub and a separate shower.
- A sizable deck is accessible from both the breakfast room and the master suite.
- Three more bedrooms and two baths share the upper floor. A balcony bridge overlooks the foyer and family room.

Plan DD-3639

Bedrooms: 4+	Baths: 3½
Living Area:	
Upper floor	868 sq. ft.
Main floor	2,771 sq. ft.
Total Living Area:	**3,639 sq. ft.**
Standard basement	2,771 sq. ft.
Garage	790 sq. ft.
Exterior Wall Framing:	2x6

Foundation Options:

Standard basement

Crawlspace

Slab

(All plans can be built with your choice of foundation and framing. A generic conversion diagram is available. See order form.)

BLUEPRINT PRICE CODE:	F

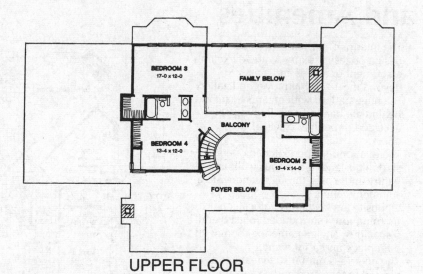

UPPER FLOOR

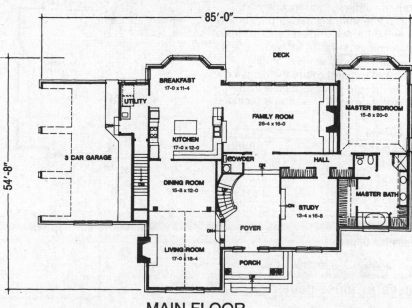

MAIN FLOOR

ORDER BLUEPRINTS ANYTIME!
CALL TOLL-FREE 1-888-626-2026

Plan DD-3639

PRICES AND DETAILS
ON PAGES 12-15

267

Exciting Angles and Amenities

- The interior of this elegant stucco design oozes in luxury, with an exciting assortment of angles and glass.
- Beyond the 14-ft.-high foyer and gallery is a huge parlour with an angled stand-behind ale bar and an adjoining patio accessed through two sets of glass doors.
- The diamond-shaped kitchen offers a sit-down island, a spacious walk-in pantry and a pass-through window to a summer kitchen.
- Opposite the kitchen is an octagonal morning room surrounded in glass and a spacious, angled gathering room with a fireplace and a TV niche.
- The luxurious master suite features a glassed lounge area and a spectacular two-sided fireplace, and is separated from the three secondary bedroom suites. The stunning master bath boasts a central linen island and an assortment of amenities designed for two.
- The library could serve as a fifth bedroom or guest room; the bath across the hall could serve as a pool bath.
- An alternate brick elevation is included

Plan EOF-59

Bedrooms: 4+	Baths: 4

Living Area:

Main floor	4,021 sq. ft.
Total Living Area:	**4,021 sq. ft.**
Garage	737 sq. ft.
Exterior Wall Framing:	2x6

Foundation Options:

Slab
(All plans can be built with your choice of foundation and framing. A generic conversion diagram is available. See order form.)

BLUEPRINT PRICE CODE:	G

MAIN FLOOR

Estate Living

- This grand estate is as big and beautiful on the inside as it is on the outside.
- The formal dining room and parlor, each with a tall window, flank the entry's graceful curved staircase.
- The sunken family room is topped by a two-story-high ceiling and wrapped in floor-to-ceiling windows. A patio door opens to the covered porch, which features a nifty built-in barbecue.
- The island kitchen and the bright breakfast area also overlook the porch, with access through the deluxe utility room.

- The master suite has it all, including a romantic fireplace framed by bookshelves. The opulent bath offers a raised spa tub, a separate shower, his-and-hers walk-in closets and a dual-sink vanity. The neighboring bedroom, which also has a private bath, would make an ideal nursery.
- The upper floor hosts a balcony hall that provides a breathtaking view of the family room below. Each of the two bedrooms here has its own bath.
- The main floor is expanded by 10-ft. ceilings, while 9-ft. ceilings grace the upper floor.

Plan DD-4300-B	
Bedrooms: 4	**Baths:** 4½
Living Area:	
Upper floor	868 sq. ft.
Main floor	3,416 sq. ft.
Total Living Area:	**4,284 sq. ft.**
Standard basement	3,416 sq. ft.
Garage and storage	633 sq. ft.
Exterior Wall Framing:	2x4 or 2x6

Foundation Options:
Standard basement
Crawlspace
Slab
(All plans can be built with your choice of foundation and framing. A generic conversion diagram is available. See order form.)

BLUEPRINT PRICE CODE: G

MAIN FLOOR

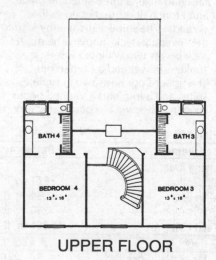

UPPER FLOOR

ORDER BLUEPRINTS ANYTIME!
CALL TOLL-FREE 1-888-626-2026

Plan DD-4300-B

PRICES AND DETAILS
ON PAGES 12-15

269

Design Leaves Out Nothing

- This design has it all, from the elegant detailing of the exterior to the exciting, luxurious spaces of the interior.
- High ceilings, large, open rooms and lots of glass are found throughout the home. Nearly all of the main living areas, as well as the master suite, overlook the veranda.
- Unusual features include an ale bar in the formal dining room, an art niche in the Grand Room and a TV niche in the Gathering Room. The Gathering Room also features a fireplace framed by window seats, a wall of windows facing the backyard and a half-wall open to the sunny morning room.
- The centrally located cooktop-island kitchen is conveniently accessible from all of the living areas.
- The delicious master suite includes a raised lounge, a three-sided fireplace and French doors that open to the veranda. The spiral stairs nearby lead to the "evening deck" above. The master bath boasts two walk-in closets, a sunken shower and a Roman tub.
- The upper floor hosts two complete suites and a loft, plus a vaulted bonus room reached via a separate stairway.

Plan EOF-61

Bedrooms: 3+	Baths: 4½
Living Area:	
Upper floor	877 sq. ft.
Main floor	3,094 sq. ft.
Bonus room	280 sq. ft.
Total Living Area:	**4,251 sq. ft.**
Garage	774 sq. ft.
Exterior Wall Framing:	2x6

Foundation Options:

Slab

(All plans can be built with your choice of foundation and framing. A generic conversion diagram is available. See order form.)

BLUEPRINT PRICE CODE: G

See this plan on our "Two-Story" VideoGraphic Tour! Order form on page 9

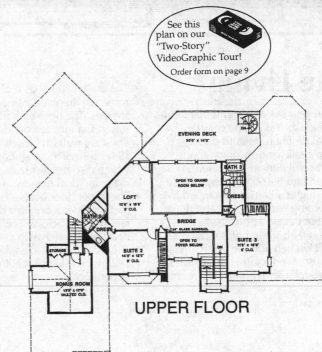

UPPER FLOOR

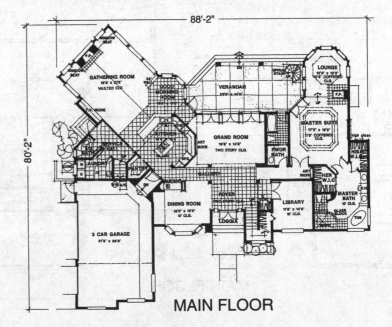

MAIN FLOOR

Plan EOF-61

PRICES AND DETAILS ON PAGES 12-15

REAR VIEW

Spectacular Executive Estate

- The unique angular design of this executive home focuses attention on the spectacular entrance, which is enhanced by two balconies above.
- Beyond the vestibule, a 19-ft. ceiling presides over the columned Great Room and the sunny dining room. A two-story window wall overlooks the expansive backyard pool area.
- The gourmet island kitchen and breakfast nook open to a side deck and offer easy service to both the dining room and the family room.
- A nice-sized media room or library boasts two walls of built-ins.
- The master suite is a masterpiece, with its 15-ft. vaulted ceiling, romantic fireplace and sliding glass doors to a secluded sun deck and hot tub. The luxurious bath offers a whirlpool tub, a separate shower and two vanities.
- A classy, curved staircase accesses the upper floor, where three more bedrooms each have a private bath. A lounge with a window seat and a central area with outdoor balconies are other special appointments found here.

Plan B-05-85

Bedrooms: 4+	Baths: 4 full, 2 half
Living Area:	
Upper floor	1,720 sq. ft.
Main floor	3,900 sq. ft.
Total Living Area:	**5,620 sq. ft.**
Standard basement	3,900 sq. ft.
Garage	836 sq. ft.
Exterior Wall Framing:	2x6

Foundation Options:

Standard basement

(All plans can be built with your choice of foundation and framing. A generic conversion diagram is available. See order form.)

BLUEPRINT PRICE CODE: I

UPPER FLOOR

Br 3 15-4x13
Br 4 15-4x13
open to below
Lounge 15x12
Balcony 14-8x15-6
Br 2 20x13

MAIN FLOOR

Pool
Dining 18x15-4
Master Suite 29-4x15 vaulted
Deck
Hot Tub
Kit/ Brkfst 16-6x19-4
Great Rm 35x35 high ceiling
Deck
Whirlpool
Wardrobe
Family 14x20-4
Vestibule
Media/ Library 16x15-6
3 Car Garage 23-8x35-4

112'-0"
88'-4"
135'

ORDER BLUEPRINTS ANYTIME!
CALL TOLL-FREE 1-888-626-2026

Plan B-05-85

PRICES AND DETAILS
ON PAGES 12-15

271

Ultimate Elegance

- The ultimate in elegance and luxury, this home begins with an impressive foyer that reveals a sweeping staircase and a direct view of the backyard.
- The centrally located parlor, perfect for receiving guests, has a two-story-high ceiling, a spectacular wall of glass, a fireplace and a unique ale bar. French doors open to a covered veranda with a relaxing spa and a summer kitchen.
- The gourmet island kitchen boasts an airy 10-ft. ceiling, a menu desk and a walk-in pantry. The octagonal morning room has a vaulted ceiling and access to a second stairway to the upper level.
- A pass-through snack bar in the kitchen overlooks the gathering room, which hosts a cathedral ceiling, French doors to the veranda and a second fireplace.
- Bright and luxurious, the master suite has a 10-ft. ceiling and features a unique morning kitchen, a sunny sitting area and a lavish private bath.
- The curved staircase leads to three bedroom suites upstairs. The rear suites share an enchanting deck.

Plan EOF-3

Bedrooms: 4+	Baths: 5½
Living Area:	
Upper floor	1,150 sq. ft.
Main floor	3,045 sq. ft.
Total Living Area:	**4,195 sq. ft.**
Garage	814 sq. ft.
Exterior Wall Framing:	2x6

Foundation Options:

Slab

(All plans can be built with your choice of foundation and framing. A generic conversion diagram is available. See order form.)

BLUEPRINT PRICE CODE: **G**

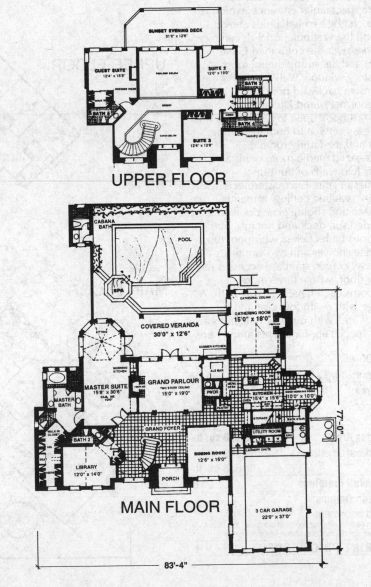

UPPER FLOOR

MAIN FLOOR

Other books available from HomeStyles:

- [ ] HOME DESIGNS FEATURING ALL-TIME BEST-SELLERS (HD22)
- [ ] HOME DESIGNS FEATURING BRICK EXTERIORS (HD24)
- [ ] HOME DESIGNS FOR AFFORDABLE LIVING (HD36)
- [ ] HOME DESIGNS FOR CONTEMPORARY LIVING (HD27)
- [ ] HOME DESIGNS FOR COUNTRYPOLITAN LIVING (HD20)
- [ ] HOME DESIGNS FOR COUNTRY-STYLE LIVING (HD8)
- [ ] HOME DESIGNS FOR ENERGY-EFFICIENT LIVING (HD9)
- [ ] HOME DESIGNS FOR FAMILY AND GREAT ROOMS (HD30)
- [ ] HOME DESIGNS FOR INDOOR-OUTDOOR LIVING (HD21)
- [ ] HOME DESIGNS FOR LUXURY LIVING (HD28)
- [ ] HOME DESIGNS FOR MASTER SUITES AND MASTER BATHS (HD31)
- [ ] HOME DESIGNS FOR MOVE-UP FAMILIES (1,500-2,500 SQ. FT.) (HD11)
- [ ] HOME DESIGNS FOR NARROW LOTS (HD35)
- [ ] HOME DESIGNS FOR ONE-STORY LIVING (HD29)
- [ ] HOME DESIGNS FOR RECREATIONAL LIVING (HD33)
- [ ] HOME DESIGNS FOR SLOPING LOTS (HD32)
- [ ] HOME DESIGNS FOR TWO-STORY LIVING (HD34)

TO ORDER, CALL TOLL-FREE 1-888-626-2026
OR WRITE TO:
HOMESTYLES
P.O. BOX 75488, ST. PAUL, MN 55175-0488

(PLEASE ENCLOSE $6.95 PER BOOK, PLUS $1.75 FOR POSTAGE AND HANDLING)

HomeStyles Designers' Network is comprised of more than 50 of America's leading residential

design firms. To create this book, our editors examined over 4,000 home designs. The final

product, **HOMEDESIGNS**, is the most comprehensive, innovative and exciting anthology of

its kind. Complete construction blueprints are available on all plans, including exterior and

interior elevations, detailed floor plans, foundation and roof plans, cross sections and other

construction details. Once you have selected your home, call our toll-free number for easy

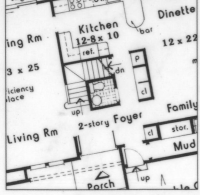

ordering and next-day shipping of your professionally drawn blueprints. HomeStyles is proud

to present this collection of: **HOMEDESIGNS**

for

ENERGY-EFFICIENT LIVING

ISBN 1-56547-063-X